PRACTICAL
parenting

baby & child
all your questions answered

PRACTICAL parenting

hamlyn

baby & child

all your questions answered

Baby & Child has been produced in association with Practical Parenting (an IPC Media Limited publication)

Practical Parenting ® is a registered trademark of IPC Media

First published in Great Britain in 2005 by Hamlyn, a division of Octopus Publishing Group Ltd 2–4 Heron Quays, London E14 4JP

ISBN 0 600 61120 5
EAN 9780600611202

A CIP catalogue record for this book is available from the British Library

Printed and bound in China

10 9 8 7 6 5 4 3 2 1

Note

This book is not intended as a substitute for personal medical advice. The reader should consult a physician in all matters relating to health and particularly in respect of any symptoms which may require diagnosis or medical attention. While the advice and information are believed to be accurate and true at the time of going to press, neither the author nor the publisher can accept any legal responsibility or liability for any errors or omissions that may be made.

contents

introduction

How many times do we call our own parents, or friends and relatives for advice?

- Why does he do such and such?
- Is this normal?
- How can I get her to do that?

Parenting is a challenge at the best of times. For first-time parents, there are the frustrations and anxieties of coping with a newborn baby whose only form of communication is a limited range of cries and body movements.

Once the second, third or fourth children come along, parents are faced with an entirely new set of concerns in dealing with sibling rivalry, gender differences and safety in the home. Not only that, but the most mundane of situations can throw a parent into near despair simply because a second child does not follow the behaviour pattern of the first.

No one has all the answers and not all answers are black and white, but it is often just enough to have someone else's opinion and to be reassured that nothing serious is wrong. So what better solution than to have all this information to hand in just one place? *Baby & Child – All Your Questions Answered* does just that. Produced in association with *Practical Parenting* magazine, this comprehensive guide addresses a host of common parental concerns in an accessible question-and-answer format.

From birth to four years, this book carries advice from a team of childcare experts and covers all aspects of day-to-day life with your baby or toddler – sleeping, eating, establishing routines, managing behaviour – discussing many of the pitfalls that arise along the way. Sections for each age group guide parents in understanding and encouraging a child's development in terms of hand–eye coordination, movement and language, and also look at emotional development in outlining how to deal with tantrums, sibling rivalry and separation anxiety. Throughout the book common concerns and problems are dealt with through questions that are often asked, with answers which prove that the many fears and anxieties we have as we raise our children are, in most cases, quite straightforward and easy to deal with, with a little reassurance and advice.

1

new baby
0 to 4 weeks

Appearance

Your first impressions of your newborn may hold some surprises, since a new baby looks quite different from one that is even a few months old. At birth, he shows signs of having just emerged from the watery environment of the womb. As well as being wet and slippery and possibly streaked with blood, being born has put your baby under pressure and stress, so he probably shows some effects of the birth process itself.

Soft spots

A baby's skull is not solid, but instead is formed of separate plates of soft bones joined by fibrous tissue. There are six soft spots, or fontanelles, which are the gaps between the bones of the head, but you will probably only be aware of the two main ones. The largest is a diamond-shaped area about 4 cm (1½ in) across, at the crown of the head. Behind that you might notice a smaller triangular soft spot. These soft spots will have closed up between the ages of nine and 18 months.

What to expect

• **Head.** A baby's head is large for his body – compared to an adult, it is proportionately four times bigger. At birth, the head may be pushed into an elongated shape, the forehead may seem short, and the head may be lopsided. This is the result of moulding, the process allowing the baby's head to change shape in order to come through the narrow birth passage safely. The effect lasts only a few hours and your baby's head will quickly become more rounded and even.

• **Limbs.** Alongside a newborn's large head and abdomen, his arms and legs may seem small and insubstantial. A baby born at full term will have fingernails to the ends of his fingers. His legs will be slightly bowed, with his feet turned in, from having been curled up in the womb.

• **Colour.** At first your baby's hands and feet may appear pale or bluish while his trunk is pink, which is a result of his circulation not yet being efficient at delivering the blood to his extremities. His immature circulation may also cause uneven colour in his body, with the top half pale and the bottom half red. Moving his position will sort this out.

• **Hair.** Some babies are born with a thick crop of hair, while others are almost bald. The colour of your baby's hair may not be permanent, as it is common for the first hair to fall out in the early weeks and when new hair grows it may be a completely different colour.

• **Skin.** Your baby's skin will be covered in vernix, a creamy whitish substance, which has protected his skin in the watery environment of the womb. The vernix continues to protect your baby's delicate skin in the first few days, so it's a good idea not to wash it off, but to let it be gradually absorbed. Dry or peeling skin at birth, usually on the hands and feet, is not a sign of eczema or other skin problems and should settle down after a few days.

• **Eyes.** Your baby's eyelids may be puffy as a result of pressure during birth. This swelling will go down in a day or two. Any small spots of blood in the white of the eyes are tiny burst blood vessels, which will soon go. Your baby will cry without tears: the tear glands only start producing tears after a few weeks.

• **Mouth.** Your baby's tongue may be anchored to the bottom of his mouth along most of its length. This won't affect his sucking and is not cause for worry. As the tongue grows, it grows mainly from the tip. There may be tiny pink spots inside the mouth, along the gums, and on the hard palate. They are small cysts and will disappear without treatment.

• **Breasts and genitals.** In both boys and girls, reactions to the mother's hormones during pregnancy temporarily affect the baby. The breasts may be swollen, and a few drops of milk may even appear. The swelling will disappear in a few days, as the mother's hormones are cleared out of the baby's system. Genitals are also enlarged, and in girl babies there may be clear white discharge, or even a few drops of blood from the vagina as a result of the hormones. This, too, will stop naturally in a couple of days.

Right: Many babies are born with red blotchy skin. This is just his skin reacting to its new world and is nothing to worry about.

Birthmarks

Many babies have small, flat red marks on the skin, most often on the eyelids, forehead and nape of the neck. These 'stork beak' marks are caused by the enlargement of tiny blood vessels and usually disappear over the first year. Mongolian blue spots are uneven blotches of bluish colouring, usually occurring on the lower back. These spots are most common on dark-skinned babies, and are caused by uneven pigmentation. They are harmless and will fade. A strawberry mark may be present at birth, or appear after a few days. It is raised, red and soft, and will grow bigger over a few months. Although it may be unsightly, it will eventually fade and then usually disappear altogether without medical treatment.

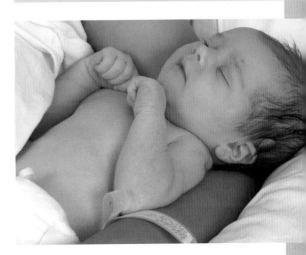

Appearance
Common questions

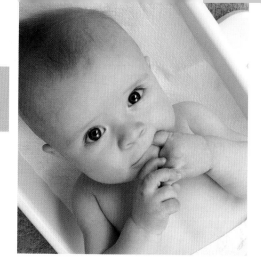

Above: Almost all babies' eyes are bluish-grey at birth because the pigment in the iris has not yet developed.

Q My newborn has fine hair over her ears, shoulder and back. Is this normal?

A This hair is called lanugo. All babies have it in the womb. It is not unusual for some to be present following the birth, especially in babies born early. It usually rubs off in a few days.

Q Should I be worried that my baby has developed tiny white spots all over her face?

A No. These are called milia and are normal. They are swollen or blocked sweat and oil glands in the skin and will disappear in a few days.

Q My baby's hands and feet are a bit blue due to his circulation, how can I tell if he is cold?

A You can check his body heat by feeling his back or tummy. If they feel the same as your own, he is fine. Don't worry about hands and feet being a bit pale or blue in the early days, but if his lips or tongue look blue, tell your midwife or doctor.

Q I gave birth two weeks ago and my baby still has a large lump on the side of her head. Is this likely to be permanent?

A This is probably a cephalhaematoma – a bruise on the outside of the skull. It is harmless and will disappear in a few weeks without medical treatment.

Q My baby's breathing is irregular. He breathes very fast for a while, and then hardly at all. Is there something wrong with him?

A It is normal for a young baby to alternate between panting, fast breaths and shallow breathing. He will be about three months old before it settles down into a more steady rhythm. A newborn baby breathes twice as fast as an adult. He may also have hiccups which can look alarming as they shake his whole chest, but which don't bother him at all.

Q My newborn baby snuffles quite a lot. Does she have a cold?

A A young baby may sound snuffly in her breathing, the result of small air passages rattling with extra mucus. The nose produces this mucus to protect the delicate nasal lining from milk which she may get into her nose in the early days. It doesn't mean your baby has a cold. If she did, she would also have a temperature or seem unwell in other ways.

Q My baby smiled in her sleep when she was just two hours old. Was this really smiling or just chance movement?

A It will be some weeks before your baby really smiles at you. Early smiles like your daughter's seem to come when the baby is contented and relaxed, such as drifting into sleep, and they probably are instinctive signs of pleasure.

Movement
Reflexes

At first most of your baby's activity is by reflex, an instinctive action that happens in response to stimulation. There are some basic reflexes that are vital to life, such as the breathing reflex, the automatic emptying of the bladder and the bowel and the hunger reflex that makes her demand food. As she grows and matures, more of her behaviour comes under her control, instead of being a reflex.

Other reflexes you might notice are blinking and closing her eyes against bright light, and pulling away from a painful sensation. Some reflexes found in a newborn will disappear after a few months.

• **Sucking reflex.** Your baby will automatically suck on something placed in her mouth, and may even have practised in the womb by sucking her thumb. A good sucking reflex is important for early feeding.

• **Rooting reflex.** If you brush something against your baby's cheek, she will turn her head to that side and open her mouth. This is called the rooting reflex, and helps her to find the nipple.

• **Grasp reflex.** Your newborn baby will grip your finger if you touch her palm, and her grasp is so tight that she can support her whole body weight if you lift with one of your fingers in each of her hands. This reflex also applies to the soles of her feet, which curl up when stroked. This reflex disappears in a few months. She has to learn to grasp something on purpose.

• **Startle reflex.** If your baby is startled by a loud noise or sudden movement she will react

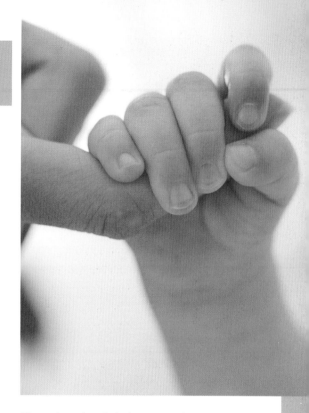

Above: A newborn baby has a natural grasp reflex and will grip on to your finger if you touch her palm.

with her whole body, in the startle or Moro reflex – flinging out her arms and legs as if to grab something, throwing her head back, opening her eyes wide and perhaps crying.

• **Crawling reflex.** If you place your newborn on her front, she will assume a crawling position since her legs are still tucked up towards her body as they were in the womb.

• **Walking and stepping reflexes.** If you hold your baby upright so her feet touch a hard surface you will see the walking reflex, where she moves her legs as if walking forwards. If her shin touches something, she will raise her leg as if to step over it. This walking reflex will disappear and is totally different from purposeful walking, which she will only master many months later.

Senses

Your baby is highly aware and sensitive, so while you are watching him and discovering all that you can about him, he is experiencing the world around him, including the part that attracts him most – you. His instinctive interest in you is his part in the bonding process, and helps get the communication between you established. From the minute he is born, your baby is using all of his senses to try and understand the world around him.

A three-day-old baby can recognize the sound of his mother calling his name.

Q What can my baby see?

A A newborn baby can see quite well, with a clear focus on objects about 25 cm (10 in) away and a more blurry image of things further off. So when you hold your baby in your arms and he looks at you intently, he is seeing you clearly. New babies show a preference for looking at a human face over any other shape, especially concentrating on the eyes. Within 36 hours after the birth, your baby can recognize the shape and outline of your own face and will prefer to look at yours rather than others. He will also follow you with his eyes as you move.

Q Is it too early to try to stimulate my baby through imagery?

A No. Babies see colours and patterns, and prefer curved lines to straight ones, three-dimensional objects to flat images. In the early weeks, they are often more attracted to patterns in black and white rather than colour. Place a hanging mobile above your baby's cot, close enough to be out of reach, but within her vision. She will love to gaze up at it.

Q What can my baby hear?

A Your newborn baby's hearing is well established, and even before birth he has been listening to your voice as well as many other noises. Your baby also instinctively responds to human speech and will subtly move his body in rhythm with speaking.

Q Why does a baby respond to his mother with higher interest?

A Because your voice is familiar, he will respond with greater interest when you speak. By only the third day of life, a baby will turn to the sound of his own mother calling his name rather than other voices. Most mothers instinctively use a more high-pitched, soft, cooing voice when speaking to their babies, and this is the voice range that a new baby hears best and prefers.

Above: Young babies are fascinated by their parents and are happy to receive lots of attention.

Q Will it spoil my baby's concentration if I talk and smile while playing with her?

A She will be momentarily distracted, but that mild negative effect is far outweighed by the pleasure she receives from your attention. And if she is happy and contented because you are showing an interest in what she is doing, she will only be encouraged to continue.

Q I feel silly talking to my baby all the time. The fact that she can't talk back and can't even understand what I'm saying to her makes me feel foolish. What should I do?

A Talk to her anyway, it's as simple as that. You may feel embarrassed prattling away to a baby who can't talk back, but reassure yourself that your use of language is good for her. Remember that she absolutely adores you and is fascinated by everything you do. So when you talk to her and she listens to the wide range of different sounds that you produce, she learns from that and eventually starts to imitate them herself. That's not silliness – that is good old-fashioned language stimulation and it only does her good.

Q What can my baby taste and smell?

A Both taste and smell are highly developed senses at the time that your baby is born. He prefers sweet tastes such as breast milk and by the time he is a week old, he can distinguish the taste and smell of your milk from that of other mothers. He is attracted to the milky smell which helps him to settle into a feed. He is also attracted to his mother's body smell. He will turn away from an unpleasant odour.

Q What can my baby feel?

A The skin and awareness of touch are the first sense organs your baby develops, and he is learning about the world around him through all the new sensations of temperature, pressure and texture. As you handle your baby, stroking, swaying, rocking, cuddling, you are getting to know each other in a unique way, since touch is in some ways the most direct language between people.

BONDING

Giving your baby the best start

At least 40 per cent of perfectly normal mothers take over a week – and sometimes months – to bond with their baby.

How soon can you expect that your excitement at seeing your new baby will become love? 'Bonding' is what we call the process of becoming devoted to your baby. So much so that you will happily give up your own sleep, take care of your baby's every need, and are prepared to put your own wishes second as long as your child needs you. Human babies need more care for a longer period than any other animal.

A strong connection between you and your baby makes her feel safe and secure, provides a solid foundation for her to build future social relationships with others, and helps her learn to trust other people. It also makes you feel good about yourself as a parent. It's a wonderful thought to know that your baby loves you and feels safe with you.

Of course, caring for your baby is demanding and you may find it hard at times. But there's lots you can do to help the bonding process. Most importantly, try to relax when you are with your baby – she will be more comfortable with you when she senses you are at ease with her.

Physical love plays a large part in her social and emotional development, too. She just adores a cuddle from you, or from any other familiar person. There is something very special about being held firmly and gently in the arms of a loving adult. The closeness, the warmth, the body contact that are all part of a caring cuddle greatly increase her contentment and confidence.

Bonding
Common questions

Q Can I expect to bond with my baby immediately after birth?

A Not necessarily. It is true that many women experience a tremendous surge of love for their baby as they first hold her in their arms, feel her soft warmth, speak to her, and see her quiet gaze taking in everything around her minutes after the birth. Some women feel in touch with their babies as individuals earlier than this, when they are still pregnant and already love them before birth. On the other hand, many women have little feeling for their baby in the beginning. It is very often two or three days before a mother feels love for her baby, and can be as long as a few months.

Q What are the reasons for not bonding immediately?

A There are many possible reasons for not having much feeling for your baby as soon as he is born. You may be physically and emotionally drained by labour and not have the energy to respond to your baby. You may feel mostly relief that the birth is over and want most of all to rest. The type of birth can affect your feelings – if it was long and difficult you might feel upset or disappointed, or if medication was used you may feel groggy yourself, or your baby may be sleepy or irritable. Other issues in your life can cloud your feelings, such as problems with your partner or other children, or money worries. Or it could just be that women react in different ways to the hormones that trigger maternal feelings, and for some the growth of that special bond is a more gradual process.

Q Should I be worried about not bonding with my baby early on? Am I failing my baby somehow?

A There is no need to worry or feel lacking as a mother if you don't feel love right away. Bonding is not a once-and-for-all event that happens just at the beginning, but a growing feeling that develops as you and your baby get to know each other. For mothers who miss out on early contact, perhaps through either mother or baby having been ill, the love that grows will be just as strong as for those who got off to a quicker start.

Q Although I felt I bonded with my baby early on, I tend to have days where I feel nothing special towards him. Is this normal?

A Occasionally a mother will have dampened feelings for her baby. It doesn't mean that you are a bad mother or that you are necessarily suffering from depression, but simply that it is taking you longer to bond fully with him.

Q Will my baby only form a close bond with the parent he spends most of his time with?

A No. There is plenty of evidence that your baby is capable of forming an emotional attachment with more than one person at a time. He can have a psychological bond with you, and also with your partner, and with his grandparents. Each of these different relationships is very special to him and each contributes in its own way to his social and emotional development.

Lifting and holding

Touching and being held is one of your baby's basic needs. He has gone from the totally surrounding contact of the womb to the frightening emptiness of space and he is reassured by being held in your arms, by movement, and feeling the familiar rhythm of your breathing and heartbeat.

As you hold him, be sure you are comfortable yourself, because if you feel tense and awkward in the position, he will too. As long as his head is supported, and he feels securely but gently held, he will relax.

Be sure to always support your baby's head when picking him up and putting him down.

When you go to pick him up, talk to him and touch him to let him know you are there, so he won't be startled by sudden movement. Raise his feet slightly with one hand to enable you to slide the other hand under his body to support his back and head. Then, with one hand under his back and head, and the other under his bottom, pick him up as you continue to talk to him. In putting him down, keep your hands supporting his head and bottom as you lie him down and then slide them out.

Left: If you always support your baby's head well he will come to no harm when you hold him.

Lifting and holding
Different positions

A variety of positions for holding your baby can give you both greater comfort, as well as providing your baby with a change of perspective.

- Used for small infants, the cradle carry lets you easily cradle your baby in one of your arms as you walk. Your baby's head is supported and he feels secure looking up at you.
- Some babies are more comfortable resting on a shoulder, and enjoy your movement as you walk about. Just make sure always to support baby's head until he can do it himself.
- Many babies like being held face down, with the comforting pressure on their tummies, and you can include soothing movement by softly swaying from side to side. Standing up, rest your baby face down along one forearm with his bottom in the crook of your elbow. Wrap your other arm around his chest to hold him close to you.

Holding your baby to breastfeed

There are a number of positions you can adopt for feeding your baby, although in the first few days, this is easier if you are sitting up. You can put a pillow on your lap to support your arm holding the baby, so that you don't have to lean forward and strain your back.

If you have had a caesarean, feeding with the baby resting on your abdomen may be uncomfortable early on. Instead lie propped up on pillows with the baby alongside you to feed, or with him turned head to toe, legs tucked under your arm.

Your baby's position is as important as yours. Hold him with his neck in the crook of your elbow and your forearm supporting his body. His back should be straight, with his head slightly higher than his body, and he should be free to turn his head or pull it back. Don't place him tummy up, because he would then have to turn his head to the side to feed – just try swallowing with your head turned. Instead, turn his whole body to face you, his belly against your belly.

If you are feeding twins, see also page 52.

Five tips on **positioning**

1 If you are sitting in a deep chair, put plenty of cushions behind you to bring you forward.
2 Put your feet on a low stool or a pile of telephone directories to make your lap flat.
3 If your baby's arms flap around a lot, try wrapping them against his body.
4 Move your baby to your breast, not your breast to the baby, otherwise you could get yourself into an awkward, uncomfortable position and your breast milk may not flow so freely.
5 If you have any doubts about getting into the correct position, see a breastfeeding counsellor before a problem develops.

Lifting and holding
Common questions

Q My baby girl seems terribly fragile and I am scared that I will hurt her when I pick her up. Is this possible?

A Although your baby seems very vulnerable, she is actually more robust that she looks. You can rest assured that you cannot harm her when you lift her, as long as you give her head the support it needs. She will have little or no control over her head for at least four weeks, so hold it firmly during this time to prevent any lolling.

Q Can I leave my baby propped sitting up when I am not holding him?

A You should wait until he is at least six weeks old and make sure that you never leave him unattended. He will not be able to support himself in an upright position, so make sure you have adequate padding to make him comfortable – pillows or cushions are ideal. Try not to have him so upright that he can fall forwards onto his face, however. You can buy a bouncing cradle to sit your baby in from this age, but an armchair or his pram will do just as well.

Q My baby often flinches when I go to pick her up. How can I prevent her being startled?

A Always make her aware of your presence before you pick her up. Touch her gently and talk to her for a few moments. Rub her on the tummy or back for a few seconds before you lift her. Always lift her slowly and gently rather than swooping her up suddenly.

Above: As well as being convenient and flexible, carrying your baby in a sling is good for bonding.

Q Our daughter is eager to pick up her newborn baby brother. She is four years old, should I let her?

A Even the smallest of siblings can hold a newborn baby, as long as you are there to offer guidance. Start by sitting your little girl in a chair that has arms. Demonstrate to her the correct way to hold the baby, stressing the need for proper head and neck support. Place the baby in her arms and encourage her to make eye contact with the baby. Do not leave the two children alone together, which may make either of them nervous and unsettled.

Positive parenting Using a sling

Q I really like the idea of using a baby sling to carry my baby – not just to the shops and back, but around the house while I do the housework. Is this a good idea?

A A baby sling can make life easier for you and is good for your baby, and there are real advantages to be gained from using one. Depending on the sling you use, you offer your child a greater range of perspectives than usually comes with a pram. For example, she can sit facing you or away from you, she can sit on your back, or to the side. Some allow the baby to lie as well as sit.

The advantages

• **Convenience and flexibility.** Carrying your baby in a sling leaves you with both hands free to carry out other tasks or manage other children.

• **Discretion.** It is easy to feed a baby in a sling discreetly while at work or eating in public.

• **Security.** If you have a baby who wants to be held all the time, this is an easy way to meet her needs while doing other things. A sling is particularly good for babies who are prone to breast refusal, as it tends to make them more alert and more likely to feed.

• **Contentment.** A baby carried in a sling for at least three hours a day tends to cry less by day or night.

• **Increased learning.** Babies see the world the way that you see it and are more involved in it, and tend to be exposed to more experiences and conversations.

• **Bonding.** Carrying your baby promotes bonding and encourages you to feel more competent as a result.

Sling safety

Although a sling offers your baby greater security by being closer to you and allows you greater flexibility to get on with other things, you should always be aware of a few basic safety rules:

• In the early days, make sure your baby's head is properly supported when in the sling. Use one or both hands to support her while you get used to it, finding out how your baby moves when you do. Once you are used to it, you will find you do not need to offer any additional support with your hands.

• If you do want to carry your baby while you do the housework, take special care in the kitchen, and do not be tempted to carry your baby like this while cooking.

• It is safe for you to eat with your baby in a sling, but avoid hot drinks.

• Always support your baby if you bend over for any reason. Bend at the knees, not at the waist, and hold your baby with one hand.

• Do not carry your baby in a sling while out riding a bike and never use the sling as a substitute for a proper seat when travelling by car.

• Read the manufacturer's instructions on the proper wearing of a sling and the maximum weight of a baby suitable for the sling.

Equipment
Common questions

When shopping to equip yourself for your new baby, you will be overwhelmed by the number of products available to you. You will be told that almost all of them are 'essential' and you may well find yourself troubling over which you really do need and which you could forgo. In actual fact, there is not very much that you have to have to start with.

Q How much equipment do babies really need? We are not well off and I am worried about overspending our budget.

A Not as much as you might think, and there are always ways to economize. You could borrow equipment from friends or relatives and most large towns have some shops that sell nearly-new clothes and equipment. But always check on the safety standards before buying. Economy is often a necessity, but treat yourself now and then. It will give you a tremendous lift.

Q What are the disadvantages in buying second-hand equipment?

A Most of the equipment available second-hand is unlikely to come with any assembly

An equipment checklist

Activity	Essential	Optional
Breastfeeding	Breast pads • Nursing bras	Breast pump • Nipple cream • Bottles with teats for expressed milk • Sterilizing equipment
Bottle-feeding	Bottles with teats • Bottle brush	Sterilizing equipment • Formula milk
Sleeping	Moses basket or cot with mattress Fitted towelling sheets Cotton blankets	Waterproof sheet • Baby monitor Cot bumper • Swaddling shawl • Sleepsuits

instructions, if relevant, and may have missing or broken parts. It may also pre-date current safety standards. For anything that directly concerns your baby's safety, such as a car seat or a sling, it is best to buy new. If you do plan to borrow or are given a piece of equipment, make sure it is from a friend or relative so that the equipment's history is known. If you are using a second-hand cot, it is advisable to buy a new mattress for it.

Q What should I look for in a pushchair?

A Pushchairs suitable from birth must be fully reclining to allow babies to lie flat until they can sit unsupported. They must have a safety harness, good brakes and a safety-locking device to ensure they do not fold up unexpectedly. They should have a deep hood to protect a baby from the wind and direct sunlight as well as a rain cover.

Q Which type of car seat should I buy?

A A newborn baby – and any under 10–13 kg (22–29 lb) will need a rear-facing car seat with an integral harness, secured in place using the car seat belt. Once the child is older and between 9 and 18 kg (20 and 40 lb) you should have a forward-facing seat, again with an integral harness, and which is secured in place by a fitting kit or a safety belt. All car seats should comply with international safety standards.

Q Is it necessary to use a baby monitor?

A A baby monitor provides a connection between you and your baby's room, even if you are in the garden. However, it is not absolutely necessary. You only really need one if you cannot hear your baby crying from the other rooms in the house, or if your baby is likely to become unduly stressed if you do not respond to his cries immediately.

Activity	Essential	Optional
Changing	Padded, waterproof changing mat Nappies, cotton wool • Baby wipes Nappy bucket	Changing unit with storage • Barrier cream Baby lotion
Bathing	Towels • Baby bath • Cotton wool Non-slip mat	Baby brush • Baby oil for massage Blunt ended scissors • Facecloth
Travel	Baby car seat • Pram or pushchair	Sling

Bathing
Early days

A new baby doesn't get very dirty, except for the face and neck from dribbled milk, and the nappy area. So a daily full bath is not really necessary. 'Topping and tailing' – cleaning the face and bottom – once or twice a day, and a more thorough wash every couple of days is sufficient.

Some babies take to being surrounded by water right from the start, while others may be unhappy and not enjoy a bath for several weeks. If your baby cries and seems frightened in the bath, there is no need to use a bath at all, but instead give a sponge bath on your lap. Or your baby may feel more secure if she has a bath with you, so she is held and supported throughout.

The 'top and tail'

For a quick cleaning of face, hands and bottom, you need warm water, cotton wool, a towel and nappy changing things. Using a separate piece of moistened cotton wool for each eye, wipe from the inner corner outwards. Wipe around each ear and the outside ear, but don't clean inside the ear or put anything in them. Wipe the rest of the face, including creases under the chin, to remove any milk, which will irritate the skin. Dry carefully by patting the skin gently. Wipe the hands and dry them. Remove the nappy and clean as in any nappy change.

Above: For a quick clean, just 'top and tail' your baby using warm water and cotton wool.

The sponge bath

For a sponge bath, you can wash your baby on a changing mat, or held on a towel on your lap. You will need a basin of water, cotton wool, facecloth, soap, shampoo (if you are washing her hair), a towel and nappy changing things. Clean your baby's face as above, then remove clothes from the top of her body while the bottom stays dressed. Gently soap the front of her body, then rinse with the facecloth and carefully pat dry. Sitting her up and leaning her on your arm, repeat on her back. If you want to shampoo her hair, wet it with the cloth, lather and rinse well with the wet cloth. Then put on your baby's vest, remove the lower clothing and clean the nappy area (see page 30). Finally wash her legs and feet and dress her.

Bathing
The full bath

To give your baby a bath, first gather everything you need, since you won't be able to leave her once you have started. You can use a plastic baby bath, which can be carried into any room, or you can use a kitchen sink or a basin in the bathroom, which may have convenient counter space. Move taps out of the way or wrap with a facecloth. You will need the same items as for a sponge bath.

Don't overfill the bath – about a hand's length of water is probably deep enough. The water should be comfortably warm, probably cooler than you would like the bath yourself. Always check with your elbow that it is about your body temperature before putting your baby in the water.

First remove the baby's nappy and clean the nappy area. Then undress her, wrap her in a towel and clean her face. A young baby gets cold quite quickly in a bath, so keep the time in the water short – you can shampoo her hair before putting her in. Hold her with her legs under your arms so that your forearm supports her back and your hand holds her head. With her head over the bath, wet, shampoo and rinse her hair.

To lower your baby into the bath, reach under her shoulders with one hand, so your forearm supports her while your hand firmly grasps her shoulder and arm on the far side. With the other hand, lift her bottom as you firmly hold one thigh, and then lower her slowly into the water. Talk to her to reassure her as she feels the water. While you maintain a grip at all times on her shoulder and arm, your other hand will be free to wash your baby. When she is clean and rinsed, lift her out onto a large dry towel and wrap her quickly. Pat dry, being especially careful in the creases.

Five tips for **bathing**

1 Make sure you have everything you need within easy reach before you begin.
2 Use a non-slip mat or small towel in the bottom of the bath to keep your baby from sliding.
3 Have a jug of hot water ready to top up the baby bath if it has cooled too much by the time you are ready for it.
4 Keep dry nappies, towel and a change of clothes handy but beyond splashing distance.
5 In the bathtub, don't pull the plug until after your baby is out of the bath, as the gurgling noise of the water might frighten her.

Bathing
Common questions

Q Although my newborn baby took to bathing readily, he hates having water poured over his head. What can I do?

A Many babies and even toddlers do not like the sensation of water being poured over their heads. You can get round this by rinsing instead with a wet facecloth, or by scooping smaller quantities of water onto his head with your hand.

Q I want to wash my baby in the bath with me. Is there a problem with this?

A Even with a very young baby, there is no problem with washing your baby in the bath with you. In fact there are benefits to gain from it. You may both enjoy skin-to-skin contact, and she may feel more relaxed in the water if you are there to hold her firmly. Remember that you will need to gauge the water temperature to suit her rather than you. For practical reasons, it is easier if your partner hands your baby to you once you are in the bath, and is there to take her from you and wrap her in a towel afterwards.

Q Can I leave my baby in a very shallow bath while I sort out her nightclothes?

A Water, however shallow, is always a source of danger, so never leave your baby unattended. Even if she cannot roll over, she is able to turn her head enough to partly submerge her face. Furthermore, you should keep a hand on her throughout the bathing process, to reassure her of your presence. Have the nightclothes ready in the bathroom or nearby bedroom before you start.

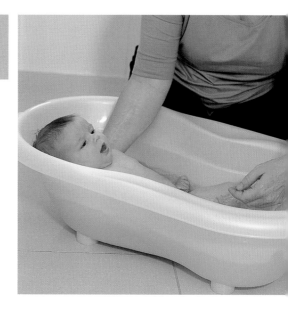

Above: You can use a plastic bath, or a sink, to give your baby his first bath.

Q My baby has cradle cap, even though I keep his hair clean. How can I clear it up and prevent it from coming back?

A Cradle cap is a common skin condition where dry scaly crusts form on the scalp, caused by overproduction from immature oil glands in the scalp. It is harmless, but unsightly, so you will probably want to remove any crusts that form. Ordinary shampoo has little effect. Never try to pick the crusts off, as you could tear the skin beneath and could cause infection. The crusts can be softened by rubbing a little baby oil or olive oil into the scalp and leaving it for several hours or overnight. Then with a fine-toothed comb you can gently remove the crusts and follow with a thorough shampoo. Washing now and then with a medicated shampoo may help prevent further cradle cap, but it does tend to come back.

Positive parenting Massage

Q I like to massage my baby as part of his bathtime routine. It keeps him warm and seems to calm him, settling him for bedtime, particularly if I keep the lights low and talk to him soothingly as I do it. Although we both find it an enjoyable activity, I would like to be sure I am doing the right thing. Is there a good or bad way to go about giving a baby a massage?

A You can learn specific techniques for massaging babies, but often there is no substitute for finding out for yourself what your baby likes. Basically this involves stroking your baby and doing what comes naturally, so you probably have nothing to worry about. You should avoid any area of broken or healing skin and leave off massaging for two or three days after your baby has been vaccinated. There are a few pointers you might find useful, and a number of established techniques for different parts of the body.

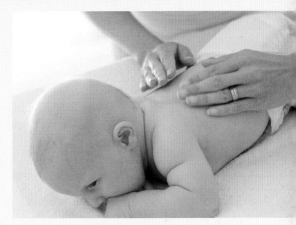

Techniques

• **Abdomen.** Massage in large circles with both hands, stroking down the centre of your baby's belly and up around the sides.

• **Back.** Stroke with both hands down the centre of his back and then up the sides. Circle with your thumbs between his shoulder blades and use your palm to rub in a circle around the small of his back.

• **Legs.** Stroke down the backs of his legs and then lightly stroke from the top of his back down his legs. On first the lower leg and then the thigh, circle up the inside and then back down along the outside.

• **Arms.** Stroke down the outer arm, and then very gently up the inner arm to his elbow.

Five steps to the **perfect massage**

1 Make sure you and your baby are both relaxed, with him lying across your lap or on the floor.

2 Massage with bare hands, and use a little vegetable oil so the strokes glide smoothly.

3 Be sure your hands are warm, and warm any oil slightly before use too.

4 Use light, steady pressure at first, and increase as you gain confidence about what your baby enjoys.

5 Make each movement slow, and repeat it several times before moving on to the next.

Changing
What is typical?

Once your baby is taking full milk feeds after the first couple of days, you can expect from six to 12 wet nappies a day. As your baby grows, she will stay dry for longer periods, because the bladder can hold more before it automatically empties. Your baby's first bowel movement produces meconium, a dark sticky tar-like substance that has been in the bowel before birth. Over the next few days, the stools gradually change to those of a milk-fed baby.

The breastfed baby

If your baby is breastfed, her stools will be soft and pasty and vary in colour from the typical mustard yellow to greenish. Because breast milk is almost completely absorbed in your baby's digestion, she may have a bowel movement only every few days. This is normal and, as long as the stool is soft, is not constipation. However, it is also not unusual for a breastfed baby to have several bowel movements a day, usually a reflex action of the gut triggered by a feed. Diarrhoea caused by gastroenteritis is rare in breastfed babies, so you need only be concerned if the stool is watery and there are other signs of illness.

Nappies what kind to use

Nappy type	Pros	Cons
Choosing nappies means weighing up the pros and cons of which are most important to you and which are most appropriate to your way of life.		
Terry	• **Cost effective:** although an initial expense, you don't have to keep buying them and they can be handed down to a later baby.	• **More fiddly to use** than disposables and some reusables.
	• **Can be folded** to fit the baby more snugly.	• **Can be bulky** to wear.
	• **Made from natural fabric** and more comfortable to wear.	• **Time consuming** in that they need sterilizing, washing and folding.
	• **Much kinder to environment** because trees are not used for their manufacture and they do not cause waste-disposal problems.	• **Also need to buy waterproof pants** and safety pins with locking heads.

The bottle-fed baby

A bottle-fed baby's stools will probably be more formed and brownish in colour, because formula milk stays longer in the gut. The baby should have at least one bowel movement per day. It is possible for a bottle-fed baby to become constipated, but again judge this more by whether the stool is hard rather than by complete regularity of motions.

Q When should I change my baby's nappy?

A A baby's urine is pale, weak and sterile. It is usually fine to leave her wet for a while as long as the nappy is not also soiled, although some babies do seem to dislike being wet, in which case you should change her. Dirty nappies need changing promptly, however, because as well as being uncomfortable, the stool is full of bacteria which act on urine to form ammonia – this irritates the skin and causes nappy rash.

Q What are reusable nappies?

A Reusable nappies are an attempt to bridge some of the gaps between traditional fabric nappies and disposables. They are cheaper and better for the environment than the usual disposables and can last more than one baby. Compared to terries they are easier to use, more attractive and offer a more snugly adjustable fit. Machine washable, they can be tumble dried, but take around 24 hours to dry naturally. Various styles are available, including all-in-one waterproof pants with cloth lining and absorbent padding, which usually have elasticated legs and adjustable Velcro waist fasteners. Although some may baulk at the effort of having to wash and dry reusables, they are the preferred choice for a growing number of parents.

Nappy type	Pros	Cons
Disposables	• **Convenient,** one-time use, with no washing. • **Come in a great variety of sizes** from low birth weight to toddler's overnight size. • **Most offer a good adjustable fit** with reusable waist tapes and elasticated legs. • **Have good absorbency,** with a one-way lining to keep a baby's skin dry.	• **Involves shopping regularly** for fairly bulky packages. • **Environmentally unfriendly,** made from plastics that take years to break down in landfill sites. • **More costly than terries and reusables** over a number of years and with more than one child.

Changing
How to do it

You need a flat, firm surface for changing your baby. A padded changing mat which sponges off easily makes the job portable, but you could use a folded towel on the floor or on top of a chest of drawers. Have to hand everything you need so that you do not have to leave your baby unattended at any point. Depending on what type of nappy you use, you will need a clean nappy, liner, waterproof and so on. You will also need cotton wool, a bowl of warm water, baby lotion or vegetable oil and possibly a barrier cream. If there has been any leakage, you will need a change of clothes.

Sensitive skin

A barrier cream is not usually necessary unless your baby has very sensitive skin or nappy rash (see page 125), in which case this can be both soothing and protective. Avoid baby powder, however, which can be breathed into your baby's lungs and tends to cake in the creases, leading to more soreness.

What to do

- Lay your baby on his back and unfasten lower clothing. Using one hand hold his ankles with one finger between to stop them rubbing together, lift his legs and slide any clothing under his back, well up out of the way.
- Unfasten the dirty nappy and if it is soiled use the unsoiled part to wipe away as much of the faeces as you can. Then fold the nappy over and lay it to one side. Water may be enough to clean the bottom, but you might find it easier to remove faeces with a little baby lotion.
- If the baby is just wet, plain water is all you need for wiping the nappy area. For a young baby cotton wool balls are softest on delicate skin, but after several weeks you could use ordinary toilet roll.
- To clean a baby girl, always wipe from front to back to prevent bacteria getting into the vagina. Never open the inner lips of the vulva to clean inside, as the vagina is self-cleaning, just clean the exposed genitals.
- For a baby boy, wipe clean around the penis and then clean the genitals. Again, clean only the exposed areas.
- When the genital area is clean, lift your baby's legs and clean the bottom. Then pat the whole area dry, paying special attention to the leg creases, which could become sore if left damp.

Changing
Common problems

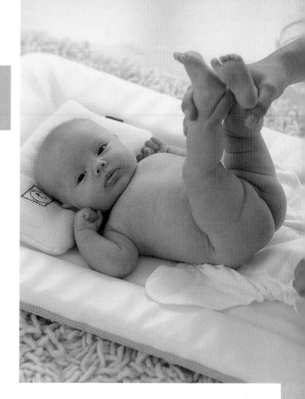

Above: A padded changing mat is ideal for nappy changes – any mess is easily sponged off.

Q My baby has very irregular stools, sometimes as infrequently as every three days, and then they are very hard. Is he constipated and, if so, what can I do about it?

A If you think your baby might be constipated, offer cooled boiled water for drinks between feeds. If he is bottle-fed, make sure you are not adding too much milk powder to bottles and, if his symptoms persist, see your doctor or health visitor to discuss any further steps you might take.

Q Whenever my baby wakes up crying, I am not sure what to do first. Should I feed her or change her?

A A young baby usually wakes up crying with hunger, in which case changing her before feeding will result in frantic crying and difficulty in settling to a calm feed. She will probably need changing afterwards anyway, so you can wait to change her later, when things have calmed down a bit.

Q Quite often, my newborn needs a change after a night feed, but whenever I give him one, it tends to make him more alert and it takes longer to get him to settle again. What can I do?

A During the night some parents like to change a baby mid-feed, so that he can doze off in the second half of the feed and won't be roused by changing afterwards. An older baby will have learned that once you are there his feed won't be far behind, and can be patient during changing first – then he can have his feed in comfort.

Q My baby hates being changed. She becomes fretful and obviously finds the whole process an ordeal. What can I do?

A Many new babies hate being uncovered, understandably since they are used to the close all-over contact of the womb. Talk to your baby as you change her and reassure her. If she becomes really distressed, just work as gently and efficiently as you are able, to complete the job quickly and get her happily dressed and held again. If she starts to kick about, making your job even more difficult, let her do so for a while: it is good exercise for her and good for the nappy area to be exposed to the air for a few minutes.

Dressing

As with all aspects of baby care, dressing your baby has, along with its practical side, the opportunity for fun. Enjoy choosing clothes, and when dressing her enjoy handling your baby and getting to know her.

Practicalities

The main purpose of clothing is to keep us warm, and keeping a baby comfortably dressed for the surrounding temperature is especially important. Your baby is able to keep her body temperature warm enough, so resist the tendency to overdress her, which is as harmful as underdressing. What babies cannot do very well is alter body temperatures quickly to compensate for rapid temperature changes around them. So your baby may need layers adding or removing as you go from room to room or as temperatures change.

You can dress your baby as she lies on her back, or sitting up on your lap. She will probably dislike being completely exposed, so wrap her in a towel if she has just had a bath; otherwise keep her partly dressed while you work on one thing at a time.

She won't like having clothes pulled over her head and drawn over her face, so be careful as you take vests and tops over her head. To remove a vest, pull the body of the vest up and stretch the armholes open as you bend her elbows to guide her arms out first. Gather up the vest, stretching the neck hole open wide. Reassure her as you slip it over the front, being careful not to touch her face. Then slide it out from under her neck. When you put a vest on, concertina it up and stretch the neck hole open. Put it on over the back of your baby's head, then stretch it wide to clear her face as you pull it forward.

To put sleeves on, reach into the sleeve from the wrong end, grasp your baby's hand and slip the sleeve on. With a stretchsuit or cardigan, you can concertina the sleeve, guide your baby's hand through and straighten the sleeve along her arm.

To put on a stretchsuit, open it up fully and lie the baby on it. Put on the arms first, then fasten the poppers for the leg fronts.

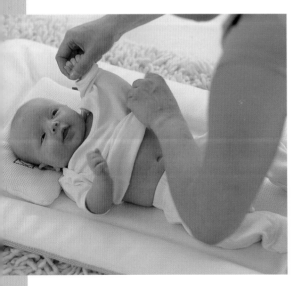

Left: Dressing your newborn is an ideal time to give her lots of love and attention.

Dressing
Common questions

Above: Socks or baby boots, rather than shoes, are all your baby needs until she is able to walk.

Q How will I know if my baby is wearing enough layers?

A In general, your baby will be comfortable in the same number of layers that you are wearing. To check that he is warm but not too hot, you can feel the back of his neck or on his body. He should feel a bit warm, but not sweaty. Don't go by hands and feet, which might be a bit cooler even when he is warm enough.

Q When I put a soft wool cardigan on my baby her skin went red. Does this mean she is allergic to wool?

A Some babies are sensitive to wool and may become irritated, but this is not an allergy. You could probably use wool if it is not directly in contact with your baby's skin and if she wears cotton beneath. Alternatively, you could choose a cardigan made from a synthetic yarn instead.

Q Should I buy shoes for my baby?

A No. Feet grow most healthily when they are not restrained in shoes and even slight distortions in the soft bones early in life can cause problems later on. Socks or bootees with plenty of room are all your baby needs until he begins to walk.

Q Is it safe for my baby to be exposed to sunshine if I cover her up with protective cream?

A Babies under six months should never be exposed to direct sunlight for any length of time, but should be well covered up by clothes and a hat with a brim. Your baby's skin does not have much pigment to protect it against the sun's radiation and will burn and be damaged very quickly. Even protective cream cannot safeguard a newborn baby and should not be used until your baby is older.

Five tips for **dressing your baby**

1 Buy three-months' size clothes rather than newborn, so they won't be outgrown as quickly.
2 Don't buy too much. You may receive baby clothes as gifts, and you can always add things later.
3 All-in-one vests with poppers between the legs keep vests from rising up and exposing your baby's midriff.
4 Take a complete change of clothes with you whenever you go out.
5 Babies like strong, bright colours so don't choose only soft pastels.

Breastfeeding

Above: Spending time learning to breastfeed when your baby is born avoids difficulties occurring later.

Breastfeeding can be physically demanding in the first few weeks: it takes time to get it right and you may feel that no sooner have you finished one feed than your baby is ready for the next. However, making up bottles is not nearly as quick and convenient as breastfeeding, especially in the middle of the night. Think of it as a skill you need to learn.

How it works

Inside each breast there are about 20 lobes, each with its own duct system. The main duct branches out into smaller ducts that end in clusters of milk-producing cells called alveoli. The ducts widen into tiny reservoirs that hold a small store of milk, then converge on the nipple. Muscle cells surround the alveoli. When the baby sucks at the breast it stimulates the nerve endings in the nipple. The nerves send messages to the brain telling it to release two hormones: prolactin and oxytocin. Prolactin stimulates the alveoli to make more milk, while oxytocin tells the muscle cells around the alveoli to contract, squeezing the milk into the reservoirs where the baby can get to it. The more the baby sucks, the more milk is produced.

Five facts about **breastfeeding**

1 Breast milk protects babies against diarrhoea, ear infections, urinary infections, eczema, diabetes, chest infections and obesity.

2 Breast milk provides babies with substances that fight infection and support their developing immune system.

3 Babies who are given nothing but breast milk for more than three months have been found to have a higher IQ than those given formula milk.

4 Breastfeeding protects women against ovarian cancer, breast cancer and hip fractures.

5 Breastfeeding uses up the fat stored during pregnancy.

Breastfeeding
Common questions

Q Why should I breastfeed my baby?

A Experts agree that breast milk is the best food for newborn babies. It is completely sterile, packed with precious antibodies and contains just the right nutrients. What is more, breastfeeding is good for women, protecting them against some serious diseases (see box).

Q What are the different types of breast milk?

A Colostrum is produced in the first few days only. It is very rich in proteins and antibodies and very concentrated. In fact, the first feed may be only a teaspoonful. Colostrum lines your baby's gut and protects him against harmful bacteria. It gradually decreases when your milk comes in on days three to five. From that point on each feed will consist of foremilk and hindmilk. Foremilk, stored in the reservoirs, comes at the beginning of a feed. There is a lot of it and it is very thirst-quenching for your baby.

Hindmilk follows the foremilk towards the end of a feed. It is rich, creamy and full of fat-soluble vitamins – like a main course after a thin-soup starter. Babies need both foremilk and hindmilk.

Q How can I tell if my baby is latching on properly?

A Often breastfeeding problems start because the baby is not attached properly to the breast. Getting this right at the beginning can avoid all sorts of difficulties. Make sure that your baby's mouth is open wide with her chin up and pressed into your breast. Her mouth should cover both the nipple and the areola, and your breast should be deep in her mouth. Check that her body is in a straight line, and that she starts sucking immediately, switching to long, deep sucks after a second or two. Make sure her nose is free from your breast so that her breathing is not hindered during the feed.

Ten tips for **breastfeeding success**

Use this checklist to make sure you are doing all you can to help breastfeeding go well.

1 Make it clear during labour – and on your birth plan – that you want to breastfeed.
2 Feed your baby as soon as possible after birth.
3 Feed on demand, day and night.
4 Learn how to attach your baby to the breast properly.
5 Get a specialist to check your feeding technique, even if you are not having problems.
6 Avoid giving your baby formula milk in hospital.
7 Do not give any bottles in the first four weeks.
8 Make friends with your local breastfeeding counsellor.
9 Get the support of your partner, parents and close friends.
10 Be patient.

Breastfeeding
How often?

Above: Breastfeeding is an excellent way to bond with your baby in the early days following birth.

Every new mother wants to know how much to feed her baby. This is not surprising since a new baby is a big responsibility and you want her to grow and be content. Unfortunately, there are no hard-and-fast rules. When you are bottle-feeding everything is measured so it is easy to see exactly how much a baby has taken. With breastfeeding, it is not so simple. Some babies want feeding every two hours; others can go four hours between feeds.

Q How much milk does my baby need?
A It is impossible to say precisely how much milk a baby needs: different babies have different needs and these change over time. A newborn baby's stomach is only the size of a large walnut or a squash ball, so he does not need much to feel full. When your milk has come in and breastfeeding is established, your breasts should produce as much milk as your baby needs. When your baby feeds it is as if he is ordering his next meal: the milk is made while he feeds and, if he is particularly hungry or his needs change, your breasts will respond by producing more as he sucks. After a month or two of breastfeeding, your breasts will learn not to make too much milk in advance and they will stop getting really full and heavy just before a feed.

Q How often will my baby feed?
A Aim to start feeding your baby immediately after birth. She will probably be sleepy for the first 24 hours and may only need to feed three times. Around days two to five, however, she may feed 10 or more times over a 24-hour period. This helps to stimulate the milk supply and to relieve engorgement, where your breasts become full, hard and uncomfortable with the new milk. By the end of the first week your baby will probably take eight feeds in 24 hours.

A feeding checklist

If the answer to all these questions is 'yes', your baby is getting enough milk.
• **Does your baby seem satisfied after a feed?**
• **Does she come off the breast of her own accord, and look 'stuffed'?**
• **Does she produce five or six wet nappies a day?**
• **Is she putting on weight?**
• **Is her skin soft and moist?**
• **Is the inside of her mouth moist and pink?**

Breastfeeding
Common problems

Q Why does my baby feed hungrily sometimes, but refuse the breast at others?

A Think before you feed. Don't automatically assume that your baby cries between feeds because he is hungry. He could be uncomfortable or bored. Check other possibilities before rushing to organize his next food intake. Also, how relaxed are you? If you are tense during feeding, he'll experience tension, too, which could put him off.

Q My baby finds it difficult to get a good mouthful of the breast and tends to come off and on during a feed. Why is this?

A It is not unusual for a newborn baby to find it difficult to grasp the idea of feeding, and it could simply be that there is not enough suction to keep her latched on. If she was born early she may need more time for her sucking action to mature. Or, in the early days, she may be feeling bruised and traumatized. Try to keep still during a feed or express your colostrum or early milk into a sterilized lidless cup, and feed your baby from this.

Q Why does my baby arch his back and scream as soon as he gets near my nipple?

A Known as breast refusal, there are several reasons why your baby might do this: he may be frustrated by a slow let-down, or a forceful let-down might be too much for him. It could be that he is unable to breathe easily while feeding, or that he has an unhappy memory of feeding. If the situation is desperate – if your baby hasn't fed at all for six to eight hours, for example – you may need to express some milk (see page 70), which can be given to him in a feeding cup. This will buy you some time to sort out the problem and prevent your breasts from getting over-full.

Q I have just started feeding my baby, and my breasts have got dramatically bigger and are quite uncomfortable. Is this normal?

A This is called engorgement and is often referred to as 'your milk coming in'. It is caused by an increased blood supply to the breasts as full milk production gets underway. This is quite normal and no cause for alarm. It usually lasts only a few days but can be very painful. There are a few remedies you can try: feed your baby as often as possible or express a little milk using a hand pump; put cold facecloths on your breasts between feeds to make the blood vessels contract. If you also experience flu-like symptoms, you could have mastitis – an infection caused by germs entering a cracked nipple, or from milk left in an over-full breast. Your doctor will tell you if you can continue to feed, and may prescribe antibiotics. You can ease the discomfort by applying a damp, hot facecloth to the sore area before each feed.

Sleep
What is typical?

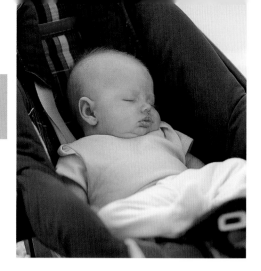

We've all heard the phrase 'sleeping like a baby', and it is true that young babies do appear to be able to sleep any time, any place, anywhere – sometimes! At others, they seem to be disturbed by the slightest noise, or show no inclination for sleep when you are about to drop on your feet. If your baby's sleeping patterns have you baffled, it is helpful to start by understanding how he sleeps.

Above: An average newborn often sleeps in blocks of four hours, both day and night.

Q How does my baby sleep?

A Everyone's sleep falls into two distinct states: REM (rapid eye movement) sleep and non-REM sleep.

REM sleep is an active state and is when we dream. It is easy to identify in your newborn: his breathing is irregular, his body twitches and his eyes dart about under his eyelids. Your baby may be easily disturbed in this state.

The non-REM stage might also be described as 'deep sleep': it is the state in which we are most restful, lying quietly with regular heart rate and breathing patterns. There is very little dreaming. In babies and young children, non-REM sleep is referred to as 'quiet sleep'. In this state, your baby will breathe deeply and lie very still. Occasionally you may see him make fast sucking motions, and now and then a sudden body jerk.

Five facts about sleep

1 It is impossible for a newborn baby to get too much sleep.

2 Young babies spend proportionately more time in REM sleep than adults, making them lighter sleepers and more easily disturbed.

3 Young babies wake several times during the night, but by the age of two months they are able to soothe themselves back to sleep.

4 70 per cent of babies are said to sleep from midnight to 5am by the age of three months.

5 Most experts agree that by six months almost all infants are physiologically capable of sleeping through the night.

Q How much sleep does my baby need?

A On average, a newborn baby sleeps for 16–17 hours per day, often in blocks of four hours spread across both night and day. This drops to 13–14 hours per day by the time she is six months old. A newborn does not know the difference between night and day, hence the need for you to find ways of encouraging your baby to sleep more at night.

Postive parenting **Sudden Infant Death Syndrome**

Q Like many first-time mothers, I am petrified that my baby might fall victim to a cot death. I know that the causes of this are largely unknown, but I would feel comforted if I thought there was anything I could do to reduce the risk to my baby. What do you recommend?

A Although in some cases cot death, or Sudden Infant Death Syndrome (SIDS), may be the result of an accident, an infection or congenital abnormality, most times the reasons remain unexplained. What is known, however, is that babies under the age of six months are the most vulnerable and the Foundation for the Study of Infant Death has outlined safety guidelines that you can follow to minimize risk.

Strategies

• Put your baby to sleep on his back on a flat mattress, without a pillow. If he rolls over during the night, turn him onto his back again, but don't feel that you need to keep checking him. When he can roll from back to front and front to back, continue to put him to sleep on his back, but then allow him to find his own position.

• Keep his head uncovered. Position your baby feet-to-foot – that is, with his feet at the bottom of his bed. This will minimize the chances of him worming his way down the bed, under the covers.

• Use sheets and blankets instead of a duvet. Make sure they are firmly tucked under your baby's shoulders so that he can't wriggle underneath them.

Vital statistics

Medically known as Sudden Infant Death Syndrome (SIDS), the words 'cot death' strike fear into every parent's heart. Although the number of babies claimed by SIDS is very small, the rates do vary around the world – from 1 in 4,000 infants in Finland and the Netherlands, 1 in 2,000 in the UK, to 1 in 700 in the United States and 1 in 400 in Italy.

• Babies find it difficult to regulate their body heat, so keep your baby's room at 16–18°C (61–64°F). At this temperature, he should be dressed in a nappy, vest and babygro, and have two to three light blankets for cover.

• Monitor the temperature of his room with a nursery thermometer. Position it near your baby's head, so that you are recording the temperature around his bed rather than on the other side of the room.

• Do not put your baby's bed next to a radiator – he may overheat. Similarly, do not put his bed up against a window – he may be in a draught during the winter, and may overheat if put down for a daytime nap in the summer.

• When checking to see if your baby is too warm or too cold, always feel his tummy or the back of his neck rather than his hands or feet, as these can appear icy even when he is too hot. Add or take off layers as appropriate.

• Do not let anyone smoke near your baby.

• Do not allow yourself to fall asleep with your baby on the sofa.

Sleep
Night feeds

If you have taught your baby that nights are for sleeping, she should be spending most of the night asleep. And if you have also taught her to settle herself when she stirs in the night, she is far more likely to drift happily back to sleep than to cry out for reassurance. So, you should find that the time between your baby's night wakings gradually increases automatically, as she is able to slip naturally into the next stage of her sleep cycle. This does not allow for the fact, however, that your newborn baby wakes once, maybe more, during the night for a feed.

Above: For the first few months your baby may wake regularly in the night for a feed.

Q Why does my baby wake for feeding at night?

A For the first few months at least, your baby's tummy simply doesn't hold enough to sustain him through the night, so he has to wake for feeds. However, as he grows, you should find the time between feeds gets progressively longer and you may even find he suddenly drops one of his night feeds of his own accord.

Q Should I always feed my baby when she wakes up?

A Although it is an easy way to settle your baby, if you always feed her when she wakes, you might find that she ends up doing so from habit, rather than because she is hungry. Before you rush to give her milk, check whether there may be other reasons why she is awake. Is she wet or dirty? Is she too hot or too cold? Is she suffering from wind? If you only feed your child when you are sure she needs it, you should find the time between her night feeds increases, until from around six months old she abandons them altogether.

Q How can I help my baby to sleep uninterrupted once his tummy enables him to go all night without a feed?

A With the right sleep training, most babies develop a clear 'night sleep' of five or six hours uninterrupted sleep from just a few weeks old. Once they have been established, you should try to avoid feeding your baby again during these 'core' sleep hours.

Sleep
Common problems

Q My baby is very wakeful throughout the night leaving me completely exhausted during the day. What can I do?

A A young baby who is awake at night for more than a quick feed will have tired parents. It could just be that he wants company during the night. You could try bringing him into your bed – your presence may calm him and as a result you may get more sleep.

There is nothing to worry about if you have a wakeful baby. Instead, just work on how you can manage. Rest when you can in the day and go to bed early. However, because daytime rest won't make up for the broken nights, try and share the load with your partner. Take turns with night feedings. If you are breastfeeding, express and store some milk so that your partner can give a nighttime bottle of breast milk while you get a little more sleep. Losing sleep with a baby is never easy, but having enough support can keep you from sinking into constant fatigue or depression.

Q Although my three-week-old baby goes to sleep quite easily, it seems just five minutes before he is awake again and crying for me. What can I do?

A Check the bedroom for comfort, as it might be that your baby is just uncomfortable. The room temperature should be pleasantly warm – neither too hot nor stuffy; if you leave a light on at night-time, make sure it is subdued; and try to keep background noise to the absolute minimum.

Q My baby wakes as early as five in the morning and will not go back to sleep. Should I stop her sleeping during the day?

A Very young babies cannot tell the difference between night and day. If you prevent her sleeping when she needs to, it will just make her overtired and she'll find it more difficult to get to sleep later on. However, you can try timing her naps so that she learns to sleep less during daylight hours. Try also to avoid letting her have a long nap before her last feed of the day.

Q My baby is inconsolable at night and I try gently rocking her to sleep, which works for my nephew, but it has no effect. What else can I do?

A Every baby is different and what works for your sister's baby might not work with yours. Some babies nod off when rocked gently or in response to soft background noise, others when wrapped snugly in a blanket or stroked gently. Be prepared to try out a variety of techniques when trying to soothe your baby to sleep (see pages 78–83). You will eventually find a method that suits her.

An evening routine that marks the change from daytime can help make nights more peaceful.

Crying
What is typical?

If this is your first baby and you have had no close contact with any new babies before, you may not know what to expect in terms of crying behaviour. Babies are as individual as adults, so you cannot expect your baby to behave in the same way as any other. However, although babies do cry most frequently during the first three months, this does not mean that you should put up with constant crying or niggling.

and months before he learns the difference between whether he is feeling hungry or cold or frustrated, and learns that you can and will help him. As he discovers other ways to communicate with you, his reliance on crying becomes less. How you respond to his cries from the beginning is part of the process of teaching him to trust that he will be all right, that you will respond to him and that he needn't cry so much.

A natural instinct

Within a couple of days of your baby's birth you will recognize his cry and your urge is to do something to get the crying to stop. This is partly due to your concern for your baby's well-being and happiness, but also to a chemical reaction in your body, which spurs you into action. Your baby's cry is a powerful stimulus, which causes stress hormones to be automatically released into your bloodstream. The effect of this is to increase your blood pressure, breathing rate and muscular tension. This feels uncomfortable and the more the baby cries, the worse you feel.

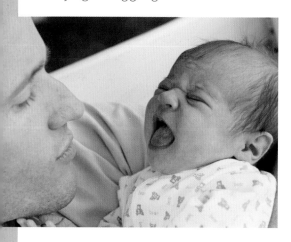

Above: Learning to interpret your baby's crying takes time, but will eventually come.

Crying is a new baby's only way of telling you that something is wrong. He doesn't know exactly what the problem is, but only that he is uncomfortable or in pain and so he expresses how he feels. It will be weeks

As your baby begins to identify his own needs and comforts, and you have had a few weeks' experience of getting to know him, you may find you are able to match a particular cry with a particular meaning; for instance, a cry that steadily builds up when he needs to be fed will be different from his more urgent, piercing cry when he is physically uncomfortable (see also page 84).

Crying
Common questions

Q How much or often can I expect my newborn baby to cry?

A Between birth and three months, your baby is likely to cry for a total of two hours a day (though not all at once).

Q Is it possible to tell why my baby is crying at this early age?

A A new baby doesn't differentiate her cries very much, but as she gradually learns that you come when she cries, it will become more as if she is calling you. Then you will hear the difference if she gives a really frantic cry of urgent hunger or pain, or a grizzly, tired cry. There are other clues as well such as facial expressions, whether her body feels tense or relaxed, and how she is breathing. You will also have some idea of what she is crying for because you know what to expect from her routine.

Q How can I help my crying baby?

A One thing you can do is try to recognize that there are times when she is likely to be more upset and to take action that might prevent her crying in the first place. For example, it is quite common for breastfed babies to want more frequent feeding in the evening, because that is when the milk becomes more concentrated and satisfying. Try to anticipate when your baby might soil her nappy – following a feed, for example – and don't let her go too long between changes. Some babies cry for two hours or more in the evening and others scream a lot, which could indicate colic and

Above: Although it can be hard to cope with a crying baby, this phase will not be permanent.

you should seek appropriate advice (see pages 46–49). If your baby is bored, she may need some more stimulation. Distract her with a favourite toy or one that makes a calming sound.

Q Is it possible to spoil a baby by responding too quickly to his tears?

A Leaving a baby to cry does not discourage a baby from crying. If he is left, he becomes more unhappy and so cries more. He becomes unsettled and insecure because he expects no help to arrive when he needs it most. As he grows older he is likely to be less content and lack confidence, and so will continue to fuss and cry as a result. Conversely, one study found that babies whose parents respond quickly when they cry in the first three months of life cry less often, and for shorter periods, than those whose mothers delay or ignore crying. By four months, the promptly-seen-to babies are less likely to cry persistently, and at one year of age they are more independent and communicate in ways other than crying.

Crying
Common problems

Q I feel as if my baby cries all the time, no matter what I do or say to try to calm her. Is this going to go on forever?

A Reassure yourself that this is a temporary phase. Babies cry most during the first three months and it usually eases off markedly after the age of one year. Take the long-term view and try some of the strategies for coping (see opposite) during the worst of your experiences.

Above: Try to remain calm when soothing your baby – she will pick up if you are tense.

Q My baby cries every night before she goes to sleep. Is this normal and should I be doing something about it?

A Many babies cry before they go to sleep, and many parents find it difficult to know how to handle this. As a parent you are best placed to judge whether your baby really is in distress or whether his cries will subside into slumber. Although this is hard during the first few weeks, you will get to know your baby soon enough.

Q I spend a large portion of the day alone with my baby. By night-time I am shattered and fear that I cannot cope with her crying. What can I do?

A You should get help. If possible, let another person spend time with your crying baby. This could be your partner, a friend or a relative, as long as it is someone you can trust. You'll feel refreshed and more able to cope after you've had a break, even a short one.

Q It is all too easy to feel guilty that my baby cries so much. Could it be that I am an inadequate parent?

A Remember, it is quite normal for newborn babies to cry for as much as two hours a day – it is their only form of communication. The fact that he cries every night does not mean you are an inadequate parent. As long as you can eliminate the typical sources of distress, then his tears are probably not related to the way you care for him.

Positive parenting **Coping with crying**

Q I spend hours trying to discover what is making my baby cry, but just when I think I have located the problem and dealt with it, she starts again. The whole ordeal is totally exhausting, and I can feel my temper rising. What can I do when it all gets too much?

A Because your baby's crying winds you up so powerfully, you may feel ready to snap when it doesn't stop. It is an unusual parent who never feels at breaking point, so don't blame yourself. What is important is recognizing the feeling and stopping before you lash out at your baby. If you feel angry at your baby's crying it is time to put her down safely in her cot and take a break. You cannot keep her calm when you are angry and upset yourself. If possible, hand over to a partner, ring a friend or go to a neighbour. If there is nobody you can go to, try a few of the following suggestions:

Strategies

• **Put on some music with headphones or use some earplugs.** These dull the sound of the crying and make it more bearable.

• **Go for walks.** The exercise will make you feel better and the jolting motion of the pram may soothe your baby.

• **Keep a diary recording times and duration of crying,** what you tried and how your baby reacted: over time you can see whether there is a pattern and you can tell when things are starting to improve.

• **Carry your baby in a sling.** This may not reduce crying but it means that you can stay close to your baby and rock her while being free to do other things.

• **Swaddle your baby.** Some babies find it very comforting to be wrapped tightly in a blanket, perhaps because it reminds them of being enclosed in the womb.

• **Let your baby suck your finger or give her a dummy.** Sucking is often very comforting for colicky babies.

• **If you are breastfeeding, cut out coffee, tea and cola for two weeks.** See if it makes a difference.

Left: To calm your crying baby try offering your little finger for her to suck.

Colic
What is it?

There is no clear agreement about the causes of colic or how to prevent it. In regular crying spells, which may last for hours and occur most often in the evenings, the baby will appear to be in intense pain as he screams. Other signs that he has colic include drawing up his knees and passing wind often. He will seem desperate to feed but may reject the breast after only a few seconds resulting in him becoming even more distressed. Or he may feed, fall asleep briefly and then wake up with more screaming. Although the crying spells are extreme, causing parents much anxiety, the baby in all other respects is thriving normally.

One opinion is that colic is caused by the immature gut going into spasm, perhaps triggered by sensitivity to a particular food. On the other hand, food is discounted as the cause because the crying tends to come at one time of day and not regularly after all feeds. It may instead be the result of tension – a sort of overdrive of your baby's immature nervous system – which would explain why it comes in the evening when you and your baby are both most tired and prone to stress.

Q When does colic start, and does it affect every baby?
A It is estimated that one or two babies out of 10 will have colic. Colic does not normally start until the baby is about a week or two old but it can last for three months, sometimes more. It may then disappear in weeks or it may develop into a good-day/bad-day pattern before it stops. A number of babies still suffer from colic at four, five or six months.

Q Could breastfeeding be to blame?
A It may be hard to believe that there is a feeding problem if your baby is piling on the weight and your nipples are not sore, but in some cases colic can be caused by poor positioning, leading to something called temporary lactose overload. This is more likely if your baby produces a lot of green, watery nappies and passes a lot of wind – top and bottom. Lactose is a sugar in breast milk that needs to be broken down by an enzyme called lactase. If it is not broken down, it passes into the lower bowel, where it is fermented by bacteria, producing gases and lactic acid (hence the wind and green nappies).

Q What may be the answer if lactose overload is the problem?
A The solution may be to slow down the rate at which milk passes through the baby's gut, thus allowing time for the lactose to be broken down. The way to do this is to make sure your baby gets a good amount of the fat-rich hindmilk (see page 35) at each feed. If you

Above: Rubbing your baby's back while he lies in your lap can help to alleviate the pain of wind.

have been offering both breasts at each feed, it is possible she is just getting foremilk – the watery milk that comes first. Increase the time that she has on the first breast to ensure that the hindmilk has come through.

Q How should I deal with wind?
A The idea is to get your baby to bring up the wind and burp. You can do this by sitting him on your lap with the palm of one hand on his stomach, supporting his head between your outstretched thumb and first finger, and with your other fingers under his arm. It is the slight pressure of your hand on his tummy that should dislodge the wind, but you can press or rub his back with your hand. Alternatively you can lay him over your shoulder and rub his back while his tummy is pressed against your shoulder or lay him down along the length of

your arm or in your lap – you might want to save this until you feel more confident handling your baby. Whichever position you use, have a muslin square or terry nappy handy – burps tend to bring squirts of milk with them.

Q Could wind be the cause of colic?
A It is unlikely that wind in itself is the cause of the problem, although there is no doubt that a screaming baby will swallow a lot of air, which can make the problem worse because the air gets trapped in the loops of the intestine during spasm. Your baby will certainly feel better after a good belch.

Q What should I do if my baby gets wind regularly?
A If you think your baby has a lot of wind, and are breastfeeding, it is possible that your baby is taking in air as he feeds because he does not have a good latch on the breast. A change of position may be all that is needed to remedy the situation. Also, avoid using bottles: bottle-fed babies tend to get more wind as they suck on the teat.

Wind

When we say a baby has wind, what we really mean is that he has swallowed some air, which is now trapped like a little bubble in his tummy or digestive system, causing him pain. This is not the same as colic and dealing with it should be a fairly straightforward affair. Having said that, some babies seem to struggle with it and have more problems than others.

Colic
Common problems

Q My baby's symptoms are so severe, I cannot believe the condition is not causing her harm. Will her colicky attacks really have no effect on her development?

A Despite much crying, doubling up and going red in the face, in most cases colic is not a serious condition. In fact research shows that babies with colic continue to thrive well, eating properly and gaining weight normally. The real problem with the condition is the effect it has on your home life. The stress and anxiety of parents and other family members who find it difficult to cope with the constant crying cause tension. It is important for everyone to take a break from it once in a while.

Q I have a history of lactose intolerance in my family and although I do not suffer myself, I am worried that my baby might. What can I do?

A You could try eliminating cow's milk from your diet. If your baby is not able to digest lactose very well, this could be partly to blame for his colic.

Q My baby is four weeks old and has just started to suffer from colic. This has completely thrown my evening routine with her and she has tremendous trouble getting off to sleep at night. Even when she does, she doesn't stay asleep for long. What can I do?

A Unfortunately, while your baby has colic you really just have to go with the flow and accept disrupted evenings for a few weeks. When she does finally settle at the end of the evening, you can continue with your chosen sleep programme to encourage her to sleep well for the rest of the night. When she outgrows the colic, you can also start moving to earlier bedtimes and a more structured routine.

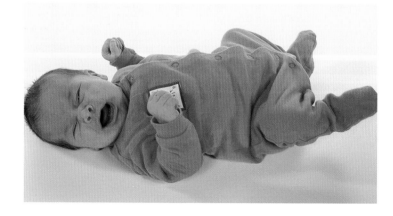

Right: A colicky baby will seem to be in extreme pain as he cries, often for several hours at a time.

Positive parenting **Coping with a colicky baby**

Q My baby suffers from colic every evening. At roughly the same time each night she cries hard, pulling her knees up to her abdomen. It is always the same and she is very reluctant to settle or feed. I realize colic is a bit of a mystery, but is there nothing I can do?

A Not much is known about colic and some experts even refute its existence. However, that's not very helpful when your baby suddenly turns into a screaming machine every evening! Although most babies grow out of it within a couple of months, there are a few ways in which you might be able to help.

What to do

Contact the doctor if there are other signs of ill-health such as vomiting or diarrhoea, or if the crying is different from normal crying. Once the baby is pronounced healthy, work out a colic strategy based on what works. If you need support, join a baby-sitting circle, explaining the problem when you join, so you can get out one evening a week with your partner.

Strategies

• **One theory is that colic is caused by a build-up of wind during the day.** Giving your baby an anti-wind treatment, such as gripe water, may help.

• **Positioning her so that she has gentle pressure on her stomach** (for example, resting her over your shoulder or face down on your lap) and patting her back may also help relieve some of the pain.

• **If your are breastfeeding, it may be worth trying to eliminate foods** that may be responsible from your own diet, such as chocolate, cabbage, onions, green peppers or milk products.

• **If your baby is bottle fed, consult your doctor** about whether a change of formula might help, although this is unlikely.

• **Try to avoid tension in the evening** by giving your baby a calming bath or a massage in the afternoon, or by going out for a walk.

• **Remove some of the frustrations of your early evening routine** by doing any meal preparations earlier in the day so there is no pressure later on.

• **Build up your energy** by having a proper lunch and a nap in the afternoon.

• **Try to soothe your baby,** making sure all your movements are relaxed and slow or place her near continuous noise or vibrations from household appliances such as the washing machine or vacuum cleaner.

Managing your time

Several things are lost when you become a mother. They may be replaced by other things that are equally satisfying, or more so, but that doesn't mean you won't have some doubts or fears about letting them go. One thing you have to let go of is your image of yourself as a childfree woman, taking on instead an image as a mother. 'Mother' means different things to different people, but you might have to reassure yourself that you can still be young, interesting, sexy and intelligent. You still need to value yourself as an individual, not just as a mother, so before long it becomes important to make sure you have time for your own interests and relaxation.

Another adjustment that can be difficult to make is to adjust to 'child time'. It is increasingly difficult to plan your day and stick to it, knowing when you'll be working and when you have free time. You are now on 24-hour call and you cannot predict exactly when you will be needed from one day to the next. Many women end up trying to do several things at once, but rarely get all of them finished. It's natural that you will sometimes find it frustrating, and feel distracted and inefficient. It doesn't help to try to impose a routine at this stage, because your baby cannot tell the time. Gradually life will fall into more of a rhythm, but it is never fixed, since your baby's needs will continue to change as he grows and develops. Flexibility is the key and you may come to appreciate a pace of life that responds to present needs, and to feel good about your ability to keep several things in your mind at once.

Strategies

- **Don't expect too much of yourself in the beginning.** Sometimes a woman who gives up work to stay at home with a baby feels she must prove herself by being a 'superwoman' – keeping a perfect house and producing delicious meals, while dealing single-handedly with every aspect of life with a baby. Instead, accept any help offered and take your time about becoming more organized and efficient.
- **Let your household standards drop so you can concentrate on the more important task of looking after yourself and your baby.** As long as the essentials are done, it doesn't really matter if there is dust on the mantelpiece or there are dishes still in the sink. Most of us have certain jobs that need to be done before we can relax, while others we can happily put off until later. Work out what your personal priorities are and do the very minimum you can feel happy with.

Managing your time
Common questions

Q I feel nervous about being responsible for my baby. There are so many things I don't know and I might get something wrong. Then people give me different advice – so who should I believe?

A There is no end to the different views on childcare and none of them are all right or all wrong. Different things work for different parents and babies and only you can find out what suits you and your baby best. You can listen to advice, but then trust your own instincts and believe your own experience. Don't be afraid of trial and error – serious mistakes are unlikely if you use basic common sense, and babies are sturdier than you think. No parent ever gets everything right but we do the best we can, and luckily that's good enough for happy, healthy children.

Q I am a single parent, and finding it hard to manage everything. Do you have any suggestions?

A Being on your own with a baby can mean extra pressures due to lack of money, loneliness and the amount of work and responsibility. Look for help from anyone willing to lend a hand and give you a break. You could contact single parents' organizations to see if there is a lone parents' group in your area, or perhaps get one started. As well as the moral support of talking things over with other parents in the same situation, you might exchange childcare to give you free time.

Q I expected to have a lot of time when my baby would sleep during the day or be contented, but instead he's awake most of the day and has to be carried or held all the time. Isn't this unusual?

A It's hard when the reality of life with your baby doesn't match your expectations. Parents who have a firm idea of what to expect, sometimes based on what their first baby or another baby they have known was like, actually find it harder than those who just take it as it comes. Every baby is different and while some have a placid temperament others are more demanding and need to be held and comforted more. The amount of sleep a young baby needs varies a lot, too. Try not to think about an average baby, or an ideal baby, but focus on your baby as an individual and what he needs.

Q If I leave my baby with my mother, could she get attached to her instead of me?

A A baby doesn't have to make just one bond, but can be attached to two or more people. Often the closest bond is to the mother, but the baby can also be attached to others who will do when the mother isn't there. It's nice if your baby does become attached to your mother, because that means she is being well cared for, but as long as you are there for important times like bedtime and your daughter knows she can trust your love, your mother won't be taking your place in her eyes.

TWINS

Coping with multiple births

Families with twins (and even triplets, quadruplets and so on) are becoming increasingly common.

Since the early 1980s, there has been a steady rise year-on-year in multiple births. This is when infertility treatment became more widespread, and births became safer because most are diagnosed early by scan. Although the prospect of dealing with twins or triplets may seem daunting at first, there is no reason why you cannot cope just as well as you would with a single child.

Strategies for feeding twins and triplets

Breastfeeding more than one baby is demanding and is very time-consuming – unless you can manage to breastfeed two babies at the same time. Avoiding formula should keep your babies healthier, which will be time-saving in the long run. In practice, many mothers of multiples use a mixture of bottles and breast – but if you are determined to give your babies nothing but breast milk it can be done.

• Get to know your local breastfeeding counsellor and enlist her help both before and after the birth – ask for advice on positions for double feeding and expressing.

• Tell everyone (and yourself) that you are going to concentrate on the babies and nothing else for the first month.

• Get help with housework, shopping and cooking so you can achieve this.

• Breastfeed early and express milk if you need to be separated from one or more babies in the early days.

• Avoid dummies early on so that you build up a good supply of milk.

• Hire or buy a double pump so that you can express milk for other people to give in bottles after the babies are a month old. In this way you can get a rest at times!

Twins, triplets and sleeping

Although their sleep may initially be more disturbed than that of other newborns, getting twins (or more) to sleep need not be any more difficult. All the sleep strategies outlined in this book can be applied just as successfully to multiple-birth children (see pages 78–83). The one big difference, of course, is that the babies may disturb one another. Most of the time this won't happen – just as siblings of different ages can usually share bedrooms without waking one another.

Behaviour

Behaviour problems are common in twins and particularly in male identical twins. A twin whose behaviour improves when they are alone with one parent may be sending a signal that they need more one-to-one attention, and the routine needs to be reorganized to allow each twin to spend some time alone with a parent every day.

Twins, especially identical twins, need to know that they are different. From a very early age they need to look different from each other – different clothes and individual hairstyles can set them apart. Other people should be encouraged strongly to call each child by their names, and not to refer to them as 'the twins', or 'the boys'. As they mature it becomes increasingly important that they have some private space, even if it is only the corner of a room.

Getting support

There may be times when looking after two or more children of the same age becomes too much. Try to get as much help as possible. There are charities that provide help for new parents, particularly those with two or more babies. The multiple-birth organizations may also be able to put you in touch with a parent who has been through a similar experience – just talking through your situation can be a big help.

Three reasons why twins and triplets may not sleep

1 They are often born prematurely, which means they require feeding even more often than other newborns.
2 They are more likely to spend time in special-care baby units, which means they get used to being touched and nursed at frequent intervals.
3 They are more likely to have different carers at night – even if they are breastfed, your partner may change their nappies because of the difficulties of dealing with two babies at once – and it can take them a while to get used to the different ways in which they are handled.

NATURE OR NURTURE?

Is personality predetermined or learnt?

As a child grows and his personality begins to become apparent, it is natural to be curious about the source of his individuality.

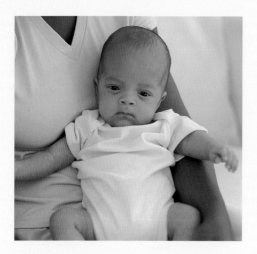

The nature/nurture debate is also known as the heredity/environment debate. The term 'nature' applies to all the characteristics and qualities that a child is born with. Many physical characteristics are inherited from parents, predetermining some aspects of a child's development. For instance, the colour of his eyes and hair, his typical height and even his natural body weight.

The 'nature' debate argues that, since many physical qualities are inherited, it stands to reason that so are many psychological characteristics. That's why, for instance, children often have the same personality and mannerisms as their parents. If physical traits can be inherited, perhaps the whole pattern of a child's development is also inherited in the same way.

In contrast, the term 'nurture' suggests that many characteristics are influenced by the child's environment, particularly by the way he is brought up within the family. For instance, bright parents make their baby's stimulation a priority and therefore tend to

have bright children; and sensitive parents teach their children to behave in a similar caring way when mixing with others. Some take this argument further, claiming that no personal characteristics whatsoever are inherited and that every child is born a blank slate waiting for his development to be written by experience.

Your position regarding the nature/nurture debate affects your interactions with your baby. If you believe in the 'nature' argument, then you'll assume that his inborn characteristics, learning abilities and personality determine what sort of person he becomes, and that your own individual input as a parent does not have much to do with it. If you believe in the 'nurture' argument, however, you'll assume that his development is dependent entirely on the way you raise him and the level of stimulation he experiences during his childhood. You might take a middle-of-the-road approach, recognizing the importance of both your baby's innate talents and also the environment in which he is raised.

Interaction

Few child development professionals adopt either extreme approach. Instead, it is widely recognized that while every child has potential based on his genetic structure at birth, the true influence on his development is the interaction that takes place between his inherited abilities and the environment in which he is brought up. The nature/nurture debate nowadays centres on the relative contribution that each influence makes to your baby's growth and progress. There is evidence to support both sides.

Studies of twins, who were adopted at birth and raised by different families, have found striking similarities between the personality and abilities of each twin despite their individual upbringing. In addition, similarities are also found between adopted children and their natural parents, even though the children were raised by others. This adds considerable weight to the inherited view of child development.

Yet there are many instances where even those physical characteristics which are undoubtedly inherited can be directly influenced by the environment. To take height as an example, a child may have the genetic potential to grow to a certain height but he is unlikely to achieve that if he is under-nourished during the pre-school years. Other factors such as health, poverty and family values have a similar impact. Evidence shows that children who are raised in a family where violence is the norm are more aggressive in their interactions with peers.

Your baby's development is a combination of all these factors and the way they interact at each point in his life. Parenting, therefore, is not about stepping back while passively waiting for the genetic plan to unfold. What you do with your growing baby makes a real difference to his long-term development.

How can I influence nurture and nature?

• **Take a hands-on approach.** Nobody can quantify exactly what impact you have on your baby, but common sense and everyday experience tell you that he is affected greatly by the way you behave towards him.

• **Have reasonable expectations.** While you can affect your baby's progress, you are unlikely to see instant changes in his development. Expect him to progress in small, steady steps and you won't be disappointed.

• **Treat him individually.** Your baby may have the same parents and the same family environment as his siblings, but he reacts to these in his own unique way. Development is not entirely predictable, varying from child to child.

• **Take pleasure from his achievements.** Whether arising from 'nature' or 'nurture', savour all of your baby's increased abilities and skills. This makes him feel good about himself and motivates him to continue to progress.

Health issues
Initial checks

All babies are given a thorough examination following birth. The doctor or paediatrician measures the circumference of the head and checks the fontanelles (soft spots), eyes and mouth. He or she will also examine the abdomen and listen to the baby's heart and breathing.

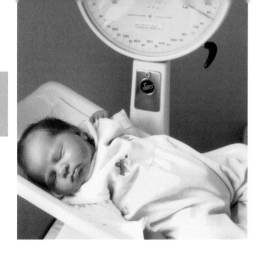

Above: Early checkups include basic functions such as breathing, weight and physical condition.

Your baby's hips will be examined to check the condition of the joints. Many babies have 'clicky' hips because the ligaments are loose as a result of pregnancy hormones the baby was exposed to in the womb. But a few babies are at risk of developing an abnormally shallow hip socket (congenital dislocation of the hip), which if not treated leads to a permanent limp and difficulty in walking. The doctor will also examine the baby's genitals, and in boys will see whether both testes are in the scrotum. The testes are formed in the abdomen and usually come down into the scrotum before birth. If the testes are not in the scrotum, the doctor will make a note to keep an eye on it.

Q What is the Apgar score?

A As soon as your baby is born, she is given a quick check to see that his breathing is established and there are no immediate problems. At one minute after the birth, and again at five minutes, an Apgar score is recorded as a measure of how well your baby is managing the transition to life outside the womb. This is a quick method of giving up to two points each for heart rate, muscle tone, body colour and reflex response. It should be noted that it is not unusual for a newborn baby to be drowsy initially, if the mother was given painkillers during labour.

Q What is the Guthrie test?

A This is where, during the first week after birth, the midwife takes a drop of blood by pricking your baby's heel. The blood sample is then examined for very rare genetic conditions where the baby is unable to break down nutrients or is unable to use them properly in the body. Other tests may also be done on the blood sample, to detect conditions such as thyroid malfunction and cystic fibrosis.

Q Why are newborn babies given vitamin K?

A Soon after birth, you will be offered vitamin K for your baby, either by injection or in liquid drops. The vitamin is important in blood clotting and is usually given routinely. It is probably more important for pre-term babies or babies who have had a difficult delivery, but discuss it with your doctor if you have any questions.

Health issues
Special care

Most babies born at full term are fit and well. But in some circumstances, a baby needs special medical care from birth. Babies who weigh under 2.5 kg (5 lb) are considered small, and may need help and careful supervision in the early days.

Some babies, even though fully mature, are small simply because their parents are small. But most small babies are either of low birth weight for their age because not enough nourishment reached the baby through the placenta, or premature, where the baby is born early and some of the body systems are not yet mature enough to function effectively.

In both cases a baby may have difficulty in maintaining body heat, and because of low sugar reserves she must be fed frequently and blood sugar levels must be monitored. Particularly with premature babies, there may be breathing problems so the baby will be put on a ventilator, which takes over breathing by gently inflating the lungs. The baby will also be placed in an incubator for extra warmth, as she loses heat so fast. In some cases, it may be possible for a special care baby to be in an incubator beside your bed. But a baby who is quite ill or needs extra help will need to stay in a special care nursery. There, the monitoring equipment and expert staff can keep a close eye on your baby and adjust treatment as necessary.

Q What causes premature birth?
A The cause of some premature births is still not understood, but it is possible that these are triggered by a common vaginal infection, bacterial vaginosis. In some pregnant women the membranes break before term, or the foetus begins to grow too slowly or stops growing altogether, and the doctor decides that they would thrive better outside the uterus. A baby may also need to be delivered early if the placenta is not functioning properly or if the mother has pre-eclampsia.

About 1 baby in 10 in the United Kingdom needs extra medical care immediately after birth.

Q How does prematurity affect a newborn child?
A All babies are different, but a baby born after 36 weeks can usually be treated like a normal term baby and will not need special care. A baby born between 33 and 36 weeks should have few difficulties, but many find coordinating sucking and swallowing too difficult for normal breast- or bottle-feeding. Babies born between 28 and 32 weeks have immature lungs, and those born before 27 weeks need more support for many of their body systems.

Health issues
Minor worries at birth

Newborn babies are prone to a number of minor ailments, which can give rise to concern if you are not prepared for them.

Birthweight

Q My baby weighed just over 3½ kg (8 lb) when she was born, but the midwife said she would probably lose some weight at first. Why is this?

A Most babies do in fact lose some of their birthweight before starting to gain weight again, and losing about 227 g (½ lb) or even up to one tenth of the birthweight is considered normal. Most of this loss is fluid, because in the first day or so your baby may not have much interest in feeding, while her urine output stays normal. And it may be two or three days before your milk production has been established. Not all babies lose weight, however. Some are born hungry and their sucking can spur on the arrival of their mother's milk in the first day.

Vomiting and mucus

Q Is it normal for a newborn baby to vomit a lot in the first week?

A A lot of mucus may be produced by your baby's stomach as a reaction to the birth, and she may vomit it up in the first day or two. It may be bloodstained and may make your baby uninterested in feeding. It may also briefly get in the way of her breathing, but she has a strong cough reflex and will clear it out of the way. Just lie her on her side if she needs to cough it up.

Q My baby brings back lots of milk. Is this doing him harm?

A See your doctor to rule out possible problems, but the answer will probably be that it is nothing to worry about. The valve at the entrance to the stomach is very loose in babies and milk can come out nearly as easily as it goes in. Some babies do bring back milk freely and although it is messy it does no harm. As long as you feed your baby when he is hungry, and he is contented, alert and sociable you can be confident no harm is being done. He will outgrow it eventually.

Pink-stained nappies

Q My baby has pink-stained nappies. Is this normal?

A A pink stain in the nappy is probably a concentration of urate crystals from the baby's urine and is normal. With a girl, there could be a little blood from the vagina as a result of the mother's hormones, which will stop in a few days.

Diarrhoea

Q My baby's faeces are very runny and I'm worried that he has diarrhoea. What should I do?

A Babies who are exclusively breastfed usually produce runny yellow faeces, but these are normal and not an indication of diarrhoea. However, if your baby's faeces are copious, completely liquid or blood-stained, then contact your doctor immediately. Diarrhoea in babies is always serious because in a few hours a great deal of fluid can be lost and the child can become dehydrated.

Eyes

Q My baby has a squint. Is this going to be permanent?

A It shouldn't be. Your baby may appear to have a squint because of a lack of muscle power in controlling the eyes. This is most noticeably the case when she is relaxed and feeding. She will be able to focus both eyes together when her muscles develop – in about three months.

Sticky eyes

Many babies develop a discharge from one or both eyes in the days following birth, which may cause the eye to run or have sticky matter in it. The lids may even be stuck shut after a sleep. Your doctor should have a look at the eye, but it is very rarely conjunctivitis, an eye infection that could be passed on to the other eye or to anyone else. Instead it is probably a blocked tear duct.

The tear ducts are tiny tubes that run from the corner of the eyes, collecting the tears which are constantly being produced to keep the eye moist, and passing them down into the nose cavity. In small babies, there can be a blockage at the bottom end of the tear duct, so there is a moist site where germs can grow, causing the discharge. A blocked tear duct needs no treatment, because it will almost always clear itself. If a baby still has a blocked tear duct at six months, treatment by an eye doctor would be considered.

While waiting for the duct to become unblocked, clean the eye, using a piece of cotton wool dipped in cooled boiled water. Wipe from the outer edge of the eye into the corner, and use a clean piece of cotton wool for each eye. If necessary, your doctor may prescribe some antibiotic drops for your baby's eye, which will not cure the problem, but may limit the stickiness while the body clears the blockage.

The umbilical cord

Q What happens to the umbilical cord following birth?

A When the umbilical cord has completed its job at birth, it is usually clamped about 2.5 cm (1 in) from the baby's abdomen and then cut. After about 48 hours, the cord stump has shrunk and the clamp can be removed. During the first week after birth the stump continues to shrivel, while bacteria soften the base so that the cord finally drops off, any time from four days to six weeks later, leaving the navel or tummy button.

Q How do I look after the umbilical stump?

A The cord should be kept clean and dry, but gentle washing with warm water twice a day is sufficient. Antiseptic cleaners will only slow down the process of the cord dropping off. It is perfectly fine to gently pull on the stump to clean in the gutter around its base. After the first day, a tiny bit of bleeding from around the stump is not a problem, but if the area around the stump looks red then there could be an infection, so it is a good idea to contact your midwife or doctor. Although infections are rare, they can happen and they spread very quickly. If the area is inflamed or tender, or if there are any signs of bad-smelling yellow pus, you should take your baby to a doctor immediately.

Q My baby's cord has fallen off, but there is a bulge under the navel that comes out more when he cries. Is something wrong?

A The swelling is an umbilical hernia, which is fairly common in babies and not dangerous. The gap in the muscle wall of the abdomen where the cord came through has not closed

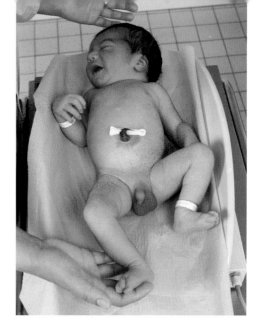

Above: Following birth your new baby's umbilical cord will be clamped by a midwife or doctor.

Innies and outies

Most people think that the reason for belly buttons being either innies or outies is down to the way in which the umbilical cord is tied following the birth. This is not so, however. An outie is in fact an umbilical hernia. As the cord begins to shrivel, the abdominal muscles surrounding it tighten, pushing the hole where the cord entered the baby permanently closed. In some cases the hole does not close fully, and part of the umbilicus pops back out again under the strain of the baby coughing or crying, resulting in an outie. They can range in size from that of a pea to a walnut, but are not harmful and do not need medical attention unless they become painful.

up fully, and so the contents of the abdomen push through, especially when the pressure is raised by crying or coughing. It is not painful for your baby, and nothing needs to be done. Almost all umbilical hernias close up by themselves before the age of five.

Skin

Q Should I be concerned if my baby develops a rash?

A Rashes in the early days are probably harmless signs of the skin reacting to its new environment. Your baby's skin may react to its first contact with clothing or other substances, producing a red, blotchy rash with small white or yellow centres. The weals look like nettle rash, and may come and go quickly on different parts of the body. The rash will clear up after a couple of days and needs no treatment.

If your baby is overdressed or if the weather is hot, she may develop a heat rash. Tiny red spots spread in the areas where the baby sweats – most often the face, neck, shoulders and chest, especially in the creases. Rinsing off the sweat will soothe the skin, but most importantly, make sure you are not overdressing your baby or using too many bed covers.

Q My baby has uneven red patches on her skin – mainly over her back and stomach. What should I do?

A Around half of all newborn babies develop these symptoms in the first two to four days after birth. At the centre of each patch there may be a little blister, which can sometimes look infected. Within two or three days the blisters and patches fade naturally. This rash, known as *Erythema toxicum*, is rare in pre-term babies.

Q Why does my baby have dry skin?

A Most babies have dry, peeling skin in the first few days after birth as the top layer of skin, which has been in contact with the amniotic fluid, is shed. It is most obvious at the wrists and ankles and on the palms and soles, but it does not cause the baby any pain and it does not mean that they will have skin problems later. It needs no treatment, although you could rub on a little good-quality oil such as almond.

Q Is it normal for a newborn baby to have bluish hands and feet?

A Sometimes the unusual appearance of a newborn infant's skin is the result of their blood flow adjusting to independent life. Some babies have greyish-blue hands and feet in the first day or two of life before the circulation ot the extremities improves. Provided they are kept warm, the hands and feet soon turn pink.

Q My baby's cheeks are red, rough and dry. They look sore and I am worried that cracks might start to develop. What can I do?

A Dry skin is caused by loss of water through the normally protective barrier of sebum or oils. The condition may be genetic or caused by exposure to cold, windy weather. Hot, dry indoor atmospheres can also dry skin unnaturally and some chemicals in soaps and bubble baths degrease the skin, dissolving the sebum layer. At the first signs of dryness, smooth on an emollient moisturizing cream or aqueous cream liberally. You can do a lot to control the condition by protecting your baby's skin in windy weather, by turning down central heating and by avoiding bubble bath and soap while the skin remains dry.

Health issues
Jaundice

Q What causes jaundice?

A Jaundice is caused by an excess of the yellow bile pigment bilirubin in the blood and body tissues. The yellow coloration of the skin and the whites of the eyes that are the characteristics of the condition are the most obvious sign of liver disease. Jaundice is normal in newborn babies, whose immature livers cannot process bilirubin quickly enough. As the unborn baby needs more red blood cells than a newborn infant, the excess is broken down in the liver and the haemoglobin converted to bilirubin. This goes to the bowel to be excreted, but if there is too much it spills into the bloodstream, causing jaundice.

Q Will it affect my baby and, if so, how?

A More than half of all babies develop jaundice three to five days after birth. There is a rapid improvement over the next two to three days and a slower fading over the next week. Two weeks after birth most babies are clear of jaundice. If they are not they should have urine and blood tests to check their liver function. Breastfed babies remain jaundiced for longer than bottle-fed babies. This type of jaundice causes the baby no problems and should not affect the decision to continue breastfeeding.

Q How is jaundice treated?

A It is important for newborns with jaundice to feed well and have extra fluids. Sunlight can help reduce the amount of bilirubin in the blood, which is why you may be advised to place the child's cot near a window for 10 to 20 minute spells, out of the glare of the sun. If there is any concern about the baby's bilirubin level it will be checked from a blood sample taken from the heel of the hand. The level will be recorded daily until it steadies or starts to decline. If the level does not fall as quickly as expected the newborn may need to have phototherapy.

Q How does phototherapy work?

A The baby is undressed and the eyes shielded before being placed under blue fluorescent lamps. The light breaks down the bilirubin, which the baby then excretes. Sometimes babies are placed on fibre-optic blankets to increase the amount of absorbed light. Treatment is usually given intermittently, for example for one hour in four.

Right: It is common for newborn babies to be born with slightly yellow skin which is caused by jaundice.

Health issues
Floppy baby syndrome

Q What is this?

A There are many reasons why a baby may be unusually floppy. In most cases there is no serious underlying cause: the infant is just slow to mature and is said to have floppy baby syndrome. Medical tests do not show any reason for the floppiness in these infants, although there may be a family pattern of later-than-normal developing in sitting, crawling and walking.

Q How does it manifest itself?

A The baby is floppy from birth, and the floppiness does not get any worse. After a few months the baby usually starts to improve and will eventually grow out of the limpness, which leaves only signs of slight muscle weakness or extra joint mobility. Premature infants are more floppy than full-term ones, but their muscle tone improves as they mature.

Q What should I look for?

A Your baby's head control may be slower to develop than in a normal baby and may need to be supported for longer. At rest, your baby may lie with arms and legs splayed out flat, and may generally make fewer movements than a normal baby would. At six months your baby may still be unable to sit upright, even with support, and may not be able to take his weight on his feet. If you hold you baby upright under the arms, he may have a tendency to slip through your grasp.

Q What can I do?

A Some mildly floppy babies have simply not had enough opportunity to move around and strengthen their muscles. This may be the case with babies who are frequently left in their car seats. Try to make sure that the infant has plenty of opportunities to move around and kick his arms and legs. This will help to develop muscle tone. For more pronounced cases, you can learn how to do exercises with your baby to improve muscle tone. And don't worry: if tests show no underlying cause your baby will develop normal muscle tone in time.

Your child may have floppy baby syndrome if, at six months, he is still unable to sit in an upright position, even with support.

2

older baby
1 to 12 months

Development
The first year

Individual children vary widely in their developmental progress, so these are general guidelines only.

From 1 to 12 months

1 month

- **Language.** Uses wide range of cries that can be distinguished as cries of hunger, boredom, tiredness and discomfort.
- **Hand–eye coordination.** Follows objects that are moved from side to side. Moves hands without much control but can connect fist with mouth.
- **Movement.** Can raise her head slightly when lying face down. Kicks arms and legs in the air. When startled will arch back and fling out arms and legs (Moro reflex).
- **Social and emotional.** Responds positively when spoken and sung to.

2 months

- **Language.** Uses a couple of identifiable but meaningless sounds. Watches people's body language.
- **Hand–eye coordination.** Hand control begins; hands are mostly open with fingers becoming more flexible. Will hold a small object for a few moments.
- **Movement.** Neck control increases and is beginning to support the weight of the head. Early reflexes are fading.
- **Social and emotional.** First smiles. May begin to sleep through the night.

3 months

- **Language.** Listening skills have improved; goes quiet when she hears a small noise. Makes at least two distinctive sounds such as 'oooh' and 'aaah'.
- **Hand–eye coordination.** Stretches out a hand towards nearby object. Stares at pictures in books and will try to touch them.
- **Movement.** Better at moving around in cot. Leg movements become quite vigorous when kicking.
- **Social and emotional.** Thrives on attention and tries to attract attention when a parent is near. Has a broad range of facial expressions to express mood.

From 1 to 12 months

4 months

- **Language.** Gives a definite laugh when amused. Makes vocalizations to attract your attention.
- **Hand–eye coordination.** In the bath will reach out and slaps hands in the water. Can focus on near and distant objects as well as an adult can.
- **Movement.** Sits in an upright position with support. Turns from side to side without help.
- **Social and emotional.** Enjoys familiar situations such as feeding, bathing and dressing. Relaxes when you sing gently.

5 months

- **Language.** Uses three or four babbling sounds at random, combining vowels and consonants; for example, 'nanana'. Observes your reactions and may imitate your facial expressions.
- **Hand–eye coordination.** Starts to look for an object that has slipped from grasp. Has a firm grip and doesn't like to let go.
- **Movement.** Pushes feet firmly against surfaces such as bottom of cot. Moves around the floor by rolling and turning.
- **Social and emotional.** May form an attachment to a cuddly toy or other comforter, especially before going to sleep. Can play on own for short periods.

6 months

- **Language.** Synchronizes speech with yours as though in conversation. Produces more different vowel and consonant sounds such as f, v, ka, da, ma.
- **Hand–eye coordination.** Uses both hands in synchrony and can pass objects from one hand to the other. Tries to feed by putting food to mouth with fingers.
- **Movement.** Sits up without requiring support. Shows first sign of crawling by drawing one knee to tummy.
- **Social and emotional.** May become anxious in strange company and start to cry. Playfully holds on to a toy when you try to remove it. Turns when hears own name.

From 1 to 12 months

7 months

- **Language.** More responsive when talked to directly and will respond to comments such as 'Look at that'. Seems to understand your different voice tones, such as happy, serious, surprised.
- **Hand–eye coordination.** Explores toys in new and interesting ways by banging them. Begins to use finger and thumb in a pincer movement.
- **Movement.** Rolls competently from back to front and vice versa. May be able to crawl.
- **Social and emotional.** Gets annoyed if stopped from doing something. Enjoys the familiarity of routines such as bathtime and bedtime.

8 months

- **Language.** Repeats the same sound over and over, such as syllables of words you use. Opens and closes mouth when watches you eat, imitating your jaw action.
- **Hand–eye coordination.** Likes to drop objects from highchair. Tries to pull a string attached to a toy.
- **Movement.** Able to crawl backwards and forwards. Takes own weight if gripping a chair for support and with effort can pull up to a standing position.
- **Social and emotional.** Initiates social contact with other adults. May be shy and reluctant to be picked up by strangers. Enjoys company of other babies, but does not play cooperatively with them.

9 months

- **Language.** Says first words, perhaps unclearly. Listens when you speak and can understand simple instructions such as 'Come here'.
- **Hand–eye coordination.** Hand movements more coordinated. May be able to build a two-brick tower. Scans surroundings and attends to small details.
- **Movement.** Can turn around while crawling. Shows an interest in climbing stairs. Makes a stepping response when held under the arms.
- **Social and emotional.** Is curious about other babies and may stare or poke at another child. Gets upset on seeing you or other children upset.

From 1 to 12 months

10 months

- **Language,** Says one or two words consistently, not always clearly. Chatters in the rhythm of speech but without meaning.
- **Hand–eye coordination,** Likes to explore cupboards, boxes and drawers. Hand preference may begin to show. Enjoys rhymes involving hand coordination such as 'pat-a-cake'.
- **Movement,** Climbs up the first step and slides down from it. Stands on own two feet, gripping something for support.
- **Social and emotional,** Gives cuddles as well as receiving them. Has no understanding of the effect of actions on older children.

11 months

- **Language.** Follows simple instructions, for example to give things to you and take them back. Will point to an object in a picture book when you say its name.
- **Hand–eye coordination.** Tries to pull lids off boxes to find whatever is inside them. Enjoys putting one thing inside another.
- **Movement.** May stand without support. Moves swiftly around the room, using furniture as supports. Slowly and gently lowers to ground with only a small bump.
- **Social and emotional.** Is frustrated when wishes are blocked and loses temper quite easily. Likes to do things that gain your approval.

12 months

- **Language.** May be able to use three or four words to name familiar objects, for example 'dog'. Has good hearing but loses interest in repetitive sounds.
- **Hand–eye coordination.** Enjoys water games and can pour from containers held in either hand. Can slot simple shapes correctly into a shape sorter.
- **Movement.** Shows the early signs of independent walking. More confident when climbing the stairs. May walk if hand is held.
- **Social and emotional.** Plays any games that involve social interaction with you. May show temper when unwilling to cooperate.

Feeding
The first bottle

Some breastfed babies simply love drinking and will readily drink from bottles. Others are very fussy and will only drink from the breast. Most babies fall somewhere between these two extremes, but a large number of women who have been breastfeeding report at least some difficulty getting their babies to take to feeding from a bottle.

The most obvious explanation for this is that babies enjoy breastfeeding: they like the skin-to-skin contact and listening to their mother's heartbeat, as well as the close cuddle that comes with it. They also quickly get used to the smell and taste of their mother's breast milk, the rate at which it flows and the control they have over that flow.

Formula milk
Formula milk is designed to mimic breast milk as closely as possible and it is just as nutritious, although it doesn't contain the antibodies of a mother's milk. Based on cow's milk, it contains carbohydrates, fats, protein, minerals and vitamins. It does take longer to digest than breast milk, however, so you may find that bottle-fed babies fall into a four-hourly routine early on. If you opt for formula, do not be tempted to round up the formula scoop or to pack down the powder too densely. This will only make it more difficult for your baby to digest. Make sure you choose a brand that is appropriate for your baby's age. During hot weather, if your baby seems very thirsty she could have a drink of cooled, boiled water between feeds. Exclusively breastfed babies do not need water or any other drinks because breast milk adapts to have a higher water content if necessary.

Expressing milk
Expressing your own milk is a useful technique to learn. It will give you a break while not depriving your baby of her mother's milk and also allows her to get accustomed to sucking from a teat.

Learning to express your milk is not always easy but it is worth persevering. Do it in the morning just after a feed, when you are feeling full. It can be stored for four hours at room temperature and for two days or more in the fridge.

Sterilizing

Everything you use in preparing formula and feeding your baby for the first four months must be sterilized, because milk is the perfect breeding ground for bacteria to grow and your baby could easily become ill if all germs are not destroyed. There are various methods you can use, including a purpose-built sterilizing unit, in the dishwasher, or in a microwave. Be sure to read all manufacturer's instructions before sterilizing equipment for the first time.

Feeding
Common questions

Five tips for **bottle-feeding**

1 Give the bottle before your baby is really hungry.
2 Get your partner or a friend to offer the bottle so that your baby cannot smell your breast milk.
3 Try softening the teat in boiling water before use (allow it to cool before giving it to your baby).
4 Start small – your baby may only take 25 ml (1 fl oz) at first.
5 Experiment with styles of teat – some babies prefer a softer latex teat rather than one made from silicone – and check that it has the right size of hole for your baby.

Q When is the best time to introduce feeding by bottle?

A There is no right or wrong time to give a breastfed baby her first bottle, but expert advice is that you should not be too hasty: if you do so in the first three weeks – before you really have breastfeeding established – you could reduce your milk supply and confuse your baby. This is because breastfeeding and bottle-feeding involve two quite different sucking techniques. For the best results, wait until breastfeeding is well established, then take things slowly, introducing one bottle a day then gradually building to two, then three and so on. Initially, you can put breast milk in the bottle so that at least the milk tastes the same.

Q If I stop breastfeeding my baby can I change my mind and start again later?

A Yes – although, depending on when you stop and restart, it can take a month or more to rebuild your milk supply. As long as your baby cooperates, you can restart after almost any interval. The more often you put your baby to the breast, the more milk you will produce. It may take your baby some time to get used to breastfeeding again after getting used to sucking on a teat. A breastfeeding counsellor will be able to help you.

Q Could my baby be allergic to formula milk?

A Your baby is fairly unlikely to have a reaction to formula milk but, if you think he has, note the date, symptoms and the brand you used. Switch to another brand, if you wish or ask your doctor to prescribe a hypoallergenic formula. Full-fat pasteurized cow's milk may be mixed with your baby's cereals or cooked food from the age of six months, but do not give as a main drink before the age of one year.

Q What other drinks can I give my baby?

A Cooled boiled water can be introduced to formula-fed babies from the age of six weeks, while breastfed babies do not need anything else to drink. Use regular tap water only, and do not add flavourings or sweeteners. Well-diluted, unsweetened fruit juices, such as apple or orange, can be gradually introduced as a drink from nine months of age. Never give sparkling mineral water or water with a high mineral content to a baby under two years of age.

Weaning

By the time your baby is five or six months old, he will have doubled his birth weight and by 12 months he may have trebled it. While breast milk or formula milk provided nutritional needs in the early months, the rapid growth and development of your baby mean that by six months he will require more nutrients than milk alone can provide.

A weaning checklist

Your baby may be ready for weaning if he is more than 17 weeks old and your answers to most of the following questions are 'yes'.
- **Does your baby still seem hungry after a feed from both breasts or 250 ml (8 fl oz) of formula milk?**
- **Does your baby wake up increasingly early, or during the night where he had been previously sleeping through?**
- **Does he chew his hands excessively or try to put things into his mouth?**
- **Does he seem generally restless and grizzly?**
- **Does your baby look longingly at what you are eating?**

Weaning is the gradual move by your baby from milk feeds to soft purées to mashed food, until he is joining in with family meals at around 12 months of age.

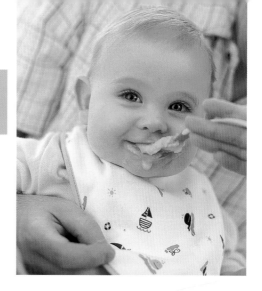

Above: Using a soft-edged baby spoon will help your baby adjust to eating his first foods.

Official UK government guidelines recommend that all babies should be exclusively breastfed until six months, but if parents choose to wean earlier than this, solid food should not be introduced before 17 weeks, as a baby's digestive system is too immature to cope.

When to introduce the first meal
Most parents find a baby is more receptive to trying his first solid food after his morning sleep. Offer your baby just a small milk feed or a feed from one breast to take the edge off his appetite – a baby desperate for food will not be easily persuaded to try a spoon for the first time. Half-fill a small, soft-edged baby spoon and offer it to your baby. Do not worry if most of the food appears to dribble back out of his mouth. Taking food off a spoon involves quite a different reflex from sucking and it will take a little time to master. Encourage your baby with face-to-face interaction and reassure him with smiles and loving sounds so that this can be a pleasurable experience.

Weaning
The first meal

Although your baby will have been fed on demand until now, it is important that the introduction of solid foods is more structured. Begin with one mini-meal mid-morning, then introduce a second two or three weeks later. Build up to a third meal two or three weeks after that. Do not be tempted to increase the amounts too quickly, as your baby's digestive system needs time to adjust.

Q Which are the best foods to start with?

A The best first food is baby rice. Sold in powdered form, this is quick and easy to prepare and, because portion size is so tiny at this stage, it is the most convenient. The taste and texture are not dissimilar to milk, so appeals to most babies. Once your baby is happy with that, you could try mixing the rice with a little puréed apple. Cooked and mashed potato or yam, butternut squash, parsnip, carrot and courgette are all great first foods, building a range of different tastes and textures. See also trigger foods (page 77)

Q What is better: boiling or steaming?

A Some water-soluble vitamins and minerals leach out into the cooking water when they are boiled. Providing you use the minimum amount of water and use the same water when puréeing the foods, they are as good

nutritionally as steamed foods. While steamed foods do not lose vitamins and minerals into the cooking water, most will need puréeing with boiled water, expressed milk or formula milk in order to get the texture right.

Q Is homemade preferable to commercial?

A There are advantages to both. When you prepare your baby's food yourself, you can use really fresh ingredients that have maximum food value. Your baby gets used to home cooking right from the start, probably with a wider variety of tastes and textures. The advantages of commercial food include convenience and reduced waste by opening only small quantities at a time. Additives and preservatives are limited and the ingredients are screened for pesticide levels.

Q My baby is now 10 months old. Can I just mash or purée small portions of what the rest of the family are eating?

A He will probably now be enjoying many of the same foods as you, but food for a baby under 12 months should not include salt or sugar, so make adjustments for that. Avoid honey and shellfish too, and remember that young taste buds are much more sensitive and acute, so strong flavours will seem overpowering.

Q Do I still have to sterilize all the equipment?

A No – washing all the utensils in hot water is sufficient. Basic food hygiene, such as washing your hands well before you begin and washing all fruits and vegetables, will help ensure safety.

Weaning
Common problems

Q My baby is not interested in eating from a spoon. What can I do to encourage her?

A If your baby is less than six months old, gaining weight well and sleeping through the night, but shows no interest in solid foods, she may simply not be ready to be weaned. Ask your health visitor or doctor for advice. For older babies, the problem may be either the idea of the spoon or what is on the spoon. Try again with a different spoon. You could also vary what is on the spoon: try a thin potato purée or, if that meets with rejection, offer a tiny taste of butternut squash purée. Never force-feed a baby and never be tempted to add baby rice to a baby's bottle. If your baby seems at all distressed by this first taste of solids, take the food away and try again after a few days.

Q My six-month-old will not touch solids at all. What can I do?

A Babies of six months or more may refuse solids because they drink a lot of milk, especially if they are still feeding during the night. Talk to your health visitor about gradually reducing the amount of milk he has, and complementing it with weaning foods. By seven months, he should be having 600 ml (20 fl oz/1 pint) breast or formula milk a day, with a little cow's milk in cooked food.

Q At nine months, my baby refuses to eat anything other than purées, and hates anything with a coarser texture. What is the problem?

A By the time your baby is nine to twelve months he should be used to eating coarsely chopped foods and raw vegetable sticks. But if foods are too thick or lumpy at the beginning, your baby will not be able to swallow them and may be put off eating from a spoon. Leave it too late, however, and he may be reluctant to move on to coarser foods. Just as your baby needed time to adjust to his first foods after breast or formula milk, he also needs to be introduced to textures gradually. As he's happy with purées, slowly move to slightly coarser mashes. Once your baby is eating these happily, offer mixtures with smooth, easy-to-chew lumps, and once he has accepted these, introduce cooked broccoli and cooked carrot sticks as first finger foods.

Left: By about 12 months your baby will be able to enjoy feeding herself finger foods.

Positive parenting **Nutritional needs**

Q Now that I have started weaning my baby, I am worried that I might be depriving her of the vitamins and minerals that are essential to her health. What do I need to know?

A Primarily, you should know that your baby's needs change with age. By the time she is six months, many of the mineral and vitamin stores your baby was born with have run out and you need to keep them topped up by supplying them in the foods you offer. If you follow the tips below, you can be confident that your baby is getting the right nutrients.

Strategies

• **Revitalize a tired child** with a miniature cheese sandwich, warm milky drink or diced cheese and sliced apple.

• **Naturally occurring fat** from whole milk, cheese and other full-fat dairy food provides concentrated energy in a form easily used by the body, plus fat-soluble vitamins A and D.

• Offer sliced fruits or raw vegetable sticks as a healthy snack between meals or slice, dice or mash them and add to breakfast cereals. Vitamin C cannot be stored by the body, so it is important to give your child plenty of fruit and vegetables every day.

• Try to vary the grains in your baby's diet and include a small portion with every meal. Offer porridge and rice cakes as an alternative to bread at lunch, and rice, couscous or millet in place of pasta.

• Fibre is important for healthy bowels, but too much will cause important vitamins and minerals to be flushed straight out before they can be absorbed. Give your baby foods containing soluble fibre, such as fruits, vegetables and oats.

Your baby's changing daily nutritional needs

up to 6 months	• Milk is still providing all your baby's nutrition. • At six months, introduce the idea of eating solids from a spoon (see page 72).
6-9 months	• Food now needs to provide the bulk of your baby's nutrition. • Iron and zinc are important because your baby's body store has now been used up. Include two portions of fruit and/or vegetables.
9-12 months	• Try to include three to four mini-servings of fruit and vegetables, served as fruit juice or cooked. One mini-serving of starchy foods per meal – breakfast cereal, rice, potato or pasta. Two protein foods: meat, fish, eggs, lentils, cheese or tofu.

FOOD ALLERGIES

Defining and dealing with allergies

A food allergy is a hypersensitive reaction to a normally harmless substance in food and can be quite common in babies and children.

Some children are more likely than others to have an allergic reaction triggered by a particular food. Those most at risk are babies from families with a history of allergy, such as peanut allergy, asthma, eczema or hay fever. An estimated one in 10 children is prone to an allergy. Although many will grow out of it by the time they are two years old, others will have a sensitivity to eggs, milk, flour or shellfish for life.

Current government guidelines suggest that infants who have a strong family history of allergy should be breastfed for at least four months, preferably longer, to provide them with protective antibodies. When beginning weaning, at six months, new foods should be introduced one at a time. A family history of food allergies may double your baby's risk of having an allergy, so seek expert advice from your doctor, who may refer you to a State Registered paediatric dietitian. If you think that your baby is reacting to a certain food – with griping pains, diarrhoea or frequent posseting after

Above: Milk and other dairy products can cause tummy aches if your child is deficient in lactose.

eating – even though you have no family history of allergy, trust your instinct and ask your doctor for advice or insist on a referral to a paediatric dietitian. Do not be tempted to exclude foods without professional advice, because a restricted diet may possibly result in malnutrition.

Trigger foods

Listed below are common trigger foods. In addition to these, you should also be wary of sesame seeds and products made from them, soya products and fish, especially shellfish – which should not be given before 12 months.

• **Peanuts and other nuts.** An allergy to any sort of nut is the most serious kind of allergy, causing anaphylactic shock in many cases. This is a particularly severe and frightening reaction in which the throat swells and breathing gets difficult. **Avoid: peanuts, peanut butter and unrefined peanut oil.** Do not offer peanuts in any form to a child under three years old if there is a family history of peanut allergy. (In any case, whole nuts should never be given to children under five years old because of the danger of choking.) Although it is usually only the peanut, a ground-grown nut, that causes the reaction, some tree nuts can also cause problems, so ask your doctor or paediatric dietitian for advice. Traces of peanut can affect shop-bought foods such as cakes and biscuits, so homemade meals and snacks are the best alternative, when you can be sure of the ingredients.

• **Dairy products.** Some children are deficient in lactase, the enzyme needed to digest milk sugar, and will suffer from tummy aches and diarrhoea. Consult your doctor if you are worried. **Avoid: cow's milk, cheese and butter.** These should be either limited or omitted completely from the diet. Alternatives include soya milk and other soya products. Yogurt may be tolerated because the bacteria that it contains produce their own lactase. Do not give unmodified (or carton) soya milks to children who are under two years old.

• **Gluten.** An allergy to gluten, a protein found mainly in wheat, is known as coeliac disease. Babies suffer from diarrhoea and tummy problems, causing damage to the intestine lining and weight loss. **Avoid: wheat – in forms such as bread, pasta, cakes and flour – barley, rye and oats.**

Alternatives include rice cakes instead of bread, rice or corn noodles instead of wheat pasta, rice or corn (maize) cereals for breakfast, and buckwheat, millet or sorghum flour. Gluten-free bread is available on prescription. If you have a family history of this allergy, your doctor may suggest that you gradually introduce oats, rye and barley from nine months and wheat from 12 months under close supervision.

• **Eggs.** Babies who are allergic to eggs may display symptoms such as rashes or eczema (see page 176), skin swellings and tummy upsets. **Avoid: eggs (especially the egg white), cakes, some breads and pastries.**

• **Tomatoes.** An allergy to tomatoes may manifest itself as a rash or eczema. There is also a possible link to hyperactivity. **Avoid: tomatoes, tomato ketchup, passata, canned tomatoes.** Alternatives include chopped carrots or red peppers. If you have a family history of this allergy, do not introduce tomatoes until your child has reached at least nine months.

• **Citrus fruit and strawberries.** The symptoms here are usually a rash or eczema. **Avoid: fresh oranges, satsumas, orange lollies, fruit yogurts, squash.** Alternatives include bananas, pears, plums, apricots, dried fruits, apple juice to drink.

Sleep
What is typical?

Sleep is a universal need, and it's not just parents who end up grumpy through broken sleep. Research shows that babies who sleep well at night are more likely to be contented during the day, while those who sleep poorly are more likely to be irritable. This is why adopting strategies to help your baby sleep soundly benefits you both.

Research suggests that babies and young children who sleep with the light on are more likely to be short-sighted than those who sleep in the dark.

There is no such thing as an 'average' baby. This becomes more obvious if you have two or more children. Your first-born may be content to be put down awake in his cot, sucking his thumb happily for half an hour before drifting off, while your second may need to scream herself to exhaustion before falling asleep. Equally, there is no such thing as an 'average' parent. Your neighbour may insist that controlled crying is the secret to getting your child to sleep successfully, but if you simply can't bear to hear your baby crying it may not be the right approach for you. Similarly, you may be keen to get your child to settle early so that you can have your evenings to yourself, but your friend may be happy for her baby to go to bed later because she is at work all day.

Below: Cuddling a safe, favourite soft toy can help a baby to settle to sleep at night.

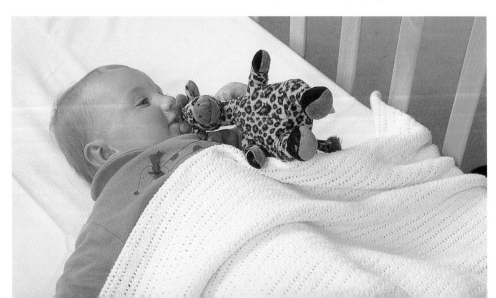

Sleep
Common questions

Q How can I create the right atmosphere for sleep?

A There are lots of factors that can make it difficult for your baby to sleep without interruption. Early morning sunlight as well as street lights or flashing headlights could disturb your baby so you could try installing a black-out blind at his window. If your heating clicks into action at 5.30am every day, for instance, it's probably no coincidence that this is when your baby wakes up. Try setting the heating to come on a little bit later. Barking dogs, car engines, other family members – there are many sudden noises that might startle your baby awake during his sleep. While you may not be able to control many of these, it could be that repositioning your baby's bed or putting him to sleep in a quieter room will enable him to sleep more soundly.

Q Should I leave a light on for my baby at night?

A Putting your child to bed confidently in the dark gives her the message that it is a safe place to be and reduces the chances of her developing a fear of the dark. What's more, your child's body produces more of its own natural sedative, melatonin, in the dark, which in turn helps to settle her. However, you may feel that a small light makes it easier for you to check on your baby during the night. Set the lights how you want them before your child falls asleep, otherwise she will wonder why it's all different when she wakes during the night and this may trigger a fear of the dark.

Q Should I give my baby a dummy at night?

A This really is up to you and your baby. Some babies need to suck for comfort, others don't. Even if your baby is a 'sucker', he may develop his own comforter, such as his thumb, a blanket or a favourite toy. Or, you may find that a dummy is the only thing that calms him. However, you should think about weaning him off it at the earliest opportunity. The longer your child has a dummy, the more of a crutch it will become for him – and you may find yourself getting up several times a night to retrieve it for him from underneath the blankets. Try introducing an alternative comforter – a suitable, safe toy, or perhaps an item of clothing that has that familiar smell of mum or dad – but make sure there is no danger of your child ending up covered by his comforter.

Q My baby and toddler have to share a room – will they disturb one another?

A Children have shared rooms successfully for generations, and there is no reason why yours can't do the same. Many parents find their children are able to sleep quite happily through any night-time disturbances from their siblings. In fact, putting your baby in with her sibling may help to settle her, as she will naturally fall in with their established, rhythmic breathing. However, if you intend to start sleep training your baby, it may be an idea to move your toddler to another room so that he is not disturbed. You should be able to put your children back in together again within a few nights.

Sleep
Forming a routine

Babies and small children love routine: it helps them to make sense of their world and gives definition and shape to their day. This is as true of bedtime as of any other part of the day. A clear routine will help your child to understand that in the daily sequence of events, the next stage is bed and sleep. Being able to understand this will in itself go some way towards setting him up for a good night's sleep. You can also take your routine with you when you go away, making it easier to settle your child in unfamiliar places.

Q How can I implement a routine?
A It doesn't matter exactly what you do, whether you tidy away toys, have a bath, read a story, it is important that you do the same things in the same order every night, preferably at the same time. Above all, your bedtime routine should be predictable and enjoyable; it should also aim to calm your child down, rather than get her excited. Once your routine is well established, you can be a little more flexible – for example, you may feel that on some nights your child is too tired for a bath – but aim to be consistent for the first few months.

Q Can I change my baby's sleeping habits?
A Yes, you can. The first thing you need to do if you want your baby to sleep well at night is to teach him that night time is for sleeping. It may sound obvious, but you'd be surprised how many new parents overlook this. It's easy to understand how this blurring of day and night arises. If you have no real experience of babies and your newborn insists at 2am that he wants to play, you may think this is what you, as a parent, should do. The problem is that after a few nights your baby will be looking forward to his early-hours play session, and will be waking up in anticipation of it.

Five tips for **a good night's sleep**

1 Keep night feeds and nappy changes functional: use only low lighting, try not to talk to your baby (if you do have to talk, keep your voice flat and low) and don't make eye contact with him.
2 Do not begin any 'daytime' activity once you have fed and changed him; instead, put him straight back into his bed.
3 If he tries to engage you in play, resettle him straight away.
4 Stimulate and engage your baby as much as possible during the day. This will not only give him the message that days are for socializing, fun and learning, but will also encourage him to be awake more during the day, which in turn will mean he will be more tired by the evening.
5 Draw a distinction between night sleep and daytime naps: put your baby to sleep in his carrycot during the day, rather than in his cot or Moses basket; draw the curtains at night only.

Where will your baby sleep?

Where	Pros	Cons
In your bed	• Some experts argue that it is the most natural solution for parents and babies. • It is very cosy. • Makes night feeds easy, especially if you are breastfeeding.	• Foundation for the Study of Infant Death (FSID) disputes claims that it reduces the risk of cot death. • Must follow safety advice (see page 39). • Not appropriate if you and/or your partner smoke.
In his own bed in your bedroom	• May reduce the risk of cot death. • Easy to respond to your baby's needs.	• May be disruptive if your baby is a very light sleeper. • Still have to get your baby used to his own room eventually.
In a bedside cot, where one long side is open and attaches to the side of your bed	• Easy to check on your baby in the night. • Cosy.	• Your baby could get trapped between the two beds. • No known value in reducing the risk of cot death.
In his own room	• No tiptoeing around your baby at night. • No need to get him used to his own room later.	• Slightly higher risk of cot death than if he is in his own bed in your room. • Means stumbling to the nursery for night-time changes and feeds.

Deciding where your baby will sleep is the dilemma that all new parents ponder over and is not an easy decision to make. However, there is no right answer, and each family works out their own solution. You may have very clear ideas about where you want your baby to sleep, or you may want to adopt a trial-and-error approach to see what works best for you.

There are different advantages and disadvantages to each of the solutions listed above, but none of them should affect your baby's ability to sleep or the strategies available to you to encourage him to sleep. However, whichever option you choose it is vital that you follow the essential safety guidelines to help keep your baby safe at night (see page 39).

Sleep
Common problems

Q My baby is six months old, and still wakes during the night for a long feed. How can I tell whether she really is hungry or is simply looking for comfort?

A If you are breastfeeding, try ending her feeds when you feel she has had her fill and insist that she goes back to sleep. Within a few nights she should come to terms with shorter, more efficient feeds and start reducing them, as she no longer has the incentive of comfort suckling.

Q My baby has been sleeping through since she was three months old, but now she is eight months, her sleeping is disturbed and she is clingy at night. How can I get back to our old routine?

A It is not unusual for babies to become clingy at eight months old, when they begin to realize that you and she are not one and the same, but different people. It is a phase that can last for a couple of months and is known as 'separation anxiety'. Eventually she will learn that although you leave her, you are not abandoning her. Meanwhile, expect to take some time guiding your baby back to sleep. If she normally sleeps well, she will want to return to unbroken nights as much as you do, once she feels confident enough to do so.

Five ways to **settle your baby**

1 Once you have put your baby to bed and said goodnight, you do not go back to her – this needs strong resolve. While this is an effective method for babies, it may not work quite so well with your toddler who may find it too traumatic. If your child becomes too distraught, you should try one of the other methods below.

2 Leave your baby to cry for increasing periods of time, the idea being that she will eventually give up and go to sleep. This is effective within a few nights, but can be time consuming initially.

3 Repeatedly reassure you baby that you are to hand, while at the same time insisting that it is time for her to go to sleep. This is usually successful within a week, but can be time consuming initially.

4 Put your child to bed with a kiss and the promise to return in a minute to give her another kiss. Return at increasingly bigger intervals until she is asleep. This is usually successful within a week, but is initially demanding.

5 Put your child to bed and sit quietly by her as she falls asleep. Gradually, over the next few days move further from the bed, until you are no longer in the room when she falls asleep. Although the most gentle technique, this can take a long time.

Positive parenting **When it all gets too much**

Q I am losing so much sleep that I am beginning to resent my baby and am worried that I may try to harm her. What should I do if I feel myself losing my temper?

A Most of us can pace ourselves through a few broken nights, but when the disruption continues, real problems can set in. Tiredness becomes exhaustion, and you may find yourself showing symptoms similar to depression: apathy, anxiety or even violence.

These feelings may be strongest in the early hours of the morning, when you are battling yet again with a wailing or wakeful child who is showing no signs of going to sleep. But no matter how frustrated or desperate you feel, NEVER shake your baby – research has shown that just one shake could cause her permanent brain damage.

If you are unable to suppress your feelings, it is vital that you get help by waking your partner, calling a friend, relative or neighbour, or telephoning a helpline. You may not want to disturb other people in the middle of the night, but they would far rather lose a night's sleep than know that you were faced with a situation that you were truly unable to manage.

Short-term solutions

If you find yourself at breaking point, try the following routine:
• Put your baby in her cot, leave the room and close the door – it won't hurt her to cry on her own for a few minutes.

• Make yourself a non-alcoholic drink (it's important you stay in control) and sit quietly while you calm down, preferably where you can't hear your baby.
• Do not return to your baby until you feel able to cope with her.

Long-term solutions

Try to take steps to overcome your sleep deprivation before it reaches crisis point:
• Catch up on lost sleep when your baby naps during the day.
• Let your partner take over during the evening while you go to bed, so that you have some reserves to see you through the night.
• Express some milk and share the night feeds with your partner, so that each of you get a chunk of unbroken sleep.
• Ask for (or buy in) help: new grandparents or friends would probably love the chance to cuddle your baby for a few hours while you get some sleep.

Crying
What is typical?

All babies cry from time to time, though some cry more than others. Crying is your baby's way of telling you that he is troubled about something: for instance, he could be uncomfortable, in pain, cold, hungry, tired, bored or thirsty. It is his natural mode of communication before he can use spoken language. Initially he cries only when he is hungry or in pain, but his cries gradually become more varied and expressive as the months pass by. Although a newborn baby will cry for a total of two hours every single day, by the time your baby is four or five months old, the amount of crying he does each day is cut by half.

Why babies cry

Your baby has different cries to express different moods and sensations. You will gradually develop an ability to tell one cry from another, enabling you to satisfy his different needs. This responsiveness to your baby's body language helps strengthen the emotional attachment between you, forming a close relationship.

• **Feed me.** A cry from hunger is an automatic response in all babies. In most instances, this is one of those cries that starts off reasonably quiet, and then gets louder and louder. There are occasionally pauses for a few seconds as he swallows great gulps of air, but the crying is relentless.

• **Change me.** Your baby doesn't like to lie in a dirty nappy, and he wriggles his body about to let you know of his discomfort. His crying is not so sharp, because his distress is not so great. He may stop his tears occasionally, but will keep crying until given a new nappy.

• **Play with me.** Your baby needs to be stimulated. True, he can amuse himself to some extent, but he really needs you to play with him, talk to him and interact with him. When bored, he uses crying almost like a shout. It's not a distressed cry, just a loud noise to attract your attention.

• **It's all too much.** A baby's senses can easily become overloaded by all the sights and sounds around them, even by being talked to and looked at, held and rocked. It often happens towards the end of the day, when you may notice your baby's body stiffening, pushing out with his arms and legs and possibly crying more when you pick him up.

Research has found that many babies cry without any explicit source of discomfort.

Crying
Common questions

Q Is it normal for a baby to cry when its mother leaves the room?

A This may certainly be the case for a very young baby. His need for the security of contact with a loving caretaker is of supreme importance during the first few months. He may cry because he cannot see or hear you, or he may need to be held and feel the reassurance of your presence. In an older baby, crying like this is usually due to separation anxiety (see page 171).

Q What is the best way to deal with my baby when she is crying from over-stimulation?

A Try to reduce the activities going on around her. Darken the room, don't make eye contact with her or speak. Use only monotonous, low sounds, like a 'sshhh' or a low hum. Lie her down rather than holding or rocking her and if you touch her at all, just place one hand on her quietly to convey the idea of stillness. She may need to cry for a few minutes to release tension, so it might be a good idea to leave her alone for a while.

Q Can babies cry from frustration and if so, what is the best way of dealing with it?

A Babies begin to show frustration from as early as six months. They have a huge drive to accomplish things and may become frustrated when they want to reach the next stage, which is just beyond their abilities. Being told 'no' is also frustrating and can lead to tears. The best thing you can do is to offer tactful help when, say, a toy will not stay upright, to ward off the frustration in the first place. If your baby persists in crying because he simply cannot do something, you might be able to distract him by finding something else interesting to do. This is also a good approach to employ instead of having to say 'no' too often.

Q Because my baby is unable to communicate with me directly, I am anxious that I may be overlooking something vital when she cries. For instance, how can I tell if she is crying because she is in pain?

A First, pay attention to the way in which your baby is crying: a cry of pain is usually abrupt, often a loud cry followed by a silence as the baby draws breath to let out a scream, while the cry of a baby who is ill is usually less intense and may be low and moaning. There are various reasons why a young baby may be in pain – she could have colic, wind, or teething problems, for example. Perhaps she has hurt herself on a toy or nearby object. If you can find the cause, do your best to soothe your baby. If her cry doesn't sound right and you think she may be becoming ill, contact your doctor.

Crying
Common problems

Q I just don't seem to be able to learn the different meanings of my baby's cries. All the other mothers are better than me at this. What am I doing wrong?

A You are doing absolutely nothing wrong. It just seems that everybody else knows what their baby wants, when in fact they are probably as uncertain as you. So have a bit more confidence in yourself. The only way to gain a more accurate interpretation of your baby's cries is by using trial and error. In other words, make an effort to soothe him and see what happens. Sometimes you'll have success and at other times it will take you several attempts before your baby settles. This is the normal learning process that all parents go through.

Q Sometimes my baby cries so much, I am sure she does it just to annoy me. Can this really be the case?

A You should take crying seriously. No baby cries 'just for the sake of it' or simply to annoy her parents. There is always a reason for her tears. No matter how fed up you may be with yet another bout of crying or screaming, she really is trying to tell you something. Do your best to find out what troubles her.

Q No matter how often I leave my child with a babysitter, she absolutely howls when I leave and stares pathetically at me. What can I do to reduce her tears?

A You will find that her heart-breaking tears gradually decrease in intensity as her experience of separating from you builds up,

Above: Placing a still hand on a baby who has become over-stimulated may help to calm her.

if you manage these moments firmly yet lovingly. However, if you make a terrible fuss over your child at the point at which she starts crying, and then prolong the moment of separation with lots of cuddles and words of reassurance, her tearful episodes will continue. That's why it is best to give her a quick, comforting hug when the babysitter arrives – whether she cries or not, then put on your coat and leave without lingering unnecessarily.

Q If my son gets upset when he is left with a babysitter, would it be better for me to sneak out of the house quietly when he isn't looking?

A This may work at first, but your infant will quickly learn your strategy and become very anxious even when you have no intention of sneaking out. It's better for you to tell him goodbye, cuddle him, reassure him, and then just go – but let him see you go.

Positive parenting **Dealing with tears**

Q I have been advised to leave my five-month-old baby when she cries, otherwise she will learn to cry in order to get my attention, but this goes against my gut instinct and I find it very difficult to ignore her. Instead I tend to cuddle her every time so that she does not feel lonely and neglected. What is the correct approach to take when soothing a baby?

A Almost certainly you will be given conflicting advice about comforting a crying baby, and although it is usually always better to comfort a new baby, as she grows older you have to be prepared to be flexible. Sometimes it may be appropriate to leave her a little longer while at other times what she needs is a cuddle. It really is up to you to do what you think best.

What is important, however, is whenever you do choose to comfort your baby that you use one technique consistently before changing to something else. If you try one thing after another your baby won't get used to any of the techniques because you don't use them for long enough. Persist until you are absolutely sure it has no effect on her tears. And don't underestimate your baby's abilities. For instance, she will learn that shouting or crying can be an effective way to get your attention, so it is always worth waiting a few seconds or so before responding. That way she will also learn how to deal with situations on her own: if she is crying from boredom then a slight delay before you go to her helps your infant learn how to seek her own amusement.

Strategies

Try the following strategies for settling your crying baby:

• **Movement.** The simple act of gently rocking her back and forth in your arms or in her buggy could have a calming effect. Sometimes she will stop crying if you just change her position in the cot.

• **She may stop if held gently but firmly in a warm bath.** Hugging her close to you could have the same effect. If she is really agitated and doesn't want to be lifted, let her lie in her cot while you gently stroke her cheeks and forehead.

• **You'll be amazed how your singing soothes her** – it's the sound of your voice, your loving tone and the familiar rhythm of the words that she concentrates on. Some babies like a steady background noise such as the sound of a washing machine.

• **Amusement.** Sometimes your crying baby can be brought out of her tears by the sight of a toy brought close to her. Her interest in the object makes her momentarily forget her distress and so she suddenly stops crying.

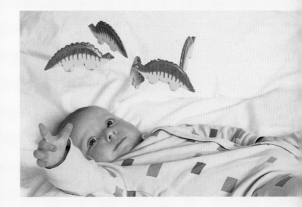

Teething

It's really exciting when you notice your baby's first tiny tooth coming through. These 'milk' teeth will need looking after and brushing regularly (see pages 96–97).

Most babies cut their first tooth around four to six months of age. In some cases a tooth appears without any warning signs. Or you may notice a light bulge on the gum or red patch on the gum and cheek, followed in a day or two by a tooth. However, some babies have great discomfort with teething and may be grizzly, wake in the night, dribble more than usual, or cry during feeding.

What are the tell-tale signs?
• **Pain.** Your baby may show signs that he is in pain and is feeling uncomfortable.
• **Being irritable.** The discomfort of teething can make your baby grumpy and grizzly, and he may seem more clingy than usual a day or two before the tooth comes through.
• **A red cheek.** You may notice a reddish patch on your baby's cheek.
• **Dribbling.** Excess saliva that is produced during teething will make your baby drool.
• **Gnawing and chewing.** Your baby may do this on anything that comes near his mouth.
• **Swollen gums.** Check for a slightly inflamed or puffy area on his gum.
• **Waking up.** Your baby may wake at night crying, even if he had been sleeping through.
• **A raised temperature.** Your baby may feel a little hotter than usual with a slight temperature.

• **Sore bottom.** It's not clear why, but some babies seem more prone to nappy rash during teething, and may also have runny poo.

How milk teeth emerge
The two front teeth at the bottom usually come through first, quickly followed by the two front teeth at the top. These four are known as the central incisors and are used for biting. The teeth on either side of the central incisors appear next, often two at a time. These are the lateral incisors. The next teeth to follow are the four back teeth – the first molars. Two appear in the lower jaw, followed by two in the upper jaw. These are the teeth your baby will use for chewing, which is why they have flat grinding surfaces. Next, the longer, pointed teeth – the canines – emerge in both jaws. Lastly, the second set of four molars erupt at the very back of your child's mouth, giving a grand total of 20.

Teething or illness?

When your baby is hot and fretful, it can be easy to put his symptoms down to teething. But while it is true that teething may cause discomfort and irritability, it doesn't actually cause illness. So it is important to be able to recognize if your baby is unwell and to act promptly. If he is suffering from any of the symptoms on pages 120–127, be sure to take him to your doctor for a check-up.

Teething
Common questions

Above: A teething baby may chew anything near his mouth, dribble excessively or have red cheeks.

Q What can I do to soothe teething pain?

A There are several methods to try: Massage your baby's gums gently with your finger (having washed your hands first); give him a quick breastfeed; try rubbing a teething gel or liquid onto his gums (up to a maximum of six times a day); rub a partly thawed ice cube over your baby's gums. Giving him a dose of infant paracetamol can also help, especially if he has a persistent slight raised temperature too; check the packaging for the correct dosage for your baby's age.

Q Can a dummy help?

A Sucking, biting or chewing on something can help soothe a teething baby. Suitable items can include a dummy, but try to limit a dummy to bed and nap times as prolonged use may result in a prominent upper jaw and protruding teeth. Other effective devices are water-filled teething rings, which can be kept cool in the refrigerator and crunchy finger foods, such as toast and lightly cooked carrot or apple slices if he is old enough (see Weaning, page 75)

Q Can I influence how or when my baby's teeth will grow?

A All of your baby's first teeth are in the jaws before birth, and the permanent teeth have even started to form. Just when they begin to appear is governed by genes and nothing in diet or habits will have much effect on when teething begins. Diet does have a large influence, though, on the strength and health of the teeth, starting with a good calcium-rich diet for the mother during pregnancy, and right through childhood for your baby.

Language
What is typical?

Your baby's use of language changes so much during the first 12 months that it's hard for you to notice all the key changes that occur. By the end of his first year he has transformed from non-verbal into an active talker who has already spoken his first clear word.

Your child uses language in two ways. First, he listens to the sounds he hears and interprets them in his own way. This is known as receptive language. Secondly, your baby has expressive skills, which enable him to make sounds of his own so that he can communicate verbally with you.

Almost certainly your baby's receptive language will constantly remain far ahead of his expressive language. In other words, he will understand a lot more words than he can actually say. For instance, you'll discover that he smiles when he hears his name even though he can't actually say his name himself. This difference probably occurs because a growing baby hears language all around him long before he is mature enough to speak, and is encouraged to respond.

What can my baby do?

2–5 months	• Your baby coos, making a meaningless repetitive vowel sound, usually when he is settled and contented.
5 months	• By now your baby can produce a wider range of sounds, known as random babbling, largely because his voice and breathing have matured.
5–10 months	• He babbles in a more controlled way, almost as though he is taking part in a conversation with you. He may tend to use the same string of sounds regularly (such as 'papapa').
10–12 months	• Towards the end of the first year, your baby makes sounds as though he is talking – he looks at you with a serious expression and varies his voice tone – but he doesn't yet use any distinguishable words.
12 months	• Around his twelfth month, your heart skips a beat with excitement on hearing his first word.

Language
Common questions

Q My baby loves bathtime and becomes excited when I start to undress him. But he now becomes excited when I open the cupboard to get the bath towel out, even before I undress him. Could he really know that this is the start of the process?

A His body language – those vigorous arm and leg movements – is clearly telling you 'I'm excited because in a moment you'll put me in the bath.' This is a sign of his increased ability to see connections between events. He may be young, but he has already observed that preparation for bathtime doesn't just start with you undressing him, that there are earlier steps than this such as getting the towel out of the cupboard. Hence, his body language conveys excitement.

Q Can my six-month-old baby tell my voice apart from other people's voices?

A Almost certainly he can identify your voice from all the other voices that he hears. Your baby has spent so much time with you and has such a strong emotional attachment to you that your voice has a special meaning for him.

Q Will sucking a dummy have an effect on my child's speech?

A Sucking a dummy doesn't make any positive contribution to her speech and language development, because it prevents your baby from using her mouth muscles, lips and tongue to make sounds. There's no harm in her using it occasionally when she is distressed or when she wants to nod off to sleep, but extensive use of a dummy will stop her from making the all-important pre-speech babbling sounds.

Q Is it sensible to use 'baby talk' with my baby? I notice that many people use words with him such as 'choo choo' instead of 'train' and 'bow wow' instead of 'dog'. Should I encourage this?

A It's really up to you to decide on this one. Some people argue that there is no point in teaching a baby a word such as 'bunny', as he will eventually have to replace it with the proper word 'rabbit'. Others, however, support the use of baby talk on the grounds that it is easier for an infant to understand and subsequently use, and therefore it is a good stepping stone in language progress. Either way, occasional use of baby talk won't do him any harm.

Q I've noticed that my infant often becomes startled when I appear in front of his cot, even though I have spoken to him while approaching. Why is he so surprised by my arrival?

A He may not have perfectly clear hearing at the moment. A baby typically uses a number of cues to prepare for someone who is about to enter his line of vision – the sounds of that person's footsteps and of their voice are good indicators of an impending arrival. One of the possible explanations for your baby's behaviour is that he doesn't hear these sounds very clearly – hence his total surprise when, from his point of view, you suddenly appear in front of him. Arrange an appointment to have his hearing checked.

Language
Stimulation

At around four to six months old your child passes from the cooing stage to the point where she begins to babble. She also becomes a more active participant in your conversations with her and she will give you the impression that she wants to join in the discussion.

Above: Singing nursery rhymes while playing with your baby helps her to learn more about language.

By the time your baby is seven to nine months old, you'll notice that her sounds seem to have a pattern to them. She might start to use the same sound combinations regularly and even use them in the same situation. This is a clear sign that her babbling is controlled, not random, and that she is using language in a more purposeful way.

How can I encourage my baby's language skills?

• **Pause when talking to her,** or when you ask her a question, just as you do when chatting with an adult. This will help develop her understanding of the concept of taking turns in a conversation.

• **Encourage her listening skills** by making a variey of sounds from different parts of a room. Each time you make the noise, wait for her to turn round to look at you, and praise her when she does.

• **Read stories with feeling and expression,** altering your voice tone to engage her interest.

• **When outside, chat to her about the things she can see.** Make a comment about the colour of the grass or the size of a bus. If she stares at something in particular, comment on it.

• **Once your baby begins to babble, pick one of the sound combinations she has just used and say it back to her** ('la') using your usual tone of voice. Your use of the same sounds makes her feel very good about herself.

• **Name everyday household objects as you use them.** Evidence from psychological research indicates that a nine-month-old child may in fact understand a lot more than she is generally given credit for. Ask her 'Where is the ball?' and watch her eyes – if she understands what you have said, she will start to look for the named item.

• **Show your baby individual picture cards,** naming each picture as she looks at it. Do this no more than a couple of minutes each day.

Language
The first words

At around nine months your child may manage to say her first word. This is a major step forward as it signifies her ability to use spoken language in a way that allows her to communicate meaningfully and precisely with you. Your child's first spoken word also marks the start of a rapid growth in vocabulary over the next couple of years.

Q My baby is close to saying his first word, how can I encourage him to make the leap?

A Provide good examples of speech for him to copy. When you notice that he tends to use the same sound to describe the same person or object, encourage him by saying the word he means. For instance, if he makes the sounds 'paneh' whenever he sees his grandmother, you could say to him 'Yes, that's right, it's grandma'. Although his utterance and your word might appear to be totally different to you, your child might think they are the same. So your speech provides a model for him to copy.

Q Will my baby say her first word earlier if I encourage her to repeat words after me?

A You shouldn't pressurize your baby into saying her first word. At this age, your child's sounds should be spontaneous, not forced, and should be made because she wants to communicate with you, not because she thinks you will be disappointed with her if she doesn't speak.

Q My friend sings nursery rhymes to her son, even though he cannot possibly sing along yet. Does this make sense?

A By the age of one, a baby can easily become familiar with words and tunes and will even try to 'sing' along in his own way. This activity enhances his listening skills and teaches him that speech follows a sequence and isn't just a random series of sounds.

Q My first language is not English and I would like my baby to learn to speak both languages. Will this just confuse her?

A Babies can be bilingual and will learn two languages much more quickly and naturally than learning one later in life. It is easier for the baby to learn different languages if they are presented to her by separate people. You could speak to her only in your first language, while her father speaks only English to her. She may be a little slower beginning to talk than if she had only one language to learn, and may mix them up slightly in the beginning, but very soon she will be at ease in both.

Q Can I expect my one-year-old to respond to basic instructions?

A By the time your baby has spoken his first word, he will recognize a wide range of sounds, even sentences. Although he cannot respond in full, he is likely to respond to basic instructions. Try asking him to give you the spoon during feeding. Reward a positive response with a smile or hug; if he doesn't understand, repeat the question, then lift up the spoon to show him.

Language
Common problems

Q I find myself instinctively talking to my baby using short sentences with large gaps between phrases and an exaggerated voice tone that I do not use when talking to another adult. Will this have a bad effect on the way she speaks?

A This is known as 'parentese', and it has been discovered by psychologists that using this style of language with young babies, in moderation, can be helpful in stimulating their language skills. However, it is important not to fall into the trap of constantly talking down to your baby, as that does not provide a good model on which she can base her own language skills.

Above: Talking to your baby, even when she's young, helps to stimulate later language skills.

Q My baby uses sounds that are unrecognizable as part of our language. He is eight months old. Could I just be mishearing what he says?

A Psychologists studying the babbling used by babies from many different countries have made a remarkable discovery – irrespective of their country of origin, babies tend to make the same range of babbling sounds. Of course, what happens during the first year of life is that they drop the sounds they don't hear used by those around them, and increase those that they hear regularly. So your son will soon stop using those sounds that are foreign to you and will only use those that are part of his own language system.

Q My son is almost nine months old and I'm sure his language is developing more slowly than his sister's when she was that age. Is that normal?

A Evidence from research suggests that in general boys develop language at a slower rate than girls at every step along the way. This is a trend, however, and doesn't mean that every boy develops at a slower rate. It does suggest, though, that your daughter's faster language acquisition is normal.

Q My 10-month-old baby is often slow to respond to my voice when I talk to her. Sometimes she does not respond at all. Could she have poor hearing, and will this affect the way she learns to speak?

A Slow responses could certainly point to a hearing difficulty, which can slow down

Above: Spending time showing your baby picture books stimulates language development.

part in body language, too. It seems as though your little boy isn't prepared to make an effort if you don't grasp his message first time. Do your best to encourage him to use the gesture again, perhaps by asking him 'Is this what you want?' as you lift different objects. You may find that if you show persistence, he will respond with persistence, too, until you have fully understood what he tried to tell you.

Q My child has said his first word, but I'm upset because it wasn't 'mum' or 'dad'. Am I being silly reacting in this way?
A What matters is that your child has said his first word, not the actual word itself. There are two reasons why 'mum' and 'dad' are often first words – parents naturally encourage their child to say these words and repeat them many times to him, and also these words are easy for a child to pronounce. You are probably upset because you think that this means he doesn't love you as much as you thought – but put this idea out of your mind completely. Whether or not he uses 'mum' or 'dad' as his first word has no bearing whatsoever on the strength of his emotional bond with you.

language development because it means the growing child can't hear the sounds she makes herself, nor can she hear the sounds that others make to her. A child who misses out on this early auditory stimulation finds learning to speak more challenging than does a child with normal hearing. With any concerns like this, check with your doctor.

Q I find that if my child gestures that he wants something, he gives up quickly if I don't understand exactly what he wants. What should I do?
A Some children are more determined to communicate than others. Personality plays a

Virtually all babies build their language skills in the same way, using the same 'building blocks' in the same order and usually at around the same time.

TEETH

How to care for them

Your baby's milk teeth are essential to provide the right foundation for the later permanent teeth.

Milk teeth have to last a long time. From the first one emerging when your baby is around six months old, it will be around six years before it falls out, to be replaced by a permanent tooth. Your child is likely to lose teeth in roughly the same order that they arrived, but this happens gradually over a long period, between the ages of six and 12. Taking care of them right from the start will give your child the best chance of having a healthy mouth and strong teeth right into adulthood.

Why milk teeth matter

There are three key reasons why milk teeth are so important. Primarily, they maintain the spaces into which the permanent teeth may grow. If one is missing, it may be necessary for your child to wear a brace or 'space maintainer' to hold space for the adult tooth. Secondly, as your baby moves on to solids, her teeth will become increasingly important as she develops the skills of biting, chewing and grinding.

Thirdly, caring for milk teeth will help to give your child a healthy mouth for the final permanent teeth. An infection of a milk tooth could cause damage to the permanent tooth that is developing in the jaw. Teeth also play a role in normal speech development.

Starting to clean

As soon as your baby's first tooth emerges you need to clean it – and the subsequent teeth – regularly twice a day, morning and at night after the final feed. As your child gets older, she will want to be involved in the toothbrushing process and you should encourage any signs of enthusiasm. It is important to remember, however, that you still need to brush your child's teeth, as she won't have the necessary skills to do a thorough job. Continue to brush your child's teeth up to the age of five, if she will let you.

Get brushing right

Using the right technique when brushing your child's teeth can make a huge difference to how effective the routine is. The aim is to get rid of as much plaque as possible, without harming the teeth or gums in the process. You need to exert even, gentle pressure when cleaning. Brushing too hard can wear away the tooth enamel over time, so encourage your child to take longer, but brush less firmly.

Here is a step-by-step guide to help you get the brushing technique right:

1 Start with the outside surfaces of the top teeth, beginning at the back molars, then slowly move around to the centre and across to the other side. Hold the brush so that the bristles are at a slight angle to the gumline and move it in a gentle circular motion over one or two teeth at a time.

2 Next, clean the inside surfaces of the top teeth, working from the back to the centre and then around to the other side. Hold the brush vertically and use the front section of the brush, again with a gentle circular motion.

3 Finally, brush the chewing surfaces. Keep the toothbrush flat so that you also clean the grooves and natural fissures in the molars.

4 Repeat for the teeth in the lower jaw.

Reluctant to brush?

From time to time, many toddlers will make toothbrushing a battleground. The tips below may help to smooth things along:

- Brush your own teeth at the same time as your child is brushing hers.
- Pretend you can see the food in her mouth that needs to be brushed away and praise her when it's 'gone'.
- Put a mirror at your child's level so that she can watch herself brushing her teeth.
- Let her choose her own novelty or favourite character toothbrush.
- Use a hand puppet as a 'friend' to brush her teeth with.
- Always tell her how shiny her clean teeth look after brushing, and praise her for being good.

As well as regular twice-a-day brushing, one of the most important things you can do to help keep your child's teeth healthy is to avoid sugary foods and drinks.

Hand–eye coordination
What is typical?

The world is a fascinating place for your young baby. There is so much he wants to learn, so many things he wants to discover – and for the first year of his life his main means of exploring is through looking and touching. He spends time watching the world around him, sometimes just taking in the information he sees, sometimes reaching out to get directly involved, and often combining both vision and touch. It is this hand–eye coordination that occupies so much of his time.

Your baby will not yet understand the implications of his actions. That's why, for instance, he happily grabs the spectacles from your face and cheerfully twists them till they fall apart. It's genuine curiosity that drives his behaviour, nothing else. It is important to set limits without losing your temper at his explorations. If you become continually angry with him, you run the risk of making your baby afraid to reach out and investigate. The same caution applies to safety. Exploration is the name of the game during your baby's first year and he runs the risk of choking, vomiting or eating dirt in his determination to discover. Keep an eye on him to make sure he remains safe.

What can my baby do?

4–5 months	• He can focus on near and distant objects as well as an adult can, has a firm grip and doesn't like to let go. He begins to play with his hands and feet.
6–8 months	• By six months, he can pass objects from one hand to the other. He plays with toys more purposefully instead of just mouthing them and tries to feed himself by putting food to his mouth with his fingers.
9–10 months	• He is now able to use a firm pincer movement to feed himself finger food such as peas and raisins. He may be able to build a two-brick tower and likes playing with toys that move across the floor.
11–12 months	• He can pull the lids off boxes to find whatever is inside them and can turn pages of a book. He can also slot simple shapes correctly into a shape-sorter.

Hand–eye coordination
Common questions

Q Is it safe for me to leave some toys in the cot so that my baby can play with them whenever she wants?

A As long as you are sure the items are safe, it's fine to leave some toys at the side of the cot. Apart from staring at them, she will also reach for them. Your baby almost certainly wakes up earlier in the morning than you would like. With a pile of toys within reach, she can play on her own without needing your attention. It's good to give her this sort of independence early on.

Q No matter how many toys are close to hand, my six-month-old quite often just stares at me as I go about the routine housework. Is this normal?

A Filling and emptying the washing machine may seem boring to you, but your young baby loves to watch you moving around the house like that. You should let your baby watch you doing routine household chores and, if possible, position her in such a way that she can see you easily.

Right: Toys and objects of different shapes and sizes can help to improve your child's hand control.

Q My 10-month-old cannot always do what he sets out to achieve. Should I help him or will this impede his progress?

A You should certainly offer solutions to your baby. If you see that he is stuck at a particular hand–eye coordination puzzle (for instance, putting a shape into the shape-sorter) you could suggest other ways for him to do this. Stay with him as he tries out these suggestions and praise him when he succeeds.

Q My niece can feed herself finger food at seven months, while my daughter, who is a month older, has not yet mastered the pincer movement. Should I be worried about her slower development?

A Avoid comparisons. Every child is different, and you may find that your niece has more advanced hand–eye coordination skills than your child even though they are a similar age.

Hand–eye coordination
Stimulation

Your baby's hand–eye coordination develops dramatically from about four to six months. She is altogether more reactive to you and to her general surroundings. There is more purpose behind her vision and touch, and your baby will become an active explorer, using her hand–eye coordination in a more focused and controlled way.

By the time your baby is seven to nine months old, her ability to sit on her own is well-established, and she can make a good attempt to propel herself along the floor by crawling: she will do just about anything to get hold of whatever she wants. Despite her increased independence, she still has more fun playing when you are involved. By all means step back a little and give her space to explore on her own, but do remember she still needs you.

How can I encourage my baby's hand–eye coordination skills?

• Ask her to look for objects that are not immediately to hand but are within her visual range. Your question 'Where's the ball?' prods her into action.

• If your baby tries to grab hold of the bottle or the spoon while having her meal, let her (though don't let go yourself). You may decide sometimes to give finger food as a snack, and this helps too.

• Let her reach for picture books. If she wants to have a closer look when you talk to her about the pictures in her book, allow her to grab hold of the thick, cardboard pages herself.

• When the two of you sit together, point to something in the room and say to her 'Look at that'; she will follow the line of your hand to the object. Then ask her to point to a specific object in the room.

• Give her direct commands involving hand–eye coordination. For instance, tell her gently 'Give me the cup'; she should be able to look round to see where the cup is, pick it up in her hand and then pass it to you.

Left: Encourage your baby to explore with her hands by giving her safe household objects to play with.

Suitable toys for your growing baby

Age	Toy/Activity	Skill
4–6 months	Soft story book	• To encourage the idea of turning pages.
	Soft play mat	• So that your baby can reach for small toys and fall without injury.
	Soft building blocks and small wooden shapes	• For your baby to learn to hold something in both hands at the same time. To start with she will hold them for a very short time before dropping them, but she will get better at it. You can also use the blocks to show your baby how to pass things from one hand to the other.
7–9 months	Small toy blocks	• So she can practise the pincer movement. Your baby can use her forefinger and thumb in a pincer grip rather like a pair of pliers. A small object can easily slip from her grasp, but the skill will improve with practice.
	Wheeled toy on a string	• To encourage an understanding of cause-and-effect toys. Show your baby how you can reach the toy from a sitting position by pulling on the string. Instruct her to do the same.
	Musical instruments, pots and pans with wooden spoons	• A fun way to develop coordination. You can arrange the pots in a row in front of your baby and ask her to hit each one in turn. Once she has mastered this, encourage her to hit the pots at random.
10–12 months	Plastic cups and jugs for the bath	• To improve your baby's hand control as she pours water from one vessel to another.
	Boxes and pots with lids	• To develop greater dexterity. You can put something inside a box or pot so that it rattles when the baby shakes it. She will not be able to curb her curiosity and will soon have the lid off.
	Stacking cubes, nesting beakers	• For a more complex task, setting the challenge of ordering items by size. Your baby will probably need a good deal of practice here, but should be able to make two or three pieces fit inside one another.
	Board books	• To develop the skill of turning individual pages. Your baby will use both hands to separate the pages at this stage.

Hand–eye coordination
Common problems

Q My five-month-old baby grabs at anything he sets his eyes on, including household objects. Should I move things out of the way or is that just giving in to him?

A It's best to remove possible temptations, especially if they present a danger or are precious. Like it or not, you may have to change the way your household is organized in order to accommodate the increasing hand–eye coordination skills of your child. It's far easier remove a fragile ornament altogether than to worry constantly that he'll get his hands on it. Once he understands 'no' you can teach him what he should not touch.

Q What other strategies can I use to keep him safe?

A Praise him when he follows the rules. There is no bigger incentive for your baby to stick to rules about touching than your approval. He'll beam with delight when you cuddle him for not going near that hot radiator, and he'll feel very self-satisfied when you hug him for staying away from the electric socket.

Q My baby is eight months old and gets angry when she can't complete a puzzle toy. What should I do?

A React calmly to her frustration. When your child simply can't manage that hand–eye coordination activity and consequently erupts with fury, don't let yourself get riled. Do your best to soothe her, then suggest she tries again. If she still doesn't succeed, put the item away and come back to it again later.

Q My six-month-old baby seems uninterested in toys and will not make the effort to reach out for them. Is there something wrong with him?

A Children differ in their level of desire to explore, some are more dynamic than others.

Left: Giving your child toys to play with in the bath is a good way to encourage hand–eye coordination, and is fun for your baby too.

Above: Toys such as this shape sorter are a good way to improve your child's hand–eye coordination.

If yours is one of those who won't reach out for toys and isn't very keen to explore, then be prepared to bring toys to him, place them gently in his hands, and play with him. This will increase his motivation. He needs you to push him gently into more activities. Also, check that he has available toys suitable for his stage of development (see page 101).

Q Is there any point expecting my baby to play quietly? She really likes to make a loud noise.

A Naturally you don't want to discourage her from playing, but now is as good a time as any to teach her that there are other people to consider. When she makes a particularly loud noise, speak quietly to her and ask her to be more gentle. She'll respond to you, at least for a few seconds anyway.

Q Is it too early to set limits for my three-month-old baby, telling him what he can and cannot play with?

A He's still quite young but you could consider setting up some rules about touching. Make a

point of warning him about small items. Your baby still likes to put things in his mouth, although he is more aware of the dangers this poses. When you see him about to put a small item in his mouth, firmly but quietly say 'no' and remove the object from his hand. Once he is a little older and more mobile, set some 'no go' areas in your home. Decide what objects you don't want him to explore (for instance, your china ornaments, electric sockets, electrical items) and tell him not to touch these. You will probably have to repeat this process again and again and again.

Q My baby doesn't seem to get very far with any activity before she loses interest. I think she gives up too easily, is there something I can do to help?

A If you think your child gives up too easily, give her gentle encouragement to complete the task, but don't force her. And make a point of setting a good example yourself. Let her see you struggle with a similar task while still smiling (for instance, pouring water from a jug to a cup) – this will persuade her to adopt a similar attitude.

Q No matter how often I show my baby how to put the shapes in his shape-sorter toy, he still can't manage them all. Should he be able to?

A Shape-sorters are incredibly difficult for little fingers to manage. Your son can probably manage the circle and square shapes but not the more complicated ones. Give him time to learn the solutions. As his hand-control increases over the next few months, he will fit more shapes into the right holes.

Movement
What is typical?

Many of the remarkable changes in your baby's control over her movements seem to occur spontaneously, without any prompting, alongside her physical and neurological maturation. For example, no matter how much walking practice you give a baby who is, say, six months old, she won't be able to coordinate her leg and body movements at that age to enable her to walk.

In contrast to this, there is evidence that practice in other aspects of movement does have an impact. A child who is allowed lots of opportunities to crawl will probably be better at crawling than a child who is denied this form of activity. The same applies to moving up and down stairs. Perhaps the best strategy to take when it comes to encouraging your baby's movement is to remember that the pace of physical and neurological development has a big impact and that this will limit the effect of practice in some areas.

What can my baby do?

4–6 months	• Your baby can sit in an upright position with support, turn from side to side and move around the floor by rolling and turning.
6–7 months	• She can now sit up on her own without requiring any support and shows the first signs of crawling. She also rolls competently from back to front and vice versa.
8–9 months	• She can take her own weight, gripping a chair for support and is able to crawl forwards and backwards. She also tries to climb up stairs.
10–11 months	• She stands on her own two feet, gripping something for support, but will shortly be standing independently. She climbs up the first step and slides back down.
12 months	• She shows her first sign of independent walking and is more confident climbing up the stairs. She may walk if you hold her hands.

Movement
Common questions

Q Could I damage my baby's legs by bending and stretching them to strengthen them?

A As long as you do this gently, without causing any discomfort, his leg muscles will probably benefit from this exercise. However, don't force your baby. If you make the leg movements very soft, and you talk happily to your baby as you do so, then he will probably have a great time.

Q Why does my five-month-old usually keep her legs off the cot mattress whereas before she used to rest them on it?

A This is just the effect of the growth in her leg muscles, and the fact that she's no longer as passive. Keeping her legs in the air like this is more comfortable for her and she can move around more freely without knocking anything. And she likes playing with her toes!

Q Should I restrain my baby when she wriggles around during bathtime?

A Your first priority must always be to keep her safe. But if you hold her steady, you can just let her wriggle and splash about. The sensation of warm water against her legs, coupled with the noise of splashing, excites her. Allow an extra few minutes for her bathing routine so that she has this special time to practise her movement skills.

Q Would my 11-month-old baby feel compelled to take her first step if I let go of her hands suddenly so that she is left standing alone?

Above: Helping your child while he is learning to take his first steps will increase his confidence.

A That could in theory motivate your child to walk, though it is more likely to terrify her. Dramatic gestures like that can backfire, making her less willing to trust you next time.

Q How old should my baby be before I can take him swimming?

A Once he has had his first set of immunizations you can take your baby to a public swimming bath. At the pool, the water and surrounding air temperatures should both be warm, but even so your baby may get cold fairly quickly so the swimming session should be short. Introduce him to the water by holding him with the water around you, and when he is relaxed you can let him float on his back in the water as you support him. Babies who are introduced to swimming early usually feel at home in water and don't have to overcome fear later.

Movement
Stimulation

Probably the most significant change in movement around four to six months is your growing baby's ability to sit up with a decreasing amount of support, and by six months he can do it on his own.

Once this has been accomplished, it is the turn of your child's lower body to become more responsive. As the early stages of crawling emerge from seven to nine months he finds totally new ways of moving himself around the house. Your baby's improved balance and body movements, coupled with his increased chest, hip and leg strength, have all been aiming towards this last section of the first year, when he might actually take his first independent steps. And even if he hasn't started walking by the age of 12 months, he will almost certainly be well on the way to that achievement.

How can I stimulate my baby's movement skills?

• Play movement games, such as softly swinging your baby from side to side while holding him firmly. His balance will improve steadily between the fourth and sixth month.
• Use easy exercises to develop your baby's back, chest and neck muscles: let your baby lie stretched out on the floor and kneel at his feet. Let him grip your index fingers ;once his hands are locked around your fingers, raise him slightly from the ground.

• When he is face down, put his favourite toys just out of his reach. Now that he knows he can move towards them, he will try very hard to reach them.
• Move around the room as you talk to him so that he turns his head to follow. This enhances his head control and balance.
• By nine months you should be able to put your baby in a standing position and let him take his own weight by gripping on to a low table or solid, heavy chair.
• Allow him time in a baby walker.
• Once he is able to stand confidently, hold his hands in yours and edge backwards slowly. He may try to take a step forward.
• Once he starts to cruise around the room using the furniture for support, gradually extend the gaps between each item so that he almost has to lunge at the next one.

I can roll

When your baby is around four months old, you'll notice that he turns from one side to the other. One moment he was side-on to the left, yet a few seconds later he faces the right. This is a remarkable feat of coordination, involving head, neck, chest, hips, arms and legs. He can change his position without waiting for you, which provides a huge boost to his independence. Similarly, your growing baby can turn from his back to his tummy completely on his own. As well as giving him more ways to explore and discover, this demonstration of body strength proves that he is getting ready for sitting up, crawling and walking.

Movement
Direction of control

Every baby is different in terms of rates of movement development, but in general, your baby's ability to gain control over his body movements in the first 12 months follows two distinct directions:

• **From the head down.** He establishes control at the top of his body before lower down. For instance, he will be able to hold his head up independently before his spine is strong enough for him to sit up on his own; and he will sit upright long before he can walk.
• **From the chest out.** Your baby gains control over the middle of his body before his hands and feet. For instance, he can raise his chest off the floor before he can reach out accurately with his hands; and he will be able to pick up something with his fingers before he can kick a ball with his toes.

Their own way

One amazing aspect of movement in babies is that although the majority of them pass their physical milestones at roughly the same age (for instance, most can sit up on their own by the age of six months), there is huge variation in the way that each stage is achieved.

Crawling and walking are two good examples of this. Your baby might be one of those who like to crawl with their hands and knees touching the floor, while your best friend's baby of the same age might prefer to crawl with his bottom high in the air and his knees raised off the ground. But

Above: By nine months babies may be able to climb stairs, but will need close supervision from behind.

they are both crawling, in their own distinctive ways. There are even some babies who dislike crawling so much that they show no interest in it, and make a smooth transition from sitting to walking with almost no crawling in between. The same applies with walking. Your baby might have gone from sitting up, to crawling, to standing, to walking. Yet there are others who have an intermediate stage of bottom-shuffling in which they sit upright on the floor, gently raising and dropping their bottom as they propel themselves along.

Movement
Common problems

Q My four-month-old baby rolls over from her stomach to her back, but cannot roll back again. Is there something wrong with her?

A There is nothing wrong with your baby. At this age your baby is more likely to roll over from her stomach to her back – because it is easier than the other way round. She is able to use her arms in a pushing action in order to start the movement off.

Q My six-month-old baby has developed a crawl of sorts, but doesn't lift his tummy off the floor. I'm worried that he is too weak. Should I be exercising his muscles in some way?

A It is more likely that his crawling movements are simply not mature enough yet. He will improve his crawling ability spontaneously, and there are no specific exercises you should do to hurry the process along. However, make sure he has plenty of opportunities to lie face down on the floor so that he can practise crawling. It won't be long before he gets the hang of it.

Q Since my baby fell a couple of times trying to walk, she doesn't try any more. What should I do?

A Give her time to restore her confidence in her walking skills. You'll find that her natural drive to walk independently will surface again after a few days, once she has recovered from this temporary upset. In the meantime, don't pressurize her into walking.

Above: Between 10 and 11 months babies can stand on both feet, holding on to you for support.

Q Now that my baby is crawling I use a stair gate, but she is fascinated with the stairs and always makes a beeline for them. When can she learn about stairs, as I am anxious she might have an accident if she finds some unguarded?

A Babies do like to climb, so she is capable of going up stairs soon after she can crawl. It is a good idea to teach her now, in case she does ever find some that are unguarded. Let her crawl up, with you behind her – and if you ever discover her going up don't call and distract her which could cause a fall, but just get quietly behind her. With you below on the stairs, show her how to go down by crawling backwards. She will continue to crawl up and down stairs for some time after she can walk.

Q My baby is nine months old. I'm worried he'll hurt himself one of these days when he tries to pull himself up. How can I keep him safe?

A The only way he can learn new movement skills is by tackling new challenges and there is always a minor risk of injury in that situation. Instead of restricting his movements, stay close to him when he manoeuvres – that way you are better placed to prevent a potential accident.

Q While other babies seem energetic and active throughout the day, mine just sits there most of the time. Is there something wrong with her?

A Remember that the act of walking requires not only good balance and body movements but also bags of confidence. Often it is this lack of self-belief that stops a child from taking her first independent step – she is afraid of falling over. That's why she needs you to be patient and supportive. Do everything you can to relax and encourage her to walk, but don't make her anxious about it or else she will prefer to remain in the safe stage of sitting.

Q My baby bursts into tears if he cannot reach what he wants, what can I do?

A Your baby's ambition outstrips his ability when it comes to movement. In other words,

he has lofty aims and is none too pleased when reality takes over and he discovers that he can't reach that soft toy just out of reach. Calm him, reassure him, and be prepared to bring the object of his despair over to him. The next time you hear his moans of frustration, try to settle him before he reaches explosion point. He is less likely to become agitated and give up when you are there with him.

Q Over a month ago my little girl took a few steps on her own, but she seems to have forgotten all about it and now she is back to crawling. Is this normal?

A Developing new skills doesn't go steadily, but rather in fits and starts. It is normal for a baby to have a spurt and do something new and then just continue practising until she has mastered it without going on to the next step, or leave it while she concentrates on something else. Your daughter won't have forgotten how to walk, but she may have put it on a back burner while she tries out something else. When she's ready, she'll probably surprise you by suddenly taking off on two feet.

Right: Even when babies have taken their first few steps, many carry on crawling for some time.

Emotional development
What is typical?

Although every baby is different, with his own special and unique set of personal traits, psychologists have identified three main types of temperament in young children.

First, there is the easy child who copes happily with new experiences. He plays enthusiastically with new toys, sleeps and eats regularly, and adjusts easily to change. In contrast, the difficult child is the exact opposite. He resists any routine, cries a lot, takes a long time to finish his feeds and sleeps fitfully. And then there is the slow-to-warm-up child who is rather easy-going and passive. He doesn't get actively involved in anything and waits for the world to come to him. You can probably see aspects of all these types in your baby! Nobody knows for sure where emotional characteristics come from. Almost certainly, though, his personality and ability to relate to others is a combination of the characteristics he was born with and the way you raise him during childhood.

How does my baby behave?

4–5 months	• Your baby starts to use facial expressions to keep your attention. He can also be shy in the company of strangers. At this age he may form an attachment to a cuddly toy or other comforter
6–7 months	• At six months he will playfully hold on to a toy when you try to remove it. He is very aware of verbal praise and enthusiasm and enjoys the familiarity of routines such as bathtime and bedtime.
8–9 months	• He will begin to initiate social contact with other adults and is curious about other babies his own age. He will cling to you in crowded places.
10–11 months	• He will now give cuddles as well as receive them. He loves interactive games, like peek-a-boo and swings from positive to negative moods very quickly.
12 months	• At a year old he likes playing any game that involves social interaction between you and him. He has a preference for playing with a child of his own gender when in mixed groups.

Emotional development
Common questions

Q By what age should my baby have formed an emotional bond with me?

A That depends entirely on you and your baby. It can take anything from a few days to a few months or, in some cases, even longer (see pages 16–17). However, research has found that a child who has not formed this type of secure psychological connection with a caring adult by the time he is around the age of four is likely to have social difficulties throughout his life.

Above: As your baby gets older he will love to play interactive games with you.

Q Should I correct my baby when she misbehaves?

A Try to encourage good behaviour from her without falling into the trap of constantly correcting her when she does something wrong. She is more likely to learn appropriate behaviour if you tell her what she should do, and praise her for doing the right thing, instead of reprimanding her for what she shouldn't do.

Q Is it true that as babies, boys tend to be more difficult to manage than girls?

A There is not a great deal of research evidence to support this idea. However, it is generally true that baby boys do tend to be more adventurous than baby girls, but this could be because parents let boys behave this way while they discourage their girls from displaying such high-spirited behaviour.

Q Should I let my daughter hold the spoon at meals? She makes such a mess.

A She makes a mess because she can't do the job properly, but the only way she can learn is through practice. Try not to dampen her desire for independence, even though you could complete feeding quicker on your own. At least let her hold the spoon for part of the time.

Q As my baby gets older, should I talk to him more, and in a more grown-up fashion?

A You should certainly increase your expectations of his sociability. Whereas when he was younger you might have chatted to him without expecting any reasonable response, it's time for you to give him an opportunity to react. So when you talk to him, leave a pause for him to babble back at you; when you ask him a question such as 'Do you want another drink?' look for an answer in his facial expression, body movements and sounds, instead of just giving him the drink anyway. Your encouragement will make him realize that he needs to get involved.

Emotional development
Stimulation

Your infant's social skills increase as her need to mix with others intensifies, usually from around seven months. She starts to become more aware of other people around her and uses non-verbal communication to interact with them; she thrives on attention.

But despite this enthusiasm to have company, her social confidence remains very fragile – the moment she sets eyes on a stranger she may well burst into tears, and will show signs of separation anxiety if she thinks you are about to leave her alone with someone else (see page 86). By the time your baby is seven months old, she is more out-going socially and makes active attempts to respond to other people. At 10–12 months her main emotional characteristics are clear and strong, and you can probably predict how she will behave in most situations. However, your baby's increased awareness of the world around her causes a temporary halt to the growth in her sociability; her attachment to you becomes more intense and her desire to mix with others slows down a little at this stage.

How can I stimulate my baby's emotional development?

• **Let her play alongside other children her age.** Although she will not play with them and might even just sit and stare at them, these other children will be of great interest to her. She watches and learns from their actions.

• **Talk to other people when she is with you.** Your young baby needs to learn that language is a key part of most social interactions. Seeing you chat to people whom you meet provides a good model for her to copy.

• **Reassure her when she is shy with an unfamiliar adult.** When she hides because a stranger talks to her, hold her hand, cuddle her and tell her not to be afraid. Your reassurance helps her overcome this dip in her confidence.

• **Continue to show your child that you love her.** Regular demonstrations that you love and value her increase her self-confidence. She soaks up every drop of parental love you put her way and she responds by acting lovingly towards you.

• **Give her plenty of praise.** Your verbal praise and approval matters very much to your baby. It acts as encouragement to persevere, while also boosting her self-esteem.

• **Use a babysitter so that you can go out without her.** Aside from the benefits to you of going out on your own, it's also good for your baby to get used to someone else's care. She'll quickly adapt to and be happy with this temporary arrangement.

Emotional development
Confidence

The foundations of your child's self-confidence are laid during the first year. She may only be a young baby but she already has a sense of what she can and cannot do. Her confidence is affected by the achievements she makes: for instance, when at the age of four months she manages to reach out and grasp a toy that attracts her attention, or at the age of one year when she takes her first step. The way others react towards her has an impact on her confidence – your love, praise and interest all boost your baby's belief in herself.

A head start

Findings from psychological research suggest that the typical baby has a very strong belief in her own abilities. That's why she is willing to explore and venture into new areas, believing no challenge is beyond her.

For instance, she'll try to reach for a new toy that attracts her attention, she'll try to move her body across the floor when she wants to get to the other side of the room, and she'll try to communicate with you even though she can't yet talk. Yet her belief in herself is easily dented by experience, and the more she fails to achieve something, the more likely it is that your baby's self-confidence will dip and she'll give up trying.

What you can do to help
• A warm, loving hug is a fundamental way of telling your baby that you love her. Contact of this sort with you boosts her self-belief.
• If she explodes with frustration when she cannot do something, reassure her that she'll soon learn how to do it.
• Break challenges into small stages that are easier to manage.
• Avoid obvious pitfalls. If you can see she is heading for a disappointment, steer her away from that activity before she fully embarks upon it.

Five facts about **confidence**

1 Self-confidence has a significant effect on your baby's development because it influences her motivation, her drive to achieve, and her relationships with others.
2 A baby who doubts that she has the ability to master the challenges that face her won't even try to play with a new toy because she thinks that it will be too difficult for her.
3 A baby with a low level of self-value is unimpressed with her own achievements and is therefore less likely to take on a new challenge with any enthusiasm.
4 A baby who receives positive feedback from people around her will feel good about herself.
5 A baby with low self-confidence has less enjoyment in life, prefers to take a more passive role, and may have difficulty giving love and receiving it from others. Challenge and adventure threaten her rather than excite her, making her reluctant to discover and learn.

Emotional development
Common problems

Above: Some babies learn quickly that crying gets their parents attention.

Q Why does my baby frown most of the time? People say he looks really grumpy when they see him, but he's actually very happy most days.

A This illustrates why you can't always gain an accurate interpretation of facial expression unless you know the baby's personality. Since parenting experience has told you that he's generally a happy, contented child, then you know that his frowns – normally associated with bad temper – don't indicate irritation. A more likely explanation is that his creased forehead is an indication of interest and concentration, and is simply his way of focusing his attention. You'll find that his use of this expression passes, and that as he matures and his other facial muscles become stronger, his furrowed brow appears less frequently.

Q My five-month-baby is hugely demanding and seems to want to play or talk to me every minute of the day. Will it harm him if I ignore him once in a while?

A No, quite the opposite. Part of social and emotional development involves your child establishing an element of independence, of managing on his own without you right beside him all the time. If you rush over to him every time he calls for you out of boredom, your baby will never learn how to amuse himself. During this period of his life, try to make sure there are times when he is left to play in the cot on his own. This will strengthen his self-sufficiency and he will soon become far less demanding on your time and attention.

Q Sometimes, when I am playing with my six-month-old daughter, I find I do something that makes her grumpy. What should I do?

A Primarily, don't pander to her grumpy moments. If your child is irritable at times, carry on talking to her and playing with her anyway. If you simply leave her alone when she is moody, her irritability will probably continue for longer.

Q My baby is eight months old but still cries extremely easily. How can I make him more robust?

A He probably cries so much because this is an effective way of getting your attention. Start to ignore some of his crying episodes unless you are sure there is something seriously wrong. His tears may flow less frequently when he realizes they don't achieve the desired effect.

Q My baby is only nine months old yet already she seems to have terrific mood swings. Is this normal?

A Babies vary greatly in their sensitivity and moods. Maybe your baby is one of those who is very dramatic when it comes to expressing her emotions; perhaps she howls loudly the minute anything goes wrong and whines and moans most of the time. Results from psychological research suggest that many of these important personality traits that are present during the early months are usually stable, in that they tend to stick with the baby for the rest of her life, so you do need to help your baby to learn to control her emotions.

Q My 10-month-old baby has had a comforter for months and I am beginning to worry that I may never wean him off it. Will this affect his emotional development?

A Using a comforter does not mean your child is afraid or timid. In fact, there is no link between comforters in early childhood and emotional instability later on – if anything, evidence from studies shows that babies who become attached to a comforter are often more confident when they start attending school.

Q Although she has no spoken language yet, my nine-month-old has no problem letting me know when she is about to explode with frustration. How can I help her release these feelings without having a tantrum?

A Frustration is common at this age, and as she can't yet express her inner tension with words, body language is the only way to release her annoyance. You'll already be aware of the situations that frequently lead to her frustration. Watch her in these circumstances, and try to defuse her temper before it builds up. For instance, distract her attention when you see her struggling with a toy – she can always return to it later on when she is calm.

Right: From about seven months some babies become shy of strangers and need plenty of reassurance to regain their confidence.

Safety in the home

It is a rare baby who never has any sort of accident, since the world around us, other people, and babies themselves are not totally predictable. In most cases the accident is a small thing such as an item dropped on a baby or a newly sitting baby toppling backward to bump her head.

Protecting your baby is one of your most important jobs as a parent, and the risk of a serious accident must always be borne in mind. Major accidents to babies do occur with tragic frequency, and although it is impossible to remove all risks, most serious accidents could be avoided with proper care.

Q What are the most common hazards for a pre-crawler?

A There are a number of everyday situations that could cause potential harm to your baby. For example, a loose rug or clutter on the floor could trip you up – if you were carrying your baby you could both go down, or you could drop or spill something hot onto her. Putting a baby down to play or sleep too close to a heat source or in direct sunlight can be harmful. Don't rely on second-hand equipment unless you know its history. All new equipment should meet safety standards and have a clear mark of approval.

Above: Keep your baby out of the kitchen when you are busy and unable to keep an eye on her.

Q What should I be wary of once my baby can crawl?

A Once your baby is on the move, even if she is only just crawling, you really need to try to think ahead of her development. It won't be long before she is able to climb furniture to satisfy her curiosity, or is dextrous enough to open a small screw-top jar. Remove anything breakable from within her easy reach and make sure all medicines or cleaning agents are kept in lockable or baby-proof cabinets. Do not have electric wires trailing across a floor or down the wall from shelving. Fit safety gates on stairs, top and bottom, and use fireguards around open fires.

The kitchen is the most dangerous room in the house, so use a playpen in the corner or a safety gate across the door. Your baby should not be underfoot when you are busy.

Five tips for a **baby-proof home**

1 If your baby is still most mobile close to the ground, make certain that the floor is clear of small objects that she will otherwise 'hoover up' and try out for taste.

2 Make sure precious heirlooms and breakable ornaments are out of reach.

3 Fit safety plugs on all low-level electrical sockets and run flexes behind furniture and fix along the base of a wall. Where there are several flexes together, run them in a plastic tunnel.

4 Place safety gates at the top and bottom of the staircase and put childproof locks on all low cupboards and doors.

5 Tuck away curtain cords and blinds that could entangle or even strangle a child. Make sure the curtains and any upholstery are made from flame-retardant material.

Q Are there specific safety guidelines for a baby's cot?

A Yes. Primarily a baby's cot must be deep enough to stop him climbing out. There should be a space of at least 50 cm (20 in) from the top of the mattress to the top of the cot, and the gap between the cot and the mattress edge should be no more than 3 cm (1⅛ in). The spaces between the bars should be no more than 6 cm (2¼ in) wide so your baby's head cannot get stuck. Make sure the clasps on the dropside are strong enough to resist inquisitive hands. If you use a cot bumper, keep the ties short, so your baby cannot twist them round his finger. Any mattress or bedding cover must be made of breathable fabric in case the baby's head gets trapped inside. Never use a pillow for a baby under the age of 12 months because of the possibility of suffocation. Instead of a duvet, which a baby could kick over his face, or become overheated beneath, use a sheet and cellular blankets.

Right: Safety gates are a good way to prevent children from wandering in to a room where there may be potential dangers.

IMMUNIZATION

Protecting your child against illness

Immunization has changed the face of childhood illnesses beyond recognition. But is it as safe as we are led to believe?

It is arguable that the most important step you can take to protect your children against serious illness is to have them immunized. Most people, including health professionals, would say that it is not arguable, it is certain. When vaccination against smallpox began on a large scale at the start of the nineteenth century, the numbers of children dying from it plummeted and the disease is now eradicated.

What vaccines do

Vaccines work by priming the body to anticipate illness. The vaccine contains a version of the virus or bacterium that normally cause the infection, or enough of it to trick the immune system into reacting as though it had met the real thing. White blood cells – B-lymphocytes – then make antibodies to the germs and these linger in the body, ready to annihilate the real thing should it ever arrive. The reason the child does not develop the infection when they are immunized is that the virus or

The MMR debate

The measles vaccination was introduced in 1968, at which time there were some 600,000 cases of measles a year, 100 of them fatal. The number of vaccinated children increased dramatically with the introduction of the three-in-one MMR vaccine (mumps, measles, rubella) in 1988, and by 1996 the percentage of vaccinated children was as high as 92 per cent. However, a study in 1998 linked the MMR vaccine with autism and parents began to opt out of having their children jabbed. Although the autism link was never substantiated and there has been no increase in autism since the MMR vaccine was introduced, the number of vaccinated children fell to 82 per cent in 2003. Should this number continue to decline, there is a very real risk that outbreaks of measles will rise, even making way for an epidemic in the not so distant future.

bacterium has been pre-treated to make it harmless. Sometimes it is heated or treated with chemicals, or only a small part of it is used. Diphtheria and tetanus vaccines, for example, only contain pre-treated toxins.

In both the UK and US, infants start their immunization at two months old, when they receive a combination vaccine against whooping cough (or pertussis), diphtheria, tetanus and Hib – *Haemophilus influenzae* type B, a cause of bacterial meningitis. At the same time they have a dose of polio vaccine by mouth. In the UK, this is repeated after one month and again one month later (in the US it is two month intervals). The next vaccines come between a child's first birthday and 15 months, against measles, mumps and rubella, either as a combination dose or as three single vaccines. The whole programme is reinforced before the child starts school with two booster doses, one against measles, mumps and rubella, and the other against diphtheria and tetanus, as well as a polio booster.

Possible complications

Vaccines commonly have minor adverse effects. For example, some babies are fretful within 48 hours of the DTP Hib injection. More worrying for parents, vaccines can also have acute adverse effects. Out of 14 million doses of vaccine given to children in the UK in 1995, there were 152 officially reported serious reactions. Some of these were probably a coincidence – illnesses that simply happened to develop just after immunization. Others were linked to the vaccine. Anaphylactic reactions are known to occur extremely rarely after a vaccine is given, which is why every nurse or doctor administering a vaccine is trained in resuscitation. In three years from 1992, there were only 87 reports of anaphylaxis out of 55 million doses of vaccine. The possibility of a severe reaction to immunization is why infants are usually kept under supervision until they are seen to be well.

When not to immunize

At the time of vaccination, you should tell your doctor if any of the following are true. He or she may want to seek specialist advice before advising you further about whether or not to have the vaccination.

- If your baby has diarrhoea, vomiting or a fever.
- If your baby is showing the first signs of having a runny nose or a cold.
- If your child has had a serious reaction to a vaccination before.
- If your child suffered any damage to the nervous system at birth or shows any signs of not developing properly.
- If you child has fits or any known allergies.

Opponents of vaccination worry, however, whether there are other effects. A research group at the Royal Free Hospital in London has raised the question of whether measles vaccination may – rarely – make the development of inflammatory bowel disease in later life more likely. In the absence of proof one way or the other, current advice is to remember the millions of lives saved by immunization and be vaccinated.

By not vaccinating a child, a parent not only leaves their child prey to the illness, but also lowers the overall level of immunity within the community. Once the overall level drops, the infection can gain a foothold again. This poses very real risks for babies too young for vaccination and for children with weakened immune systems, such as those being treated for leukaemia.

Health issues
Basic first aid

This health section covers minor accidents only. First aid cannot be taught from a book, and to be able to deal with resuscitation, severe bleeding and burns or head injuries, you should enrol on a first-aid course. Otherwise you should get your child seen by a doctor or take her to an accident and emergency department. (See also pages 174–175 and 244–245.)

Above: A fever strip is the easiest way to take your child's temperature.

Q How should I take my baby's temperature?

A It is not usually necessary to know the exact temperature, because a baby's temperature can go up and down quite rapidly and not necessarily give an accurate indication of illness. You can tell when your baby is feverish because her forehead and abdomen may feel hot to the back of your hand and her eyes may look burning and shiny. She may also lose interest in food and be more irritable and clingy than usual. As well as fever, a temperature that is lower than normal can be an important sign of illness. A normal temperature is 36–37.5°C (97–99.5°F). A fever strip that you hold on your baby's forehead is the easiest way to take her temperature. Otherwise you can hold a thermometer in her armpit, with her arm pressed against her side to keep in her body heat, for two minutes.

The family medicine chest

Keep all medicines in a child-proof medicine chest, well out of reach of even a child standing on a chair. The following are essentials:

- Children's sugar-free paracetamol or soluble tablets for older children. The brand doesn't matter, so choose the one your child prefers.
- Oral rehydration sachets. These are useful for making up balanced drinks should your child develop diarrhoea.
- Calamine lotion to soothe itchy rashes such as those that occur with chickenpox.
- Aqueous cream to moisturize dry skin.
- Vaseline or petroleum jelly to protect noses, lips and chins during a cold.
- Any prescribed drugs that do not need to be kept in a fridge.
- A fever strip and mercury or digital thermometer.

Q What should I do if my baby develops a fever?

A When your baby is feverish, feeling burning hot to the touch and shivery or shaky, try to cool him by using only lightweight clothes and bedcovers and keeping the room pleasantly warm but not too hot. Give extra drinks and you can give a dose of paracetamol syrup. Sponge his arms and legs with lukewarm water, or put him in a lukewarm bath.

Q How should I deal with a fever fit?

A Fever fits (also known as febrile convulsions) may happen if your baby's temperature goes very high. Though very frightening to witness, the baby will come out of the fit on her own and almost always recover completely. Stay with her, lie her on her side and be sure nothing is against her mouth or nose to block her breathing. When the fit has finished she will be drowsy or fall deeply asleep. Ask someone to call a doctor when the fit starts or ring yourself afterwards if you are on your own. See also pages 180–181 (febrile convulsions).

Q What should I do if my baby starts to choke?

A Your baby might choke on an object he has put in his mouth, or on some food that he has not chewed properly. He may be unable to breathe, cry or speak and could start to turn blue in the face. Lay your baby along your forearm, facing downwards, supporting his chin. Give five sharp downward thrusts. If there is still a blockage, send someone for medical help. Do not be tempted to see if you can hook the object back out of his mouth with your finger, as you will risk pushing it further in.

Emergency situations

Call the doctor immediately if:

- You cannot rouse your child. Being difficult to rouse is not the same as being sleepy: on this occasion, when you handle your child or talk to her, she does not respond.
- Your baby or child turns very pale or blue. If you notice a bluish-grey tinge around the mouth or tongue, this is an emergency.
- Your baby becomes quiet and lethargic or droopy and hot.
- Your child's temperature rises to over 39.5°C/103.1°F and paracetamol doesn't keep it under control.
- Your child has any difficulties in breathing or has noisy, grunting or fast breathing or cannot speak or drink.
- Your child has a pain severe enough to stop them in what they are doing. The child cannot be comforted.
- Your baby has a pain on breathing in.
- Your baby or child cannot keep drinks down.
- Your baby or young child has diarrhoea and is vomiting.
- Your child is vomiting and the stomach looks swollen.
- There is any blood in the vomit.
- Your baby or child has a convulsion.
- Your child vomits for more than one hour.
- Your child develops a rash of violet spots that do not fade when you apply pressure.
- Your baby cries in a very odd, weak or high-pitched way.
- You are worried, even if you cannot explain why you are worried.

Health issues
General illness

Q What should I do if my baby develops a regular cough or cold?

A Give your baby plenty to drink and provide extra moisture in the air with a water vaporizer or by boiling a kettle in his room (stay with it and be sure it is out of reach if your baby is mobile). Don't use cough medicines unless prescribed by your doctor. See your doctor if a cold starts to get worse after the first few days, since a bacterial infection may have developed.

Q Should I be concerned if my baby develops a runny nose?

A Most runny noses are the result of a cold or other viral infection and not usually serious, except a baby who needs to suck to feed, and who may be unable to do so if her nose is blocked with mucus. In early summer a runny nose, sneezing and sore eyes could suggest hay fever. Children who have these symptoms all year round may have an allergy to a substance such as house dust mite or pet fur. A runny nose on one side could mean that an object such as a bean has been pushed up the nostril. The best action to take is to see if there are any other signs of illness, such as noisy or rapid breathing, or if the discharge from the nose turns a thick yellow-green, in which case you should consult a doctor. If you suspect a foreign body, don't be tempted to try and remove it – you could end up pushing it to the back of the nose where the child could inhale it – seek medical help instead.

Q What is bronchiolitis?

A This is a chest infection in which the bronchioles, the tiny airways in the lungs, become inflamed and blocked. It is usually caused by the respiratory syncytial virus (RSV), which is most common in the winter months. The condition is most common in babies between the ages of two and five months, whose bronchioles are quite narrow and can therefore become obstructed relatively easily.

Q What are the symptoms?

A The illness usually starts with a cold. Over the next day or two the baby develops an irritating dry cough. He may be breathless and have difficulty feeding. Other symptoms include a moderately high fever (rarely higher than 38–38.5°C (100.4–101.3°F), restlessness and wheezing. In a severe case, your baby may develop rapid, laboured breathing, seemingly struggling to pull in his chest with each breath.

Q What should I do?

A First, contact your doctor. Meanwhile, keep your baby warm, comfortable and as calm as possible – crying makes it harder for him to breathe. Cuddle him on your shoulder or prop him in a carry seat – he will breathe more easily in an upright position. Encourage him to drink, even if it is only in small amounts, and check his temperature. Your doctor will examine your baby and listen to his chest. Infants who have mild symptoms can be nursed at home as above. Those who need help with feeding or breathing will be admitted to hospital.

Health issues
Whooping cough

Q What is it?

A Whooping cough (pertussis) is an infection of the lungs and airways by a bacterium, and is highly infectious. Babies do not inherit immunity and so are vulnerable from birth. It is much less common now that babies are routinely vaccinated against it, but immunization doesn't give complete protection and is not permanent. Whooping cough can vary from a slight cough to bouts so severe that the child can hardly catch breath and vomits as he coughs. For very young babies there is a risk that lack of oxygen during the breathless spells will cause brain damage. The incubation period is seven to 10 days. A child is most infectious while the first signs show and remains infectious for three weeks after the coughing fits begin. The cough may continue for up to two to three months after the infection has responded to treatment.

Q What can I do if my baby has whooping cough?

A Stay with her while she is coughing. Sit her up on your lap and try to calm her. If she stops breathing, hold her still, she will start again. Consult your doctor regardless of whether your baby has been immunized. He or she will probably prescribe antibiotics for your baby and for any other children in the family. The drug will not cure the cough, but it will probably make it less severe, and will help to prevent other babies and children from catching the disease. Very young babies may need to be observed in hospital, where their breathing can be monitored, the airways cleared and oxygen given if necessary.

The three stages of **whooping cough**

1 Early symptoms may resemble those of an ordinary cough or cold – sneezing, runny nose, sore throat, slight fever, poor appetite. Following this, a dry irritable cough develops that may be worse at night and after eating.

2 After a week or two, the child has bouts of coughing. He may appear to choke and his face may turn red or blue. When the child manages to breathe in you may hear the characteristic crowing 'whoop'. Despite this, between coughing fits the baby seems well. Younger babies may not whoop, but may have spells when they stop breathing for a few seconds before spontaneously starting to breathe again. Older babies may also stop breathing after a coughing fit. They may also vomit.

3 In the third and final stage, the cough becomes less severe. However, the child may still be weak.

Health issues
Eyes

Q My three-month-old baby has a persistently watery left eye, even when she isn't crying, and her eyelashes are often stuck together with discharge after she has been sleeping. What is the problem?

A Your daughter may well have a blocked tear duct (see page 59). You can gently massage a blocked tear duct to allow the tears to flow away. Make sure your hands are clean, then, using your fingertips, gently massage the tear ducts between the inner corner of the eye and the bridge of the nose. Repeat twice a day. You also need to bathe your baby's eyes regularly by wiping from the outer corner to the inner corner with a cotton wool pad dipped in warm, boiled water. If the discharge looks infected your doctor may take swabs to discover its source, and then prescribe eye drops or an ointment to clear it.

Q My baby has a pink and swollen eye, which she constantly rubs as if it is itchy. Could this be conjunctivitis?

A Yes. Along with an eye that waters or has a thick yellow discharge, these are common signs of conjunctivitis, an inflammation of the transparent membrane that covers the eyeball and the inside of the membrane. You can ease the symptoms, and prevent them spreading from one eye to the other, by laying your baby down on the side with the infected eye to stop tears infecting the other eye. Wash your baby's hands frequently with soap if she tends to rub her eye. To prevent it spreading to other family members, keep all face cloths and bath towels separate.

Q Can my doctor prescribe a treatment for conjunctivitis?

A Yes. If symptoms persist, or if both eyes are infected, consult your doctor, who may prescribe antibiotic drugs or ointment. You should continue to use these until 24 hours have elapsed since the baby's eyes have cleared. The eyes should improve within a day, but if they are no better in two or three days, take your child to the doctor again.

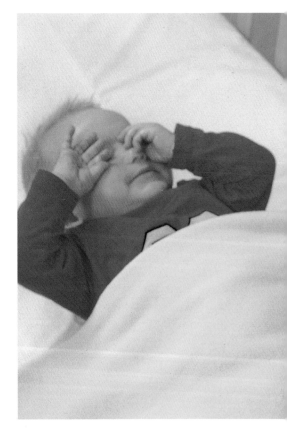

Above: If your baby is constantly rubbing her eyes it may be a sign she is suffering from conjunctivitis.

Health issues
Skin irritations

Q What is thrush?

A Thrush is a common infection in babies, children and women. It is caused by a yeast-like fungus, *Candida albicans*, which lives naturally on the skin, in the vagina, the mouth and the bowel, in harmony with a range of natural bacteria. When the immune system is upset, symptoms of thrush can occur. Once it starts to flourish, it multiplies quickly, damaging mucus membranes and triggering the typical symptoms of intense inflammation and irritation.

Q What should I look out for?

A Most babies develop thrush in the mouth and one of the first signs is a reluctance to feed. There will be spots inside the cheeks that look like the remains of milk. Wiped very gently with a tissue they may stay stuck or they may come off to reveal a sore red patch.

Q How should the condition be treated?

A If you are breastfeeding a baby with thrush, tell your doctor who may prescribe an antifungal cream for your nipples. Your doctor will also prescribe an antifungal gel or liquid containing the drug nystatin or miconazole. This should be dropped onto the sore patches in your baby's mouth after every feed. Make sure that the medicine reaches right round the mouth, including between the gums and cheeks. You may also be given cream for your baby's sore bottom if he also has a vivid red nappy rash that does not respond to the usual remedies. When you change a nappy, make sure your baby is perfectly dry before applying the cream. It

should start to work in two to three days. Leave the nappy off whenever you can.

Q Are all nappy rashes caused by thrush?

A No. The most common type of nappy rash is usually caused by a reaction to urine and faeces, and is evident from red patches or spots on the skin that is in contact with the nappy. Babies with sensitive skin are more prone to suffer and, in most cases, the condition is cleared up without the need for medical treatment. If your baby develops a rash, change his nappy frequently and leave him nappy free whenever possible. At each nappy change gently but thoroughly wash his bottom. Instead of astringent wipes, use warm tap water with aqueous cream or bath oil as a cleanser. Be extra vigilant if your baby has a cold, diarrhoea or is on antibiotics.

Q How does heat rash come about and how should I treat it?

A Heat rash develops because a baby's sweat glands are not yet working efficiently and so they are not able to cool down if they become overheated – perhaps because she is dressed too warmly in hot weather or her room is too hot. The sweat glands leak sweat under the skin, and this causes a mild inflammation, which usually disappears within a few days. Keep your baby cool by undressing her and bathing her in tepid water or wiping her all over with a damp sponge. Dress her in cool clothes and check the temperature of the room. Offer the baby drinks to keep her fluid levels up.

Health issues
Meningitis

Q What is this?

A Meningitis is an inflammation of one or more of the three thin membranes that cover the brain. It can be caused by a number of micro-organisms, including viruses and bacteria. Viral meningitis is usually less serious than bacterial meningitis, and although bacterial meningitis is quite rare, it develops quickly and needs urgent treatment with antibiotics. Meningitis can occur at any time of year, although it tends to peak in winter.

Q I know there are different types of meningitis. Which one is most likely to affect my baby?

A *Haemophilus influenzae* meningitis was the most common form in children until the introduction of the Hib vaccine for infants. Meningococcal meningitis is caused by the bacterium *Neisseria meningitides*, and there are two major types – group B and group C. Group C, which accounts for one-third of cases, is often linked with outbreaks in schools and other closed communities. Group B, which accounts for some two-thirds of cases, usually affects only one person in a community, although sometimes there is a cluster of cases. This type of meningitis is especially common in babies under 12 months and in older teenagers.

Q How does the infection spread?

A The bacteria that cause bacterial meningitis do not live for any length of time outside the body, so they are not passed on in public places. Instead the bacteria are transmitted in nasal discharge during coughing or sneezing. When the bacteria are breathed in they reach the lining of the upper respiratory system and from there pass into the bloodstream. They are carried in the blood to the meninges, the protective membranes that cover the brain, where they cause inflammation.

Q What should I do if I suspect my baby has meningitis?

A Call the doctor immediately and describe your baby's symptoms. You will either be told to take your baby to hospital straight away or to wait for the doctor to visit. If the doctor suspects meningitis your baby will be given an

Symptoms of meningitis

Babies show some of these signs:
- Reddish-purple spots anywhere on the skin, which grow quickly into larger marks or bruises. Pressed under an empty glass, the spots don't go white, even for a few seconds.
- Drowsiness and difficulty waking
- Fretfulness and irritability
- Vomiting or food refusal
- A dislike of being handled
- Fever
- An odd, staring expression
- Neck stiffness
- Fontanelle may be tense or may bulge
- Odd shrill or moaning cry
- Pale or blotchy skin.

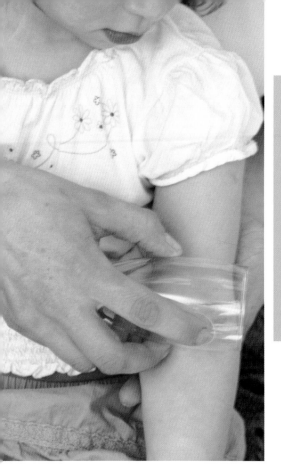

In people who carry the bacterium responsible for bacterial meningitis the microorganism, present in their throat and nasal passages, can be transmitted in exactly the same way as a cold.

Above: Reddish-purple spots that do not go if pressed under a glass are a sign of meningitis.

intravenous injection of penicillin before going to hospital. The doctor will also take a swab from the baby's nose and throat to help identify the organism that has caused the illness. Once meningitis has been confirmed you must contact all relatives, friends and child carers who have been in contact with your baby during the last 14 days. (The incubation period for meningococcal disease is 2 to 10 days.)

Q What treatment will my baby receive at hospital?

A Treatment will begin the minute your baby arrives. Depending on how ill she is, an

intravenous drip will be set up to give your baby antibiotics to kill the bacteria, and possibly steroids to reduce the inflammation and pressure inside the skull. If your baby needs drugs to stop convulsions, they can be given in the same drip, as well as fluids to keep her hydrated and analgesics for pain relief. Your baby will have blood tests and almost certainly a lumbar puncture (insertion of a hollow needle between the vertebrae into the spinal canal to draw off a small quantity of cerebrospinal fluid) to confirm the diagnosis.

Q What is the outlook?

A It might be a few days before your baby's condition starts to improve. In the meantime, she may need intensive care, with her breathing and heart supported. Although three-quarters of children recover completely from bacterial meningitis, some are left with permanent handicaps such as deafness and brain damage. There may also be temporary damage to the nervous system, which usually clears up within a month.

3

toddler

1 to 2 years

Development
The second year

From 12 to 24 months

12–14 months

- **Language.** Shouts at you when doesn't like what you are doing. Makes tuneful sounds when hearing familiar music. Begins to learn the names of body parts. Listens avidly when other children talk to each other. Understands many more words than can say. Can follow a broader range of instructions: 'Let go of the toy', 'Take the biscuit'.

- **Hand–eye coordination.** Is able to hold two items in each hand at the same time, and enjoys making marks on paper with crayons and pencils. Hits pegs into a peg board with a hammer. Puts hands up when you bring out a jumper or top to wear. Likes playing with moving objects, watching them as they roll, and may even be able to throw a medium-sized, lightweight ball.

- **Movement.** Spends a lot of time trying to climb up stairs but finds coming down is harder. Is determined to walk on own, despite frequent falls, and insists on walking unaided when outside with you. Is able to stop and change direction when walking and can bend over to pick up an object from the floor. Masters the challenge of climbing in and out of highchair.

- **Social and emotional.** May have a temporary attachment to one person in particular, and will give you a big cuddle when happy. Plays alongside rather than with another child of the same age. Has increased sense of self-awareness of being an individual with particular likes and dislikes. Is very determined to get own way and has a tantrum when frustrations become too much. Begins to show signs of jealousy when you give attention to others.

From 12 to 24 months

15–18 months

- **Language.** Consistently uses approximately six or seven words, but understanding extends to many more words. Combines language and gestures to express needs. Enjoys songs and nursery rhymes and may join in with some sounds and actions.

- **Hand–eye coordination.** Sees a connection between hand movements and the effect this causes – for example, knows to pull at a string to make the attached toy move. Starts to feed with hands and a spoon. May want to help when being dressed. Hand preference may become apparent. Claps hands together. Successfully completes a simple inset board activity.

- **Movement.** Walks unsteadily with support up and down stairs. Walks confidently about the home and outside. Trots towards you across the room, but may become unsteady when starting to run. Starts to climb playground equipment, but will need constant supervision. May enjoy splashing and kicking in the swimming pool.

- **Social and emotional.** Wants to do more, especially feeding and dressing. Learns good eating habits by sharing mealtimes. Begins to learn basic social skills like passing a toy to another child. Expresses preferences for particular foods or for certain toys.

From 12 to 24 months

19–21 months

- **Language.** Has extended vocabulary to dozens of words, mostly nouns that describe a general class of object such as 'car' for all vehicles or 'house' for all buildings. Tries to join in songs. Is interested in conversations and begins to learn conversational conventions, such as giving and waiting for answers. Puts words together to form two-word phrases. Develops an understanding that speech is about social contact as well as communicating basic needs. Spots familiar characters and objects in picture books and photographs and tries to name them.

- **Hand–eye coordination.** Enjoys playing with modelling materials like playdough or clay, and sand and water – making shapes and drawing 'pictures' into the surface. Likes rolling, throwing and perhaps even catching balls, both large and small, though will find large ones easier to grasp. Stacks small wooden blocks on top of each other to make a tower of perhaps five bricks. Pours water accurately from one container into another one without too much splashing. Makes increasingly deliberate marks on paper with a crayon.

- **Movement.** Is able to undertake another activity while on the move – for example, can trail a pull-along toy while walking along. Likes to clamber over furniture. Climbs up and down from a chair. Improved balance and coordination leads to fewer instances of tripping over and unexpected falls when walking and running. Can walk backwards a few steps. Is able to use a wider range of playground equipment. Enjoys running freely in a park and in the garden.

- **Social and emotional.** Appreciates your company and makes an effort to engage your attention either through talk or play. Shows signs of being nearly ready to begin potty training, although full control is unlikely at this age. Persists in challenging decisions. Begins to interact with other children but needs lots of basic social guidance. Is able to understand simple rules, although may not always comply with them. Enjoys the security of a regular daily routine.

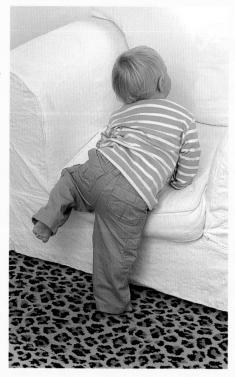

From 12 to 24 months

22–24 months

- **Language.** Accurately identifies everyday objects. Experiments with different (perhaps 'incorrect') word combinations. Tackles most sounds but often mixes up or mispronounces certain consonants such as 'c' or 's'. Names the main parts of the body. Listens with interest to other people talking to each other. Vocabulary is at least 200 words, often combined in short sentences.

- **Hand–eye coordination.** Looks at books for several minutes studying each picture, pointing to images that are of interest and turning the pages. Can participate increasingly in helping to dress and undress. Combines index finger and thumb effectively in a pincer grip to pick up small objects. Receives and passes objects from your hand and then back again. Is able to eat with a spoon effectively. Makes increasingly rhythmic sounds with simple musical instruments such as drums and tambourines.

- **Movement.** Pushes a pedal toy along using feet, though probably cannot yet turn the pedals. Can stand on one foot while using the other to kick a ball. Runs confidently and rarely falls, although this activity still requires quite a lot of concentration. Moves fast when going in a straight line. Is able to throw and catch a ball from a sitting position. Dances to music. Can adjust balance well on a swing.

- **Social and emotional.** Enjoys the company of other children, but has trouble sharing toys and does not yet play cooperatively. Potty training is probably underway but bladder and bowel control may not yet be totally reliable. Wants to help wash at bathtime and to clean teeth. Enjoys the responsibility of carrying out small tasks. May cry when separated from you temporarily, although soon stops when you are out of sight. May be shy with strangers.

Feeding
Introducing foods

By the time your baby is one year old, milk will probably still provide at least half of the calories and nourishment needed each day, and perhaps much more, because not all one year olds are eager to eat much in the way of solids. From now on, the solids you give at breakfast, lunch and tea can gradually begin to take over from milk as the main source of nourishment, although for most young children milk will continue to be an important food for several years.

A balanced diet

Plan the day's food to make sure you give your child enough foods containing calcium, iron and vitamins. Avoid too many foods that contain added salt and sugar. At this age a good, balanced diet should be based on the following daily recommendations:

- 3–4 helpings of starchy carbohydrate foods (bread, pasta, rice, cereals)
- 3–4 helpings of fruit and vegetables
- 1 helping of a non-dairy protein-rich food (meat, fish, beans)
- 2–3 helpings of full-fat or other dairy produce

Ten foods to **introduce from 12 months**

1 Raw fruit and vegetable finger foods.
2 Mashed portions of the family meal, providing that no sugar or salt is added.
3 Fresh fruit juice, diluted by measuring 1 part juice to 10 parts water.
4 Well-cooked whole egg, mashed or finely chopped.
5 Finely ground nut or seed butters, if there is no history of allergies.
6 Tiny portions of oily fish, such as salmon, making sure all bones are removed.
7 Canned tuna in water – avoid brine because it will be too salty.
8 Fresh or canned tomatoes.
9 Tiny amounts of unsmoked low-salt/sodium ham.
10 Small amounts of hard cheese such as Cheddar and Gouda.

Feeding
Common questions

Q How can I introduce my toddler to foods with more texture?

A There are a number of ways to introduce more texture to your baby's food: offer more finger foods; put a little grated cheese straight onto the highchair table; stir some soaked couscous, some tiny soup pasta or some cooked rice into a finely mashed or puréed baby meal; mix finely chopped cooked vegetables into some smooth, cheesy polenta; mix some finely chopped melon into smooth, sieved raspberry or strawberry purée.

Q Should I always offer my toddler fresh foods?

A Fresh foods may be best, but it is not practical to shop every day, or even two or three times a week, if you have a young family. A well-stocked freezer and store cupboard can be a lifesaver and may also work out cheaper. Handy store-cupboard meals include: just-cooked frozen mixed vegetables and grated cheese; eggy bread – sliced bread dipped into beaten egg, fried in a tiny amount of oil and served cut into strips with apple slices; macaroni cheese – cooked macaroni or other small pasta mixed with cheese sauce and frozen mixed vegetables.

Q My 13-month-old toddler grabs at the spoon whenever I try to feed her. Should I let her feed herself now?

A As your baby grows, you will discover that she is very keen to feed herself. Encourage her: the more she practises the better. Try not to worry about the mess too much – just have a damp cloth at the ready, to wipe her sticky hands and face with. It is good practice to give your baby a spoon and a small amount of food in a bowl while you feed her the main part of the meal from a separate bowl and spoon.

Q Will it benefit my toddler to start eating meals with the rest of the family? I am anxious that it might get too chaotic.

A Eating is a social experience – it's not just about your toddler satisfying his nutritional needs. The different schedules of those in your family might mean that it's more convenient for your toddler to eat on his own than to wait for everyone else. However, you may find that he enjoys eating together with the family. True, this might make the mealtime more hectic – and probably noisier as well – but your toddler learns from the eating habits of others and has more fun than when eating alone.

Ten foods to **avoid at 12 months**

1 Salty, sugary or fatty foods.
2 Whole or chopped nuts.
3 Soft ripened cheese, such as Brie and Camembert and blue cheeses.
4 Smoked or salted fish.
5 Smoked or unsmoked bacon.
6 Pâté.
7 Liver more than once a week.
8 Strong, hot spices, such as chilli.
9 Fizzy drinks.
10 Tea or coffee.

Feeding
Common problems

Q My toddler gets us so worked up about food that mealtimes usually end in tears. What can we do?

A You need to force yourself to take a more relaxed approach to mealtimes. Since tension is highly infectious, you will make your toddler anxious before he sees the food. Try to hide your tension. Chat calmly to your child while he eats, and set a good example yourself by eating whatever is on your plate.

A recent study suggests that if a baby is not introduced to new textures and tastes until she's six months or older, she is more likely to be a fussy or difficult eater when she is a toddler.

Q Our toddler insists she will only eat snacks, and not proper plates of food. How can we overcome this?

A Be creative. Present the foods you want her to eat in snack format. For instance, if she barely touches a whole pizza that is put on a plate in front of her, simply cut it up into small pieces and serve these on a small side plate. Varying the presentation in this way makes the same food seem quite different, changing it from a formal meal into an informal snack.

Q Should I force my toddler to eat the meals I give him, rather than give in every time he makes a fuss?

A You cannot force your child to eat what is placed in front of him. No matter how much pressure you put on him, he has to choose to eat. In fact, the more stressed he becomes, the less likely he is to eat, so challenging him about it will probably make the situation worse. Instead, a calm, planned approach is required. Try letting him eat at his own pace.

Q My toddler has a very short attention span when it comes to eating. As soon as I place a meal in front of her she wants to get down from the table and play. What should I do?

A Is your toddler eating alone? Her behaviour could be the result of plain boredom. She is by nature sociable and she likes contact with others in the family. You can hardly blame her for wanting to leave her meal and play with her toys if she has no one else to talk to while eating. You should try to sit with her while she eats, at least for some of the time. She is more likely to clear her plate when you are nearby.

Five reasons for **food rejection**

1 The taste isn't good.
2 The food is too hot.
3 The portion is too large.
4 The cutlery is the wrong size.
5 The food is out of comfortable reach.

Positive parenting **Coping with a fussy eater**

Q While my little girl was happy to eat everything I gave her from six months on, at 16 months she has suddenly become very picky about what she eats. Mealtimes used to be fun, but now I find myself dreading her refusal of yet another meal. I desperately want to avoid this becoming a long-term problem. What can I do now to prevent that happening?

A Toddlers tend to assert their independence on food choices from the age of about 15 months onwards. Although fussy eating is often a passing phase in a young child's life, it can also develop into a long-term trait. There are ways you can target fussy-eating at this age, successfully in most cases.

Strategies

• **Give your child some choice.** She will be more interested in eating what is in front of her when she has selected it herself. If you can, let her pick from a very limited range of meal options.

• **Involve her in preparing the meal.** Much will depend on her age and stage of maturity, but try to find some way to connect your child with the food preparation. The more she invests emotionally and physically in the meal, the more likely she is to eat it.

• **Offer small portions.** Your child may be put off by a portion that seems very large, so offer a small portion at first and if she clears the plate she can have a second helping.

• **Introduce new tastes slowly and subtly.** Start by mixing a small amount of the new food with something else, such as potatoes.

Gradually increase the amount you disguise in this way. When your child eats this amount without comment, show her the new food and put a very small amount alongside her favourite food. Explain that she will find the taste familiar. Encourage her to try it and give her lots of praise when she puts some of it in her mouth.

• **Provide subtle positive reinforcement.** Do not talk directly about how much she ate. Instead, at the end of the meal tell your child how much you enjoyed having a relaxed time with her.

Above: Tempt your toddler with small pieces of fruit and a bowl of chocolate sauce for dipping.

BODY LANGUAGE

Learning to read your child's emotions

This form of non-verbal communication is another key to understanding your child's thoughts and feelings.

Five facts on **body language**

1 The more you and your growing child understand each other's non-verbal communication, the closer your relationship becomes.

2 Body language is used more than spoken language. Studies comparing the amount of spoken with non-verbal language exchanged between two people in a relationship have found that body language dominates.

3 Results of such studies show that less than 10 per cent of emotions are expressed in words, whereas more than 90 per cent are expressed in body language.

4 At three years old, your child is more likely to use words to communicate facts and body language to communicate emotions.

5 Body language is less controlled than spoken language. Smiles, body posture, leg and arm movements, eye contact and other features of non-verbal communication occur without deliberate planning. This means that your child's body language seeps out, even though she doesn't realize it.

You use body language all the time and so does your child, even though you probably don't consciously think about it. You smile at your child when you are happy with her and she smiles back; that's body language. And you frown when you're annoyed at your child and she pouts in response; that's body language. In other words, body language – the meaning conveyed by body movements, such as gaze, facial expression and touch – is part of your daily life.

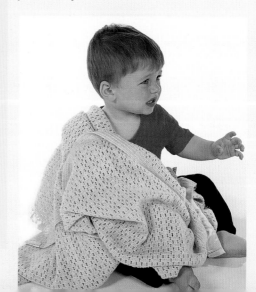

Dimensions of body language

Although the interpretation of body language is often very complicated, there is nothing to stop you understanding the basics. And that alone will improve your relationship with your child, right from the start. The elementary components of non-verbal communication include the following:

• **Face.** As soon as she is born, your baby starts to make facial expressions that reflect her inner feelings. By the time she is three years old your child has a wide variety of expressions that tell you something about her underlying emotions.

• **Eyes.** Eye contact is a natural part of human communication; instinctively, we look into each other's eyes during a conversation. Variations in the rate of eye contact can indicate anything from fascination to guilt.

• **Stance.** Once your toddler starts to move around, you'll notice she adopts various postures – for instance, the one that tells you she is sad because she moves slowly with hunched shoulders.

• **Hands and fingers.** If you notice that your child's hands are gripped tightly shut in a fist, you can be sure she's angry and upset. But if they are open, dangling casually by her sides, then she is probably relaxed.

• **Legs.** A child who shifts backwards and forwards from one foot to the other is usually concerned about something. She may feel guilty about what she is saying at the time, or perhaps she is afraid.

• **Breathing.** Rate of breathing often changes as a result of emotional state. Quick, shallow breathing is associated with nervousness, whereas deep, slow breaths can be a reflection of your child's relaxation.

People watching

Another way to improve your ability to understand non-verbal communication is by looking at other people. For instance, you could watch a television programme with the volume turned off, so that you can see the main characters without hearing their words. Try to work out what they 'say' to each other, solely on the basis of their body language. Or watch other people in the street. You'll be amazed at how much you can deduce from body language alone once you build up your confidence and experience.

• **Distance.** When she is in a bad mood, your child creates distance between you and her, perhaps by sitting on the opposite side of the room. On the other hand, she likes to snuggle up close to you when she feels anxious about something.

Making a start

When trying to understand your child's body language, remember that this is not an exact science! You probably won't get it right every time. The best way to improve your skill in this area is through accumulated experience of watching your child closely in a variety of situations. For instance, when she is a baby you'll soon know when you have interpreted the meaning of her cries accurately, because you'll be able to ease her distress. When she is older, you can test out the accuracy of your interpretations by simply asking her what she feels. So, spend time observing your child.

Sleep
What is typical?

Your toddler plays a much more active part in her bedtime routine now that she's older, more independent and more able to make choices. She has her own favourite toys to accompany her and her own set way of getting ready for bed. Your child needs to have a stable sleeping pattern at this stage in her life – if she doesn't get a good night's sleep with regularity, she'll be tired, fractious, demanding and bad-tempered the next day. She may need help to establish good bedtime habits because she prefers to remain in your company.

Below: Reading your toddler a story at bedtime can help her to relax, ready for sleep.

The average 18-month-old toddler needs between 12 and 14 hours sleep, mostly at night with a nap or two during the day. Around this age you can expect her to cut out her daytime nap as her overall sleep requirements fall. When she is ready to cut back from two naps to one, you can expect her no longer to show signs of tiredness in the morning, but to fall asleep in the afternoon. Dropping her last nap can be a bit more of a problem. Your child may push her nap back later and later, until it begins to interfere with her bedtime. At this stage you may need to take the initiative to eliminate the nap, either by creating gentle playing time to stimulate her or by starting your child's bedtime routine earlier as she drops her daytime nap.

Waking Up

Research confirms that at least 15 per cent of all children around the age of 18 months still wake up regularly during the night. There are good reasons why your child might wake up and call for you during the night, perhaps because she had a bad dream, which may have been caused by a particular food or a scary story or video. When she wakes up crying, calm her and soothe her until she settles. You'll find that your reassurance helps her to get back to sleep quickly.

Sleep
Common questions

Q When is the right time to move my baby from a cot into a bed?

A Once your toddler shows signs of being able to climb out of her own cot, it may be time to move her to a bed. This can be a major challenge, a complete non-event or a new adventure that will make her feel very grown up. Explain to her what is happening and allow her to feel that she has some say in the matter: perhaps she can help to choose her bed or a new duvet cover. If she has difficulties settling in her new bed, try playing games on it with her during the day so that she associates it with fun.

Q Can I reason with my toddler when he refuses to go to bed?

A Now that your child is able to communicate with you verbally, it is certainly important for you to discuss things with him. Explain what is happening and why, making it clear that you are not going to be swayed in your resolve when and where he should go to bed. If your child has a long history of difficulty getting to sleep or broken nights, he is likely to resist a new sleep strategy more stubbornly than a young baby, so it will probably take you longer to get results. It may take you a couple of weeks to see significant results, but the important thing to hang onto is that you will get results, as long as you remain steadfast.

Q What is the best approach for settling a toddler at bedtime?

A You can help her settle before she goes to sleep by specifically involving her in calm, sedate activities at least 20 minutes before her bedtime routine normally begins. A predictable pre-bedtime ritual is advisable; this could be that she has a bath, puts on her pyjamas, brushes her teeth and is then read a story by you. Once this pattern becomes firmly set in her mind, she'll know that the first stage means bedtime is fast approaching. If possible, stick to the same bedtime each night as this will get your toddler used to a fixed sleeping pattern, physically and psychologically. Of course, there will be evenings when this time varies, and that's fine. Once you have tucked her in, read her a short story in a quiet voice to relax her. After that, give her a cuddle and a kiss and leave the room.

Q If I bring bedtime forward to avoid my toddler having a late nap, won't he just wake up earlier in the morning? If so what should I do?

A You should not have any cause for worry. Although his sleep requirement has fallen, he will still need to add some of his former day-sleep time to his night sleep in order to compensate for his lost nap, so he should in fact sleep longer at night. If he does tend to wake up early in the morning, you can encourage him to play on his own, rather than seek your attention. Try leaving a pile of toys and books in the cot or by the bedside so that he can keep himself amused until you get up.

Sleep
Common problems

Q I have had considerable difficulty getting my toddler to settle into any kind of routine. He just resists and gets out of bed the minute I try to leave the room. What can I do?

A Resist any urge to pick him up, look sympathetic or even reason with him about why he needs to be in bed – it is important not to 'reward' him in any way. Instead, insist firmly that he goes back to bed. It is important to maintain an unruffled neutrality even if your child throws a tantrum. When he sees that he gets no response from you, he will soon get bored and begin staying under his covers.

Q Over the last few weeks, my toddler has developed a habit of waking two or three times a night. How can I discourage this?

A Above all, keep your toddler in her bed when she wakes during the night. Naturally you should go to her when she cries or calls out, but try to prevent her from leaving her bedroom. If she insists on rising, say, to go to the toilet, take her back to bed as quickly as possible. Tell her that she'll soon fall asleep, and then leave the room once more. Don't go back in immediately if she calls out again – wait at least five minutes before responding to her.

Q No matter what I do, my toddler always finds some way to drag bedtime out for longer. One night he says he's hungry, the next he insists he needs a nappy change. How can I break this habit?

A Build any essential needs into his bedtime routine. Bedtime often follows soon after tea for

Above: A milky drink before bedtime can help to settle your child.

young children, so you know he's not hungry. Give him a last drink of water or milk before he begins his bedtime routine. Change his nappy just before he gets into bed. If you are sure that his claims are merely an attempt to manipulate you, you can confidently refuse to indulge them. Don't get sidetracked into long negotiations: tell him simply that he has just had a meal or a change and repeat your bedtime phrase to him. He will soon get the message that you are not to be worn down.

Q Should I offer my toddler a snack or something to drink if she wakes in the night?

A There is no doubt that if your child continues to wake up and that if you then make the decision to take her downstairs for a drink or snack, or perhaps to play with her, she will probably wake up at the same time the following night, too. After all, as far as she is concerned waking up during the night is great fun – there's food, games and loads of attention from you! Stick to your original plan of action and you'll discover that her waking at night soon becomes a thing of the past.

Positive parenting **It's never too late**

Q I have never been able to establish a regular bedtime routine with my baby. Now that she is a 17-month-old toddler, I feel it might never happen. Am I wasting my time?

A If you've had a year or more of broken nights, you may feel that the goal of uninterrupted sleep is an unattainable dream. But even the most persistent poor sleeper can be taught to go to bed and stay there in a comparatively short space of time. The fundamentals of getting a toddler to sleep through the night – even one who has never achieved this before – are essentially the same as training a baby to sleep well.

Below: A last kiss and cuddle from you are an important part of your child's bedtime routine.

Strategies

• Your child needs to understand that nights are for sleeping: if you let her run around after you've put her to bed, she is never going to understand that you really want her to stay there until morning.

• You need to establish a positive, structured bedtime routine to calm her down and act as a physical and mental trigger that bedtime is the next, immovable, part of her day.

• You need to teach her to settle on her own. If she relies on your presence in order to get to sleep, she is going to suffer the same anxiety as a younger baby when she stirs in the night and realizes you are no longer there. The ideas for settling a younger baby (see page 82) can be applied to a toddler too.

BIRTH ORDER

Linking birth position with personality

Research has shown that there is a link between your baby's birth order and her subsequent development.

In other words, her progress during childhood is to some extent affected by whether she is your first born, your middle child, an only child or your youngest. Evidence from research confirms that some characteristics – including temperament, learning skills, social skills and confidence – are linked to each of the major birth positions. However, birth order is only one of the many influences on your baby's development, and its effect can be offset by the way you raise her.

If you understand how birth order can mould your child's development, you can ensure that she doesn't become unduly affected by this potential influence. Look at your child's life from her point of view and imagine what it's like to have that particular family position. Consider the following:

Your first-born baby has you all to herself for the first part of her life – she may be two years old or more before the next one arrives – which means you spend all your child-focused time with her. The effort you put into stimulating her development doesn't have to be shared around with any other child. With that level of attention from you, it's hardly surprising that she's so bright, alert and highly motivated.

Later-born children probably like to bend the rules and seek the outrageous rather than the traditional because they want to be different from their older brother or sister. Your second-born child wants to carve her own destiny; she doesn't want to be in the shadow of her high-achieving older sister and the best way to avoid that trap, as far as she is concerned, is to follow a different path altogether.

Your youngest will tend to be the most independent largely through necessity. There's nothing like living with the prospect of being always at the back of the family queue to sharpen your youngest child's survival skills!

Do what you can to make sure that birth order doesn't have a disproportionate effect on any of your children. For example, make a specific point of spending time stimulating your second child even though you now have two to look after; don't always assume that your older child should be responsible for her younger siblings when they play together; let your younger child sometimes be the one to choose the television programme the family watches.

Strategies

• Take an interest in each child's progress. Each one needs to feel valued by their parents. Your youngest child's achievements are special to her, even though you have been through that stage already with her older siblings.

• Let your child's natural characteristics show through. Your second born, for instance, might be desperate to achieve as good grades at school as her bright older brother. If so, she deserves your support in this.

• Make turn-taking a hallmark of your family. Older children often think they have an absolute right to come first in the queue every time. But your youngest child can be the one who gets the new toy occasionally.

• Listen to your children. Take your middle child seriously when she says that her older

brother has more freedom and her younger sister is spoiled. Let her express her feelings and show that you are listening.

• Praise effort as well as achievement. What matters is that each of your children tries their best. Of course you are delighted when one of them has high achievements, but that shouldn't detract from your pleasure at the others' efforts.

Five facts about **personality**

1 First-born babies tend to be more intelligent than their siblings, and they tend to think clearly and rationally. They are likely to be the most successful in life, compared to their siblings.
2 Second children frequently are less concerned with following rules. They prefer to go against the grain and to challenge conventional thinking. Your second-born baby may push your rules to the limits.
3 Youngest children are the most able of all the children in the family to cope with the stresses and strains of everyday life. Your youngest child is likely to be confident, and to be able to handle problems on her own without seeking help.
4 Middle children are usually the most even-tempered, and are adept at solving disputes peacefully. Your middle child is also likely to be protective towards her older and younger siblings – she may occasionally feel left out of things.
5 Only children typically mix well with adults. The chances are, though, that your only child is self-sufficient, and when she mixes with others she shows good leadership qualities.

Language
What is typical?

If you gasped in amazement at your baby's language development during the first year – when he changed from a baby who could only cry into someone who could say his first clear word – then you will be stunned by the language explosion that occurs during his second year. His language takes a tremendous surge forward, enabling him to take part in conversations, to relate his experiences and to voice his feelings.

Having spoken his first word at around the age of nine to 12 months, your toddler will use about six clear words by the age of 15 months, most often names of people in the family or familiar objects. The ability to combine words together to form phrases and short sentences develops, and by the age of 18 months, your toddler is able to combine two words together to form a meaningful phrase, such as 'me teddy', meaning 'I want my teddy'. Your toddler will use most consonants and vowels, although at times he becomes confused. Word beginnings, in particular, often get mixed (for example, 'lellow' instead of 'yellow'). Your child becomes a better listener during this time too, which aids his language development because it is through listening that he hears language spoken, and this enables him to interpret instructions and take part in conversations.

What can my toddler do?

12–14 months

- He can say five or six words in the appropriate context. He listens avidly to other children when they talk to each other. He understands many more words than he can say.

15–18 months

- He is able to follow and act on simple instructions and combines language and gestures to express his needs. He starts to learn the names of different parts of the body. He enjoys songs and nursery rhymes and will perhaps join in with the words or actions.

Language
Common questions

Q What is my toddler most likely to say when she starts to speak?

A Psychologists studying the types of words that children first acquire when they start to speak have found that over 50 per cent of these early words are general in nature, referring to objects within a general class, such as 'ball', 'car' and 'house'. And a word such as 'dog' may be used for all animals. Less than 15 per cent are specific, referring to particular people or objects, such as 'Mummy' and 'teddy'. Another finding from this area of research is that many of a child's first words are connected with things she can actually use in some way or another, for instance, words like 'spoon', 'juice' and 'cup'. This is further proof that your child's language growth reflects closely her everyday experience.

Q Why is it that my child says 'f' for 's' and also says 't' for 'c'?

A Say these sounds slowly yourself – you'll discover that 'f' and 't' involve your teeth, lips and the tip of your tongue, while 'c' and 's' involve the back of your mouth. Your child finds front-of-mouth sounds much easier at this age and hence makes these substitutions. He will gradually master the whole range of sounds.

Q Is it true that boys are somewhat slower in learning to speak than girls?

A Evidence from psychological studies confirms that, in general, girls acquire spoken language at an earlier age than boys and they also develop more complex language structures before boys. This is only a trend, though; it doesn't mean that every boy says his first word later than every girl. Much depends on the individual child.

19–21 months
- He has extended his vocabulary to dozens of words, mostly nouns that describe a general class of object such as 'car' for all vehicles or 'house' for all buildings. He can put words together to form two-word phrases. He begins to develop an understanding that speech is about social contact as well as communicating basic needs.

22–24 months
- Now that he is nearly two he can accurately identify everyday objects placed in front of him. He will experiment with different (perhaps 'incorrect') word combinations and tackles most sounds but often mixes up or mispronounces certain consonants such as 'c' or 's'. His vocabulary is at least 200 words, often combined in short sentences.

Language
Stimulation

Your toddler's vocabulary starts to build steadily as she listens to conversations around her. If she's not talking before a year old then she certainly will be by 15 months. She can say several words herself and understands the meaning of hundreds more. Progress in language continues and your child realizes that speech is not just for the purpose of communicating her ideas and feelings – it's also a good way to make social contact.

She is increasingly interested in two-way conversation. By the time she reaches her second birthday your child is much more communicative and has a better grasp of vocabulary, grammar and sentence structure. In particular, she enjoys mixing with other children of her own age, even though they can't always make themselves understood to each other.

How can I stimulate my toddler's language skills?

• Encourage your child to talk to you about events as they occur – don't wait until the end of the day to recap as she may have forgotten about the incident. Bear in mind that she is fascinated by everything going on around her, and has an inherent desire to speak to you about her experiences. Whether it is putting on her vest and pants in the morning or going out for a walk in the afternoon, she will want to chat to you about it and needs you to respond. Try and use words that she can easily understand.

• Introduce pretend play to your toddler, using her cuddly toys. Set them up in a circle and talk to them. A child aged between 13 and 15 months may stare at you in amazement but she'll soon realize it's good fun and want to join in.

• When you bath or change your toddler, start to name her body parts. Make this a fun activity each night.

• Arrange for your toddler to spend some time in the company of other children who are approximately the same age. She will be fascinated by their use of language.

• Make a tape of familiar sounds and see if she recognizes any of them.

• Miss out the last word of her favourite song. Look at your child in anticipation to encourage her to say the missing word.

• Demonstrate the meanings of new words with which she is not fully familiar, raising your hands to describe height, for example. Ask her to name objects. Point to an object she knows and ask her what it is called. Extend this to new objects she hasn't named before.

• Try to make the language you use with your child basic but varied. Instead of using the same words each time, offer alternatives with the same meaning.

• Place her in front of a mirror and show her how to wiggle her tongue about, blow through her closed lips, and make 'p', 'b' and 'd' noises. This improves tongue and lip control.

Positive parenting **Coping with mistakes**

Q My toddler makes a good number of mistakes when speaking. She will mix up words sometimes, get confused occasionally, mispronounce initial letter sounds from time to time, and even make up words and constructions of her own. I am anxious that, unless I correct her, she will fail to learn the language properly. Is this the right approach to take?

A No. You should expect your child to make plenty of mistakes with the language she uses – it's a normal part of the learning process. If you tend to correct her when she makes language mistakes, she may become anxious or unwilling to express herself freely.

Strategies

• Reiterate what she has tried to say, using the correct words or construction, as if you were agreeing with her rather than pointing out her mistake. If she watches a dog walk away from her and says, for instance, 'Doddy gone away' you could say 'Yes, that's right. The dog has gone away.' Modelling language in this way shows her how to say the words correctly, without weakening her self-confidence.

• Similarly, your child expects everybody to understand her – she knows what she is trying to say and so she assumes you do as well. And she may explode with frustration when she suddenly thinks that you don't grasp her meaning. The more you ask her to repeat herself, the angrier she becomes. In this situation, use a variety of strategies. You might decide to distract her attention onto something else altogether, or you could just nod your head as though you have understood exactly what she has said.

Right: Take time to talk to and explain things to your child – this will help to improve their language skills.

Five ways **to keep your toddler interested in language**

1 Show excitement at every new word your toddler says.

2 Use lots of repetition.

3 Make good eye contact when chatting to your child.

4 Remove distractions when trying to attract her attention.

5 Respond when she talks to you.

Language
Common problems

Q Should I be worried that my toddler is 17 months old and still hasn't said her first word?
A Every child develops at their own rate and although the majority of children have said their first word by the age of 15 months, there is a significant number who don't achieve this until a few months later. There is no need to be unduly concerned, especially if there are other signs that her speech is developing in a normal way. For instance, the presence of babbling is a positive sign that her language development is progressing satisfactorily, as is her active involvement in songs and nursery rhymes.

Q My toddler stammers. He starts to say a word, but doesn't complete it, then starts to say it again, and so on. Is this likely to develop into a long-term problem?
A Stammering or stuttering is common in children as young as two years old. Repetitions and uncertainty like this occur frequently when a child's language development is beginning to accelerate. Fortunately, most two-year-olds pass through this phase without any help as their confidence grows. However, if your young child stammers or stutters, make sure that nobody (including older siblings) makes fun of him, tries to mimic him, or attempts to hurry him along. He needs your time, patience and support to get through this temporary phase.

Q My 21-month-old child has a stilted way of talking, as though abbreviating what she is saying. Is that typical for a child this age?
A Her language sounds abbreviated because it contains only the key words, such as 'want milk' or 'me sleep'. Over the next year she will start to add in other types of words such as prepositions and adjectives. This is the way in which language development normally progresses over the months.

Q My toddler speaks so hurriedly I can't make out what she says. What should I do?
A She is just impatient to express herself. Over the next few months she will naturally slow down her speech and it will become easier to understand what she is saying. In the meantime, if she is over-excited when she speaks to you, try to encourage her to speak more slowly. But there is absolutely no cause for concern.

Left: Communicating with your child, one-on-one, will boost her confidence in her language skills.

Q How can I get my toddler to speak instead of pointing at what he wants?

A Your child will still use gestures as part of his communication, even when his verbal skills have improved. You can help his speech progress by resisting the temptation to respond to his gestures alone. For instance, should he point at his cup of juice, ask him 'Do you want the cup of juice?' or even better 'What is it you want?' Repeat the question if he continues to point. Eventually he will try to communicate his desire using spoken sounds instead of gestures alone.

Q Should I be concerned that my child talks to himself?

A No. One of the best ways for him to improve his language skills is through regular practice and what better way to practise free from interruption than by talking to himself? You won't understand most of what he says during these self-directed monologues, but remember that his words are not intended for you to hear.

Q There are times when my toddler is much less talkative. For example, she tends to clam up when out with other people. Why is this?

A It is not unusual for a child to go quiet when in company and it's nothing to worry about. Despite her instinctive desire for attention, she may suddenly lose her confidence to speak when she is confronted by a sea of faces, and may not speak again until she is alone with you once more. At other times, it may be that she is tired or in a bad mood. Whatever the reason, let her have quiet times and don't try to force her into having a conversation with you. You'll probably find that she becomes more communicative again later in the day.

Right: It is common for a toddler to still use gestures to communicate with you even when his language skills have improved.

Hand–eye coordination
What is typical?

Your growing toddler has matured to the point where her vision and hand control combine effectively to enable her to focus keenly on a small toy that attracts her attention and then put her hand out to grab hold of it. Games that previously were too demanding for her, such as jigsaws, now hold great interest.

Improved hand–eye coordination combined with more mature learning and understanding allows your child to begin the early stages of drawing. Drawing adds an extra dimension to your child's life and is something you should encourage whenever she shows an interest. At around 15 months, your child's hand preference will start to become apparent, and you'll notice that she generally uses the same hand for most tasks involving manipulation.

What can my toddler do?

12–14 months

- By a year, she can hit pegs into a peg board with a hammer, she knows how to use crayons appropriately instead of mouthing them and is more adept at fitting difficult pieces into a shape sorter. She will also automatically put her hands and arms up when you bring her jumper towards her.

15–18 months

- As she approaches a year and a half, she is able to hold two items in each hand at the same time. She sees a connection between her hand movements and the effect this causes, for example, she pulls at a string to make the attached toy move towards her. She starts to feed herself with her hands and a spoon.

19–21 months

- She enjoys playing with modelling materials like playdough or clay and likes rolling, throwing and perhaps even catching balls. She can pour water accurately from one container into another and begins to make deliberate marks on paper with a crayon.

22–24 months

- By now she likes to help to dress and undress herself. She also makes increasingly rhythmic sounds with simple musical instruments such as drums and tambourines.

Hand–eye coordination
Common questions

Q Should I give my toddler toys that present a challenge, rather than those that he is able to do relatively easily?

A Your toddler will naturally tend to play with toys that he can manage without too much difficulty. For instance, he'll play with inset boards he has already mastered, even though they are no longer a challenge. You may need to encourage him to persist with new toys and puzzles – he may prefer familiarity to novelty. Once you are aware of his level of hand–eye coordination, buy him an inset board that is difficult for him to complete but not too demanding. If he puts it to one side at first, sit with him and suggest that you do it together.

Q What size of ball should my toddler play with, big or small?

A Ideally she should have a range of sizes. Different sizes require her to use different visual and manual skills. A small ball helps her strengthen her grip because she can hold it in one hand alone. A larger ball requires her to coordinate both hands in order to grasp the ball.

Q Why does my toddler's hand often tremble when he concentrates on putting shapes into the correct holes?

A This is a normal occurrence during an activity requiring great concentration. His desire to fit the shape in the hole is so strong that his hand and arm muscles start to tense up, and his whole hand begins to shake. It stops shaking when he relaxes.

Above: Playing with a ball requires your child to coordinate both hands in order to grasp it.

Q Now my toddler is able to pick up small, delicate things, these are what she seems to go for. I am terrified she will swallow something dangerous, but am I being over-anxious?

A Your toddler will enjoy manipulating small objects such as zips, tiny buttons, pins lying on the floor, small wooden beads and bits of dried food that she discovers – they all fascinate her. She will want to pick them up and explore them, and perhaps even put them in her mouth. Although she needs this sort of hands-on experience to develop her hand–eye coordination even further, there is a risk of injury if she is unsupervised. You have to balance your safety concerns with her need for varied play opportunities. Keep all sharp items out of reach altogether and watch over her very carefully when she plays with permitted small items. See also Safety in the home (pages 172–173).

Hand–eye coordination
Stimulation

Your toddler is able to do much more for himself during his second year. His improved attention span enables him to cope with more complex hand–eye coordination challenges. At times he is totally preoccupied with a task and his face is a picture of concentration as he persists in his attempt to complete the activity. His increased confidence motivates him to try harder with more difficult games and puzzles. As he approaches the end of his second year, your toddler has a strong fascination with other children his own age. Although he does not yet play cooperatively, he watches his peers closely and will try to imitate their style of play. This can act as an incentive for him to play with toys and games that he was not particularly interested in before.

Above: Drawing with pencils and crayons will help your child to improve his fine motor skills.

How can I stimulate my toddler's hand–eye coordination skills?

• **Make a special display area for his drawings.** There is no better way to express your admiration of his drawing skills and this will encourage him to do more.

• **Play clapping games.** By now he is able to clap his hands together, but you can encourage him to clap less randomly, say to music.

• **Wiggle his fingers.** Demonstrate how you can stretch your hands wide open and wiggle your fingers in the air. Your toddler will try to imitate you.

• **Play 'pointing' games.** Name specific objects in the room and ask your child to point to them. He'll then scan the area, spot the object you have named and point his index finger towards it.

• **Use household items.** His hand–eye control benefits when he plays with everyday items. Whenever possible, arrange for your child to play with others his own age – he learns from and is motivated by their actions.

• **Allow him to choose some of his clothes.** He'll be more enthusiastic about trying to dress and undress himself if he has chosen the items to wear.

• **Encourage him to clear up.** For instance, once he has finished his meal, he can lift his plate and cutlery and carry it to the sink.

Suitable toys for your growing toddler

Age	Toy	Skill
12–14 months	Shape sorter	• To encourage your child's ability to differentiate between shapes and colours and to improve dexterity.
	Ball	• Rolling a ball back and forth will develop your toddler's control.
	Toy telephone	• Provides a chance to imitate real-life activities. A telephone with a dial will improve your child's dexterity.
15–18 months	Inset board	• To develop your child's ability to manipulate smaller, irregular shapes.
	Coloured crayons and paper	• Drawing is one of those activities that he never tires of because he is able to create something new every time.
	Building blocks that lock together	• Learning how to connect two locking pieces will teach your child to carry out tasks with more accuracy.
19–21 months	Doll with zips or buttons on its clothing	• Toddlers love to imitate adults. Dressing and undressing a doll is good practice for dressing themselves later on.
	Modelling materials	• Your toddler will use his hands to make different shapes and forms, encouraged by the fact that he can start again if he doesn't like the results.
	Construction blocks of varying shapes and sizes	• Building towers of up to five bricks or more will improve your toddler's hand control.
22–24 months	Toy musical instruments	• Your toddler's improved hand control allows him to make more planned use of toy musical instruments, becoming more rhythmic with practice.
	Jigsaw puzzles	• Simple jigsaw puzzles with lugs present a challenge and improve your toddler's concentration.
	Colouring books	• Although he won't be able to colour neatly between the lines, this is good early practice for writing skills.

Hand–eye coordination
Common problems

Q No matter how often I show my one-year-old how to put the shapes in his shape sorter toy, he still can't manage them all. Should he be able to?
A Shape sorters are incredibly difficult for little fingers to manage. Your son can probably manages the circle and square shapes but not the more complicated ones. Give him time to learn the solutions. He will improve as his hand control increases over the next few months.

Q My toddler doesn't seem to understand how cause-and-effect toys work. What should I do to encourage her?

Above: Your child will soon get the hang of how a toy works if you show him what to do.

A It may be that her hand–eye coordination simply isn't good enough yet to operate the toys you give her. If she doesn't understand how to make a toy work, then just show her what to do with it. You may need to do this a few times.

Q My toddler won't let me help him when he struggles with undressing. What should I do?
A Although he won't let you give you a hand, you can still talk to him and can give helpful directions (for instance, 'Pull that sock off first, not both at once'). Once he starts to listen to your comments, he'll be more willing to let you give practical help.

Q Why does my toddler often fall over when she bends down to pick something up from the floor?
A Picking something off the floor involves both hand–eye coordination and balance at the same time, and this may be too demanding for her. Putting all her concentration into coordinating her thumb and forefinger reduces her focus on balance – and hence she topples.

Q My toddler is showing signs of being left-handed. Is there something I can do to persuade him to use his right hand instead?
A Don't be tempted to force your toddler to use his right hand if his natural preference seems to be to use the left hand. This could cause difficulties in other areas of his development. For instance, there is some evidence that since hand preference is controlled by the part of the brain that also

controls speech, forcing a left-handed toddler to use his right hand could create language difficulties. In addition, pressuring your toddler to go against his natural preference will result in confrontation and frustration and could create a problem where none existed before.

Q My toddler is 19 months old and she is still 'mouthing' toys. Is this normal?

A Most children this age play more purposefully with toys instead of simply putting everything straight into their mouths. However, if yours continues with this habit, do your best to avoid confrontation over this as toddlers can be determined to get their own way. Because you run the risk of drawing her attention to the habit, which could make it persist even longer, attempt to distract your child with another activity when you see her about to mouth toys, and while she is distracted, gently remove the item from her hands. She will soon grow out of the habit anyway, even if you do nothing about it at all.

Q My toddler often throws puzzles away in frustration if he cannot put them together immediately. What can I do to help him?

A The typical toddler this age likes to get things right first time. And if he doesn't, temper and

Above: Fitting complex shapes into a shape sorter takes a great deal of concentration and patience.

tears may follow. This often shows through with activities involving hand–eye coordination because they need concentration and patience to achieve steady hand movements. Encourage your toddler to practise again and again with any hand–eye coordination task that he finds particularly difficult. Explain to him that everyone learns gradually and that the more he tries, the easier it will become. An alternative, but common reaction, is to get upset, but refuse to give up. In this case, it often works if you suggest he temporarily leaves the challenge that upsets him and then returns to it later once he is calm. When you see him struggling, distract him with another activity – perhaps give him a drink of juice – and then let him go back to the activity.

One boy in 10 and one girl in 12 is left-handed; over 90 per cent of children are obviously left- or right-handed by the time they reach school age.

Movement
What is typical?

By the time your child is two years old, his movement skills will have improved considerably with a number of significant changes taking place. He has probably attained half the height that he will be as an adult. His legs are longer and his muscles are stronger and firmer, enabling him to move in a more agile manner and at a greater speed.

During the same time, your child's brain, which was approximately 25 per cent of its eventual adult weight at birth, has grown to approximately 75 per cent of its full adult weight. And this increased brain size is accompanied by maturation in part of the lower brain (called the cerebellum), giving him more control over his balance and posture. Furthermore, you child's vision improves and he is able to focus his sight more accurately.

What can my toddler do?

12–14 months

- He is determined to walk on his own, despite frequent falls and is able to stop and change direction when walking. He climbs stairs either on all fours or by shifting his bottom one step at a time.

15–18 months

- He walks confidently about the home and outside and can pick up toys or other objects from the floor without toppling over. He will start to climb playground equipment, but will need constant supervision. He may also enjoy splashing and kicking in the swimming pool.

19–21 months

- By now he is able to undertake another activity while he is on the move. For example, he can trail a pull-along toy behind him as he walks. He climbs up and down from a chair and his improved balance and coordination leads to fewer instances of tripping over and unexpected falls when he is walking and running.

22–24 months

- Towards the age of two years, he can stand on one foot while using the other to kick a ball. He is able to move fast as long as he goes in a straight line and he can throw and catch a ball from a sitting position. He may also like to dance to music.

Movement
Common questions

Q Is it normal for a toddler to walk a bit, then crawl, then walk another bit, then crawl?
A Yes. A child rarely abandons his earlier mode of travel as soon as he learns to walk. He knows that crawling is a very efficient and rapid form of movement that isn't tiring, whereas walking is slower and more exhausting to start with. That's why he still crawls to cover longer distances.

Q Do socks and shoes give my toddler confidence with walking?
A For outside the house, your toddler needs to wear socks and shoes to protect her feet. Inside the house, however, let her toddle about in her bare feet. This gives her foot muscles maximum grip on the floor and allows her to use her toes more effectively for maintaining balance.

Q My toddler has a fat tummy. Could this slow his progress with movement?
A At this age your child's liver is very large in proportion to his overall body size and also his bladder is still quite high in the abdomen. These physical characteristics may make you think he is overweight – even though he is not – and they have no negative effect at all on his movement.

By the age of two, the rapid early growth rate has slowed down and boys are generally taller than girls.

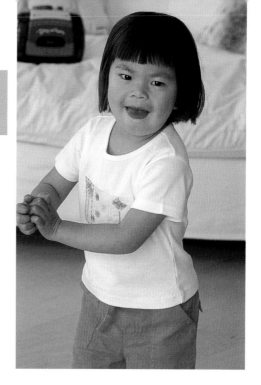

Above: Dancing is a great way for your toddler to learn balance and coordination while having fun.

Q My toddler is 21 months. Should she be able to walk backwards at this age?
A Most children can manage this by 21 months, though it can take time to learn. When your toddler faces you, she can probably take steps to go backwards, but if she half turns around to look over her shoulder as she moves in the reverse direction, she may tumble over. She should practise this on a carpeted floor.

Q Will dancing improve my child's movement?
A There's nothing like dancing to music for getting a toddler to twist and turn her body. The dance won't be systematic or follow any set pattern, but it will require lots of movement, plenty of coordination, and loads of balance. This is a great way for your child to develop her agility while also having fun.

Movement
Stimulation

The majority of children take their first few walking steps before they reach the age of 15 months (the average age is 13 months) and then they become increasingly adventurous as confidence grows. Your toddler's natural curiosity, coupled with his new coordination skills, opens up a whole new range of play experiences for him.

Above: Once your toddler has learnt to walk he will become more confident and adventurous.

The most significant change in your toddler's movement skills at this stage is his ability to concentrate on more than one action at a time. For instance, he can stand on one foot while kicking a ball with the other. As he reaches the end of his second year, your child's improved balance and body movements, coupled with his increased chest, hips and leg strength, give him the ability and confidence to attempt physical tasks that he could previously observe only passively, such as running, jumping, kicking, throwing and catching.

How can I stimulate my toddler's movement skills?

• Reassure him when he falls. The occasional tumble may upset him. All it takes to get him on his feet again is a cuddle from you, and reassurance that he is unlikely to fall again.

• Let him climb in and out of his chair without help. The twisting, kneeling and turning involved provides excellent practice for his balance and movement skills.

• Ask him to pick up toys from the floor. When toddling about, your child will be willing to lift a toy from the floor, and will improve with practice.

• Play kicking and catching games with him. His balance will be shaky at first, but he will improve over time.

• Hold his hand when he attempts to walk quickly – in this way you both know that there is no risk of him toppling over, and therefore he'll be prepared to try harder.

• Demonstrate actions if necessary. Your toddler learns by experience and he will watch you closely and then try to do the same himself.

• Begin to give him simple movement challenges that have more than one element in them.

Clumsiness

Q I am aware that my toddler has difficulty tackling most playground activities, where other children of the same age seem to have no problem at all. He is accident-prone and quite often stumbles or trips over his own feet. Is he clumsy?

A There is huge variation in the rate at which children acquire coordination skills and individual differences in the development of movement are perfectly normal. Take a closer look at the other children and you will see that some are clearly more agile than others. So there is no need to worry if yours is always the one who seems to trip most or who is last to manoeuvre himself onto the first step of the climbing frame.

Statistics reveal, however, that between five and seven per cent of young children are clumsy, in other words, they have difficulty with every activity involving arm, leg and body movements. Anything involving balance and coordination proves to be an overwhelming challenge for a clumsy child.

The dividing line between a child who is slow to acquire new coordination abilities and a child who is clumsy is unclear. This lack of a clear definition doesn't really matter because every child – clumsy, average or agile – requires stimulation and encouragement to improve. Bear in mind that the root of clumsiness lies in the way the child perceives the world and in the way he is able to coordinate a number of processes – it is not due to any physical problem with his arms or legs.

The biggest hurdle facing a clumsy child – and in fact any child who struggles with a physical challenge – is that he may lose confidence in himself and may start to give up too easily when it comes to physical activities. A child with poor coordination often expects to fail and so doesn't try hard. He needs your support to overcome the difficulties he experiences so that he can maintain his self-confidence and continue to enjoy healthy physical play.

The ratio of clumsy boys to clumsy girls is about 2:1.

Above: Toys that encourage your child to walk will help to improve agility and coordination.

Movement
Common problems

Q My toddler is 15 months old now and still is not walking. Should I be concerned?

A If your 15-month-old child hasn't taken his first step yet, don't worry. There are some children who don't walk until a few months later and yet whose subsequent development proves to be perfectly normal. It's just that their genetic blueprint has pre-programmed walking to occur at a later time than usual. What does matter, however, is that the other positive signs of progress are there, such as he is crawling comfortably, he kicks his legs when lying in his cot, he pulls himself to standing, and he reaches out for toys. If he shows these positive signs, you can be sure he'll walk very soon.

Q While my first child used to climb stairs on all fours, my second tends to go up and down on her bottom. Is she doing it wrong and can I help to correct her?

A Toddlers have an amazing ability to improvise. There is no 'right' way to do this; your toddler will use the technique that best suits her and her level of physical development. The best help you can give is plenty of encouragement, because her enthusiasm can quickly be dampened by repeated failure and she may be tempted to give up trying completely.

Q My toddler took his first few steps at 13 months but, five weeks on, he has made little progress. I worry that he may never advance any further. Is this normal?

A Yes. You can expect occasional lulls in his progress. There will be temporary phases during which he makes almost no advance in his movement skills. This happens with most children. He will start to progress once again when he is ready for change.

Q My 13-month-old looks odd when she walks. She tends to have her arms stretched out on either side and her body movements are very jerky. Is something wrong?

Above: As your child becomes more confident, she will begin to use furniture to pull herself up.

Above: When outside, your newly walking toddler should wear socks and shoes to protect her feet.

A No, this is fine; she's just feeling her way very carefully and letting her balance system adjust to the new sensations. Within a month or so you will find that her arms are closer to her side and her forward steps are smoother, less shaky and altogether more relaxed.

Q Although my toddler was making good progress with his walking, he had a bad fall last week and this has made him reluctant to rise to any challenges. What can I do to help him?
A The most important help you can give your child at this stage is to increase his confidence and stability when walking. Despite his determination to stand on his own two feet, he may be nervous about being in such an

exposed upright position. And all it takes is a minor fall or bump to give him a little setback. That's why he needs bags of praise and encouragement from you when he starts to walk. Be there with him when you can, smiling at him, telling him how terrific he is and giving him a big cuddle when he manages on his own.

Q My two-year-old girl seems a long way behind her contemporaries when it comes to catching and throwing a ball. Should I be concerned?
A There is wide variation in athletic ability among two-year-olds. This is largely due to different rates of physical and neurological maturation. For your toddler to achieve complex movement skills, she must have developed the important underlying muscular and neurological structures. If her development hasn't reached this point, she won't be able to master skills like running, throwing and climbing, no matter how much she practises these actions. So be careful not to push your child too hard if she struggles physically – it's probably that her body just isn't ready. Try again in a few weeks.

Q My child makes the same movement, climbing up on the chair then climbing down, only to climb up again one minute later. Why does she do this?
A This is her instinctive way of mastering a new skill. It's not that she is easily amused or that she can't think of anything else to do. She instinctively knows that repetition is the best way to improve her movement, balance and coordination, and she keeps going until she feels that she has got it right.

Emotional development
What is typical?

During your child's second year, her social and emotional development enters a new phase as her own identity begins to develop. She wants to make choices, to do things by herself, and she can be extremely assertive. From the age of about 15 months onwards, she becomes very self-absorbed.

Although this type of behaviour in an adult would be described as selfishness, that description doesn't apply when it comes to a child of this age. Her behaviour is 'egocentric' in the true sense of the word, rather than 'selfish'. She literally cannot understand anybody else's point of view. There have been many psychological investigations that confirm that children of this age struggle to consider how other people think and feel.

How does my toddler behave?

12–14 months	• From the end of her first year, her innate desire to become independent will begin to show. She will play alongside rather than with a child of her own age. She will give you a big cuddle when she is happy and may have a temporary phase of attachment to one parent in particular.
15–18 months	• She may have a tantrum when she doesn't get her own way and wants to do more for herself, especially with feeding and dressing. She begins to learn basic social skills like passing a toy to another child and may become jealous when you pay attention to others.
19–21 months	• She appreciates your company and makes an effort to engage your attention either through talk or play. She persists in challenging decisions that she disagrees with. By now she will begin to interact with other children but needs lots of basic social guidance.
22–24 months	• She enjoys the company of other children, but has trouble sharing her toys and does not yet play cooperatively. She may cry when separated from you temporarily, although she soon stops when you are out of sight.

Emotional development
Common questions

Q Is it sensible to criticize my toddler whenever he misbehaves?

A Regularly criticizing your child for his misbehaviour reduces his self-confidence and creates a bad atmosphere for everyone at home. When you want him to change his behaviour, merge your negative observation with a more positive comment. For instance, instead of saying 'You're naughty for making such a mess' you could say 'I'm surprised you've made such a mess because you normally eat so nicely.'

Q When I take my 17-month-old to parent-and-toddler group she doesn't say a word, she just clings to me like a limpet. Should I push her away so that she is forced to cope more independently?

A Her body language is telling you 'I'm afraid of these other children and I want to stay beside you because that makes me feel safe.' Put like that, the strategy of forcing her away from you probably won't work – it could make her feel even more miserable. Give her time to adjust to this new social context. Several visits may pass before she feels confident enough to leave your side, but her natural social instinct takes over eventually and she gradually takes a few hesitant steps away from you.

Q Every time I visit friends with other children, mine gets clingy for most of the time we are there. Is this normal?

A The typical toddler feels very secure with his parents and also has an increased awareness of strangers. The ironic effect of these two trends is that you might find that your child is happy to play with you but more anxious with unfamiliar people, even though recently he was more socially adventurous. Don't be irritable with him when he clings tightly to you – this apparent increase in his emotional dependency on you will pass in a few months. He needs your patience and support at this time.

Q How can I encourage my toddler's sense of self?

A Make a special point of using her name when you talk to her. She knows this word is just for her and that when you look at her and say her name, you are referring to her alone. You can also help by starting to teach her the names of her body parts, such as hands, feet, eyes, ears and so on. She's much too young to say these words but she can start to understand them.

Q What are the best ways of providing social contact for my child?

A A good idea is to take him to a local parent-and-toddler group. Your presence will give him enough confidence to attend without tears, and going regularly gets him used to being in larger groups of people, which in turn builds his social confidence. If there isn't a local group, invite parents of children the same age to your house so that all the toddlers can play together.

Emotional development
Stimulation

At the turn of her first year, your toddler wants to do more on her own and does not like it if you set limits on her behaviour. Tantrums may be frequent when she can't get her own way. She is curious about other people, and will stare uninhibitedly at anyone who attracts her attention.

Your child's developing sense of self makes her increasingly determined to challenge the rules that you set for her at home. Yet all it takes is a small disappointment for this apparent self-confidence to crumble, sending her rushing to you for a reassuring cuddle. As she approaches two, your child becomes much more sociable, although contact with other children may still end up in squabbles over toys. She may be shy with strangers and may greet relatives she hasn't seen for a while with a blank silence.

How can I stimulate my toddler's emotional development?

• **Take her with you outside,** when at all possible. People fascinate her and she loves watching them.

• **Tackle jealousy** when it arises.

• **Try to include your toddler at a family meal occasionally** – she will love the social nature of it.

• **Provide opportunities for her to mix with others of her own age.** She will learn from watching other children's behaviour and from the different ways in which they play with toys.

• **Enjoy her company.** Listen to her as she tries to tell you her latest exciting piece of news, and play games with her. She needs to know that you care for her as much as ever.

• **Structure her day.** Routine makes your child feel secure.

• **Comfort her when she is distressed.** She may quickly become upset by something that seems trivial to you but seems huge to her.

• **Let your child see that you value her achievements.** Her self-confidence depends greatly on how she thinks you view her.

• **Encourage her to think of others.** She will become more sensitive to the feelings of other people if you specifically suggest this to her.

• **Give her small tasks of responsibility.** Even at this age, small amounts of responsibility will increase her maturity and level of independence.

• **Teach her how to take turns.** Practise this very important social skill with her at home.

Left: As a child gets older, she becomes more emotional and can easily become upset or frustrated by the smallest thing.

Positive parenting **Coping with egocentricity**

Q I am finding it increasingly difficult to control my child. He is prone to frequent bouts of anger and frustration whenever something doesn't go his way. I don't want to discourage him completely, but there are times when he simply cannot do or have what he wants. What can I do?

A Your toddler has reached the stage where he finds it impossible to see anything from any viewpoint but his own. He is totally shocked the moment his wishes are blocked, whether by you or because he simply can't achieve his target, and he experiences a sudden surge of frustration that overwhelms him – he just can't believe that he can't get what he wants, when he wants it. It can be very hard to stand by as he thoughtlessly snatches a toy from another child's hand without asking simply because he wants to have it, and when you do try to step in you bear the brunt of his anger. He can't accept that you have set rules for him to follow; from his perspective, his feelings come first and it doesn't matter to him that you are the parent and he is the child.

Strategies

• **Remember that your toddler is still a wonderful, loving child who gives much love to you and to others in his family.** Despite an increase in tantrums and other frustrations, there are plenty of times when he is settled and when you have great fun just enjoying his company. Enjoy these frequent moments, and do your best to avoid them becoming overshadowed by the more challenging episodes.

• **Remember that, despite this surge of determination and independence, your toddler remains vulnerable socially and emotionally.** This same child, who only a few minutes ago howled at you angrily because you had the nerve to ask him to stop playing with his toys in order to prepare for his bath, now clings to you sobbing because he can't find his favourite cuddly toy. Self-confidence is easily rocked at this stage, turning happiness into distress, laughter into tears.

• **Handle his changing moods sensitively.** On the one hand, his temper tantrums will push you to the absolute limits of your tolerance and you will need plenty of resolve to withstand his demands. On the other hand, he needs your affection and support when he is upset.

• **Teach your child to recognize what is acceptable behaviour and what is not** by giving him lots of love to increase his sense of security, by offering him help and advice when he faces challenges that are too demanding, and by suggesting ways that he can learn to mix better with other children.

Emotional development
Common problems

Q My toddler insists on having a night light. Should I discourage this?

A There's no harm in having a night light, although you can gradually reduce his reliance on it by fitting a dimmer switch. Make the light slightly dimmer each night, in such small stages that he doesn't realize you are doing this. You'll soon reach a point when he falls asleep without any light.

Q Our 14-month-old has insisted recently that he only plays with me, not my partner. Is that normal?

A Phases of attachment to one parent in particular happen occasionally, but are temporary. Arrange for your partner to play with your toddler, to bath him, feed him and so on, even though he prefers your company. This will help the attachment remain strong to both of you.

Q What can I do about my toddler who refuses to leave my side at toddler group?

A Be patient with her, despite your embarrassment at her behaviour. She's obviously not ready yet to venture into the playroom alone. In the meantime, let her stay at your side. Almost certainly her natural curiosity will eventually take over and she'll soon start to drift slowly away from your side towards the exciting activities on offer elsewhere.

Q My toddler is 22 months old and still uses a comforter when he is upset or wants to go to sleep. Should I try to wean him off it?

A Some children form an attachment to a cuddly toy or blanket, continue to suck a dummy or develop the habit of sucking their thumb. This is a normal pattern of behaviour, and is nothing to worry about. Psychologists believe that comforters of this sort can give your child extra security at times when he particularly needs it, perhaps when he's tired, in unfamiliar surroundings or when going to bed. Most children grow out of this behaviour by the time they are three or four.

Q I feel as though I'm in confrontation with my toddler every day. What can I do?

A Try to take a more positive approach. Start to use more praise for good behaviour instead of reprimands for misbehaviour; make a point of spending time together just having fun; and

Left: Toddlers do not have the appropriate social skills to ask for a toy – they just tend to snatch.

Above: If reassured, a clingy child will eventually want to join in the exciting activities on offer.

do your best to keep any disagreements short so that anger between you and your toddler doesn't carry on for hours.

Q What can I do to curb my child's aggression to others? When I take him to parent-and-toddler group, he grabs toys from other children without saying a word.
A The problem he faces is that he wants to play with a toy but he doesn't have the social or language skills to ask politely for it. He is only able to to express his wishes non-verbally, hence he snatches the object without any concern for his peers. Help him become more sensitive by discouraging this habit. Remove the toy from his hands and let him see you return it to its original owner. Explain to him why you are doing this and try to calm him.

Q How can I make my child less timid when he is with other children?
A Do not allow him to avoid social interactions; reassure him that the other children will like him and will want to play with him; and arrange for him to play with only one child at a time instead of a group. These strategies may help to reduce his timidity.

Q My toddler changes her mind often at mealtimes, asking for milk to drink, then juice, then milk again. Is she being deliberately awkward?
A No. It's just that she is beginning to think for herself. Her drive for independence can be difficult for you, especially when she starts to make choices that clash with your own plans. However, the development of her individual identity is an essential part of the growing process and is something to be encouraged. Naturally your child can't have everything she wants. Yet you can help her in her drive for self-reliance by giving her the chance to make small choices.

Q There are times when my toddler throws a terrible tantrum that I feel totally unable to control her. Am I failing her as a parent?
A You have to remember that your daughter expresses her ever-growing desire for independence in many ways and can be extremely forceful in trying to get what she wants. Try to maintain a positive perspective no matter how despairing you may feel at times with her behaviour. Reassure yourself that this behaviour – albeit infuriating – is normal and that it does not mean you are an inadequate parent or that you are doing anything wrong.

CHILDCARE

The right option

Trying to find the right kind of childcare for your child can be difficult as there are so many factors to take into consideration.

The benefits of childcare

- His independence increases. Without you by his side, he learns to become less reliant on you to do everything for him.
- Social skills improve. Mixing with a range of other children his own age on a regular basis provides an opportunity for him to develop new social skills.
- He learns more. Children learn from each other. Shared games and activities provide new daily learning opportunities.
- Friendships increase. Common sense tells you that the more children he mixes with each day, the more friendships he is likely to form. These friendships boost his self-esteem.
- His routine is varied. Instead of following the same routine at home every day, childcare creates welcome variety in his daily pattern of activity.
- Your relationship becomes more focused. When you and your child spend time away from each other, you are likely to use time together more effectively.

Some parents are lucky enough to have a trusted relative who lives close enough to look after their young child while they are out at work. In cases when this is not possible, the most popular childcare options for toddlers are nannies, who look after the child in the home, or childminders, who look after one or more children in their own home, perhaps alongside their own children. There are also various types of nurseries and crèches, in which several carers look after children in a separate premises, but not all of these cater for under-threes on a full-time basis.

Criteria to consider
- Qualifications in childcare and education. These demonstrate the carer's seriousness about their job and their knowledge of child development and education.
- Previous experience in childcare and education. You will probably be more comfortable knowing that your child is under the supervision of someone who is used to

Separation anxiety

The first day without you can be challenging for both of you, as your toddler presses himself against you, refusing to let go of your hand. This reaction is completely normal and there is much you can do as a parent to help your child adjust to a new carer and a new environment.

Five steps to separation

1 A week before he is due to start with his carer, tell your child about the arrangements you have made. Be ready to answer any questions he might have, and adopt an upbeat attitude about it.

2 A few days before your child is due to start with the carer, arrange for the two of them to meet. This lets your child grow accustomed to the idea. Meeting his carer in advance reassures and excites him.

3 Find him something to play with as soon as he arrives. Your child will settle more easily at the start of each session when he targets a specific activity straight away.

4 Discuss your return. You know you are coming back but your child might not realize this. So, make a specific point of telling him: for example, say 'I'll see you very soon, before lunch.'

5 Praise on collection. Tell him how proud you are that he enjoyed herself and played with the other children there. He loves you to take an interest and he glows under your obvious approval.

The facts about separation

• A child's anxiety about being away from his parents typically declines after a couple of weeks, and usually vanishes altogether after a month at the most.

• There is no connection between tears at separation and later psychological problems – apprehension is a normal reaction to temporary separations.

• Separation anxiety often occurs in a confident child, too – even one who has been to a carer or crèche before starting at this one.

• Children who experience separation anxiety from their parents are often more alert, curious and assertive once they settle into the new environment.

dealing with children of a similar age to that of your child.

• References from other parents. Try to talk to at least a couple of parents who have previously used this carer for their own children. This will give you a clearer idea of whether the carer is suitable.

• Registration. Check that the carer you are considering is fully registered.

Questions to ask yourself:

• Am I at ease with this carer?

• If I was a child, would I want to spend time in the company of this person?

• Do the carer's views on child development coincide with mine?

• What will the carer offer my child?

• How does the carer link with parents?

• What kind of social life will they provide?

Safety in the home

The majority of child accidents happen at home, typically to young children who can often be one step ahead of expected abilities. While many aspects of home safety depend on you as a parent being reasonably vigilant, others require equipment that can be expensive and difficult to install.

Kitchen safety

For a young child the kitchen is the most dangerous room in the house and it is safest to keep a toddler outside the kitchen altogether. If this cannot be avoided, however, don't let her sit on the floor between you and the work surfaces, and don't allow her to spread toys over the floor where you may trip over them. If you are preparing a meal, chances are you are not able to keep a close eye on her all of the time, in which case you might be better off putting her in a playpen with some toys or sitting her in a highchair and giving her her supper while you prepare your own.

Fires kill more children in the home than any other single hazard.

Safety in the living room

The greatest single danger in the living room is heating devices. Even radiators can burn, so use room thermostats to control temperature. Shield children from solid fuel, wood-burning stoves, electric and even decorative gas fires with a fireguard. Turn off the electricity supply of an electric fire and remove the plug when not in use.

Bathroom safety

It is never a good idea to leave a toddler alone in a bathroom. You might think it is fun for her to play with water, but she can come to serious harm. At best she runs the risk of slipping on a wet floor or scalding herself on hot water. At worst, a toddler can drown in even very shallow water. If not playing with water, your toddler might find any number of cosmetics, aftershaves, perfumes or cleaning materials, many of which are poisonous.

Safety in the garden

Gardens and playgrounds are exciting places for children to play. Of course they are also hazardous. It is unrealistic and unreasonable to try to think of every possible danger that could befall a child outside and to protect them from injury. However, taking sensible precautions and teaching basic outdoor safety rules from the start allows children to gain confidence and allows parents to build up trust.

Checklist for the **living room**

• Remove any tablecloths and use mats instead. A child can pull the tablecloth and the entire contents of the table on top of herself.
• Lock all bottles of alcohol away. Never leave hot drinks, glasses or alcohol within reach on a coffee table, low shelf or television.
• Fix a fireguard around an open fire and use a spark guard for extra protection. Never leave a young child alone in a room with a fire.
• Don't assume your child can't climb; the chances are that if she is inquisitive enough she will view all shelves or tables and chairs as a challenge to her ingenuity.
• Keep houseplants out of reach of young children. Some are poisonous or can cause an allergic reaction.
• Fit corner protectors to sharp corners on tables and cupboards.
• Apply safety film to patio doors and glass tables. Put stickers on large areas of glass.
• Keep any toys belonging to your toddler within reach, not on a high shelf; she may try to climb up to reach them.
• Position light chairs with their backs to the wall so a toddler cannot pull them down on herself.
• Cover electrical sockets when not in use. Ideally use only one plug per socket.

Checklist for the **garden**

• Remove garden or building rubbish.
• Secure garden gates and fences so children cannot get out onto the road.
• Put garden tools away out of reach. Store garden chemicals in a locked shed.
• Make sure that garden furniture and play equipment is safe and correctly anchored.
• Prune back prickly plants and remove those known to be poisonous.
• Ensure that paving is even and remove any moss so that children don't slip.
• Cover all water butts, dustbins or ponds in which water collects.

Checklist for the **bathroom**

• Keep the temperature of an electrically heated towel rail low.
• Position the door lock out of a toddler's reach so she cannot lock herself in.
• Apply safety film to a glass shower.
• Set the hot water thermostat to a maximum 54°C (130°F) to avoid a child being scalded.
• If you have a very inquisitive toddler, use a toilet lid lock and don't use a toilet block as children sometimes chew on them. Also, remove the toilet brush if you have one.

Checklist for the **kitchen**

• Always use the back rings of the cooker and keep pan handles turned inwards so they cannot be grabbed.
• Keep a baby away from the oven doors, which can get hot enough to burn.
• If you have a kettle on the worktop use one without a cord or one with a short curly flex.
• Empty spare hot water after boiling.
• Turn off and unplug the iron after use, leaving it to cool well out of reach. Store it at the back of work surfaces, and never leave a trailing flex.
• Fix child-resistant safety catches on doors and drawers to prevent access to sharp knives, matches and cleaning materials.

Health issues
Basic first aid

This health section covers minor accidents only. First aid cannot be taught from a book, and to be able to deal with resuscitation, severe bleeding and burns or head injuries, you should enrol on a first-aid course. Otherwise you should have your child seen by a doctor or take him to an accident and emergency department. (See also pages 120–121 and 244–255.)

Above: Unless a cut is gaping open, clean it and cover it with a plaster or non-stick dressing.

Q What is the best way of dealing with regular cuts and grazes?

A Minor cuts and grazes with broken skin, tissue damage and bleeding are very common in children and can be treated at home. First, wash your hands thoroughly, then sit or lie the child down while you examine the wound. Wash the wound gently until it is clean and pat dry. Press gently with a clean cloth or pad to stop any bleeding. Cover with a non-stick dressing and adhesive tape or a plaster larger than the wound. If the edges of the wound gape open or it is on the head, take the child to hospital.

Q How do blisters come about and how should I treat them?

A Blisters form when the skin is rubbed or burned but not broken. Serum from the tissues gathers under the bubble of skin. New skin gradually re-forms under the blister and the serum is reabsorbed into the tissues. The skin from the blister eventually peels off. Do not burst a blister, but clean around it with water and pat dry. If it is likely to be broken or rubbed, cover it with a non-adhesive dressing larger than the blister.

Q What is the procedure for treating a burn?

A The first thing to do is to remove the child from the cause of burning and to rinse the affected area under cold running water for at least 10 minutes. Remove any clothing from the area, as long as it is not stuck to the skin. Loosen tight clothing because the burnt area might swell. Cover the area with cling film, or put a plastic bag over the hand, arm, foot or leg. Do not apply lotions, creams or fats. Any child with a burn larger than 25 mm (1 in) in diameter should be seen by a doctor or taken to the accident and emergency department.

Left: Protect your toddler with a hat, T-shirt and sun cream to prevent him from becoming sunburnt.

Q Can you give me advice for treating a toddler with sunburn?

A You will recognize sunburn as soon as your child has been over-exposed to the sun because the skin becomes red and extremely painful. It may also blister. You should cover your toddler immediately and move him to the shade. Give him something cool to drink. Gently cool the reddened skin with cold water for 10 minutes and apply calamine lotion or an after-sun cream. Dress him in loose, soft clothing. If the skin has blistered, take advice from your doctor.

Q What should I do in the event of heat exhaustion or heatstroke?

A A child who has been in strong sunshine for too long or who has over-exerted himself can lose so much water from the body that his temperature rises; he feels dizzy, and develops a headache and nausea; and his skin becomes very clammy and pale. The pulse will become weak very fast. To begin with, move your child to somewhere that is cool and shady. Lie him down with his feet slightly raised and make sure he is cool. Give him a drink of water, juice or a rehydrating drink. If he is not better within an hour call a doctor. If his condition gets worse, call an ambulance. If he is suffering from heatstroke, his skin will feel hot and dry. Remove his clothing and sponge him with tepid water to cool him down.

Q What should I do if my toddler receives an injury to the mouth?

A A blow to the mouth can cause cuts or bleeding from the tooth socket. Bleeding may be profuse, as the blood supply to the mouth is rich. A blow or fall may even knock out a tooth. Sit with your child after the accident and hold her head over a bowl to catch any blood. Press a pad in place over the wound for 10 minutes or until any bleeding stops. Look for a tooth that has been knocked out to make sure your toddler has not inhaled or swallowed it, and have her gum checked by a dentist.

Q How should I treat an eye injury?

A An injury to the eye needs prompt attention. Any blow could cause burst blood vessels, causing a black eye. Lay a clean facecloth that has been wrung out in cold water over the eye to limit bruising. If a sharp object enters the eyeball or makes a cut in the region of the eye, then the child will need emergency treatment. Bandage a pad over the eye for protection and bandage the other eye to limit movement. Then take your child to hospital.

Health issues
Skin complaints

Q What is eczema?

A Eczema is the most common skin problem in young children, affecting at least one child in eight. It can be very mild, consisting of just one or two red, scaly patches, or it can cover the entire body with an intensely itchy rash. It is usually impossible to pinpoint the specific trigger that initiates eczema in a young child, but it may be contact with house dust, animal fur, pollen or all of these. Overheating, dry air and cold weather make the condition worse, as do teething, colds and other infections. Sadly there is no cure for eczema, but in almost all affected children it does go into remission, in 40 per cent by the age of two and 90 per cent by the teens.

Q What should I look for?

A A baby or young child may become restless, sleeping poorly and rubbing her face. There may be small scratches on the face and arms where she has rubbed or scratched the skin. There may be patches of rough, red itchy skin on the face and arms, which may spread, affecting the skin creases at the wrists, elbows and knees. Sometimes skin all over the body becomes dry and rough.

Q What can I do about it?

A In caring for a child with eczema, avoid using soap, baby lotion or bubble bath, all of which can irritate the skin. Keep the affected skin smooth and supple by moisturizing it regularly with an emollient cream that you can buy from the pharmacist. After bathing, pat the child gently dry and leave the skin slightly moist. Spread the emollient cream thickly over her skin. Your doctor can prescribe soothing skin preparations, and if eczema keeps your child awake at night, the doctor may also prescribe a sedating antihistamine drug to be taken an hour before bedtime. To keep potential triggers to a minimum, keep family pets, soft toys, soft furnishing and carpets to a minimum and choose absorbent, non-irritating materials such

Above: You may notice an early sign of eczema if your young child is scratching red and itchy skin.

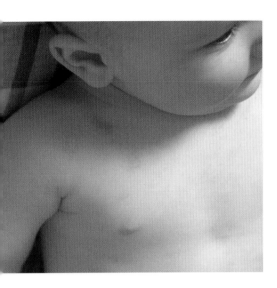

Above: Not all eczema is severe. Mild eczema can consist of just one or two rough, red patches.

as cotton for clothes; make sure clothes are not too tight to prevent rubbing; use pure cotton towels and bedding. Try out non-biological washing powders until you find one that suits your child's skin. Always wash and cream your child's hands after she has played with sand, playdough and water.

Q What should I do if my toddler develops a cold sore?

A At the first tingly cold sore sensation, apply cold sore cream, lotion or petroleum jelly. To ease the tingle, hold a piece of wetted, frozen cotton wool to the sore. Sterilize everything that goes into the child's mouth and keep his facecloth and towel separate from the rest of the family's. A child with a cold sore on the mouth will find it hard to eat. Give him soft foods such as ice cream, yogurt, mushy vegetables or even baby food. If drinking is uncomfortable, it may be easier for him to use a straw. Keep a child with a cold sore away from anyone with eczema, because the herpes virus that causes a cold sore can produce an extremely unpleasant rash.

Q What is roseola and how should I treat it?

A Roseola is a mild infection caused by the herpes virus and is very common among babies and young children, especially between six months and two years. It starts with an abrupt fever, which is often accompanied by a sore throat and slightly swollen neck glands. As the fever drops, after three to five days, a rash of splotchy rose spots appears over the chest, abdomen and back before spreading to the arms and neck. On the thigh and bottom, each spot may be surrounded by a fine halo. The rash rarely lasts more than two days. The first thing you should do is contact your doctor to discuss the symptoms and rule out the possibility of rubella or measles. The child will recover completely within two to three days, during which time you should give him paracetamol to keep the fever down and offer cool drinks regularly to prevent dehydration. You can also sponge down the skin with tepid water to cool him. Your child may lose his appetite, but it will only be for a couple of days.

Coldsores are more likely to develop when a child is run down.

Health issues
Ears, nose, throat

Above: It is best to avoid using cough medicine unless prescribed for your child by a doctor.

Q What is glue ear?

A Also known as otitis media with effusion (OME), this is a form of fluctuating deafness that is extremely common in young children. It is usually caused when, in response to an infection, the lining of the middle ear produces excess mucus, which can block the Eustachian tubes, leaving the mucus to collect in the middle ear. This thickens and becomes gluey, making the child's hearing muffled. Bouts of glue ear can start in early infancy and most children recover within six months. In many cases the condition can be cleared with a course of antibiotics. On some occasions your doctor may recommend a minor operation to drain the glue.

Q How should I treat a nose bleed?

A Sit your child down with his head forward over a basin or sink. Tell him to breathe through his mouth and not to sniff. Meanwhile pinch the soft part of the nose just below the bone. Lay a facecloth that has been rinsed in cold water, and possibly containing some crushed ice (or a half-full packet of frozen peas), over the bridge of the nose. Tell the child to spit out any blood into the basin. After 10 minutes check if the bleeding has stopped. Don't look any earlier than this or a clot that has formed may rupture or be dislodged. Once the bleeding has stopped, wipe away any blood from the face with cotton wool or kitchen paper and warm water. Tell the child to sit quietly for a while, and to resist the urge to sniff, pick at his nose or blow it for the next few hours, or the bleeding may start again.

Q Should I be worried if my toddler develops a cough?

A Most coughs are a healthy symptom of a passing cold, but if the cough occurs with other signs of illness, a chest infection may be the cause. There are two types of cough – a dry cough when nothing comes or is brought up, and a productive cough, when phlegm or

Children with glue ear show a marked inability to concentrate when expected to listen in a group.

mucus is brought up. If the child has a cold, wipe her nose regularly to limit the mucus dripping down and irritating the throat. For an irritating night cough with a cold, raise the head end of the mattress. Give the child warm, soothing drinks to loosen mucus and avoid any cough medicine unless prescribed by your doctor. Make sure the air is warm but moist and keep your child away from smoky atmospheres. Take your child to a doctor if she develops any of the following symptoms at the same time as she has the cough: difficulty in breathing; a high temperature; wheezing; barking; vomiting.

Q How can I tell if my toddler has croup rather than just another cold and what should I do about it?

A Although your child may have a cold before developing croup, you will notice a harsh barking cough, like that of a seal, and her breath will come in noisy, rasping gasps. She may also wheeze. You will also see that she has difficulty breathing and will suck her chest in. The condition is serious and you should call your doctor immediately. While waiting for help to arrive take your child to the bathroom, close all doors and windows, and turn on all the hot taps. The steamy atmosphere will help ease

your child's breathing and the coughing should stop in 10 minutes or so. Once the child is breathing easily again, prop her up in bed. Your doctor may prescribe a steroid drug to inhale from a nebulizer or to take by mouth. If the child does not respond quickly, she may have to be taken to hospital.

Q Is it normal for a toddler to wheeze?

A By the age of six, almost all children have experienced at least one episode of wheezing – a characteristic high-pitched musical whistling that is heard as the child breathes out. In most children under the age of three the wheezing occurs as the result of chest infection, and because the child's airways are still small. Most toddlers grow out of wheezing, but in some cases the condition may be caused by asthma, hay fever or some other allergy and it is worth getting the opinion of a doctor. If the wheezing comes on very suddenly, it may be because your child has inhaled something – a nut, a small toy, a leaf or a seed – in which case he will need immediate attention.

Above: If your child suffers from an ear complaint he may need treatment from a doctor.

Health issues
Febrile convulsions

Q What are they?

A Fits or seizures occur when there is a sudden increase in the strength of electrical impulses in the brain, which disrupts the surrounding nerve cells and sends uncontrolled signals throughout the body, which in some cases causes the muscles to twitch and jerk. Convulsions in children aged between six months and five years are often brought about by a sharp rise in temperature. These fever fits are very common and about a third of children who have had one febrile convulsion can expect to have another. Fits that are not caused by a sharp rise in temperature are much less common and could be linked to epilepsy.

Q What should I look for?

A The following signs are most likely in a child aged six months to five years. The signs may last for only a few seconds or for up to 10 minutes.

- The child becomes stiff or rigid.
- Arms and legs tremble or twitch.
- The eyes roll up, fix or squint.
- The child stops responding to you and loses consciousness.
- The child turns blue or becomes pale and limp.

Q What should I do?

A Stay with your child. If you can, lay him face down over your knee, or on the ground with his head resting on something soft and turned to one side. If he is sick, clear out his mouth with your finger. Gently try to remove any clothes that will come off easily. If the room is heated, turn off the heating and open a window or door to cool the air in the room. Your child will probably regain consciousness in a few seconds or minutes. Meanwhile lay your child in the recovery position (see below). Call a doctor if this is your child's first fit, particularly if it lasts more than five minutes or if it recurs. Once the child is fully conscious give him a paracetemol and a small drink.

The recovery position

A child who is unconscious but who is breathing should be placed in the recovery position so she cannot choke on vomit or swallow her tongue.
- Check for a clear airway and that your child is breathing, and that she has a pulse.
- Keeping the arm nearest you straight, put it under her thigh with the palm facing up.
- Place the back of the other hand against the child's nearest cheek and hold that hand (palm to palm) to protect the head as you roll her over.
- Bend the knee of the furthest leg from you until the foot is flat on the ground.
- Pull the thigh of the bent leg towards you. The child will roll over onto her side. Support her against your knees to stop her going right over onto her front.
- Tilt her head back to keep the airway open.
- Bend the upper leg at right angles to the hip and knee to support the child.
- Ensure that she is not lying on her lower arm and that her palm is facing upwards.

Health issues
Breath holding

Q What is breath holding?

A Breath holding can occur as a result of shock or pain following an injury, or during a temper tantrum. In the latter case it can be the most alarming expression of frustration in your child's repertoire. While it is upsetting for the parent, particularly if the child holds her breath for so long that she loses consciousness, she will not come to any harm.

Q What should I expect?

A At the moment of high anger or frustration, the child draws in a deep breath. You wait for the scream but it does not come – the child is silent and her face turns red, then blue. Within seconds the child may lose consciousness and start to breathe again. Seconds later the child comes round. Occasionally the child has a brief fit or convulsion. The body becomes rigid, before the child regains consciousness.

Above: Temper tantrums can result in a child holding her breath.

A child in the middle of a full-scale temper tantrum may hold his breath, and hold it for so long that eventually he loses consciousness.

Q What can I do?

A Pull your child away from any hard-edged furniture or toys so that she won't come to harm if she falls. If you can, lay her on the floor, put her in the recovery position once her body is relaxed. Don't leave her alone, but call a doctor immediately to confirm that breath holding is the cause of loss of consciousness.

Q Is there any way I can prevent my child from breath holding in the future?

A Next time you see the signs of frustration mounting, try distraction tactics. If they don't work and your child starts to hold her breath, blow on to her face. If she still doesn't relax, then walk away – she is less likely to breath hold without an audience. But keep her in sight.

4

child

2 to 4 years

Development
The third year

From 2 to 4 years

2–2½ years

- **Language.** Adores you reading stories at bedtime. Asks questions and listens attentively to the answers. Has a vocabulary of several hundred individual words. Enjoys simple conversations with familiar adults and other children. Uses language to extend the complexity of imaginative play, such as dressing up. Starts to use pronouns, such as 'he' or 'you' and prepositions, such as 'in' or 'on'. Recalls small amounts of personal information, such as age and full name, and is able to relate that information.

- **Learning.** Begins to match colours, for example, by finding two bricks of the same colour. Understands that coins are 'money', but still has little concept of their value. Sorts objects according to specific characteristics – able, for example, to divide toys according to type – say, animals or cars. Begins to develop a broad sense of time – for example, can probably distinguish between 'today' and 'tomorrow'. Identifies own face in a photograph. Is hungry for new experiences beyond the home and enjoys visits to new places such as the zoo. Ascribes human qualities to inanimate objects as an expression of an active imagination and perhaps as a means of understanding the world around.

- **Hand–eye coordination.** Manages to thread large beads onto a lace. When painting and drawing grips the crayon or brush and is able to make a controlled mark – for example, may be able to copy a vertical line that you have drawn. Copes better with construction toys and games and puzzles that have pieces that fit together. Can start to learn how to use pieces of cutlery other than a spoon. Has firmly established hand preference.

- **Movement.** Is able to jump a short distance off the ground from a standing position and with practice may be able to jump over a low obstacle. Successfully manoeuvres around obstacles while performing another task. Is able to take short walks on foot rather than being wheeled in a pushchair. Walks up stairs in your house without your support. Stands on tiptoes for a couple of seconds.

From 2 to 4 years

2½–3 years

- **Language.** Issues instructions confidently to you. Frequently uses pronouns such as 'I', and 'me', although not always correctly. Discovers that questions (mainly 'Who?' and 'Where?') are a good way to gather information. Has a vocabulary of at least a thousand words. Is ready for more complex stories with multiple characters. Asks frequent questions about the meaning of unfamiliar words when hearing them. Shows an understanding of grammatical rules, and applies them in speaking.

- **Learning.** Compares two objects in terms of size or height, albeit not always accurately. Makes up simple stories from imagination. Remembers something you both did yesterday and may be able to recall exciting events in the more distant past. Completes jigsaws with three or four large pieces. Is able to commit information, such as the name of an object, to memory by repeating it over and over. Anticipates the consequences of actions. For example, if a cup is knocked over the drink will spill.

- **Hand–eye coordination.** Benefits from the wider range of play equipment and craft activities at a playgroup or nursery. Can build a tower of eight or more blocks. Begins to be able to cut paper with a pair of child-safe scissors, although finds this difficult. Completes simple jigsaw puzzles. Due to improved control, drawings are less random and their subject is often recognizable. Can copy simple shapes you draw. Carries out simple household tasks like putting cutlery on the table or toys in a box.

- **Movement.** Jumps from a small height, such as a single step, without losing balance. Will attempt challenging balancing activities such as walking along a log or hopping, although may not succeed. Balances for several seconds while standing on one foot only. Is able to negotiate ladders and slides on large outdoor play equipment. Runs fast with great confidence. Carries out more than one physical task at the same time through improved coordination.

From 2 to 4 years

3–3½ years

- **Language.** Loves listening to stories and becomes more involved, perhaps discussing it with you as you read, trying to turn the pages and pointing to the pictures. No longer uses the minimum amount of words to convey meaning but instead uses a string of four or five words. Uses adjectives to describe everyday objects or people; at this stage only uses two or three regularly. Can understand and carry out verbal instructions that contain up to three pieces of information.

- **Learning.** Develops an elementary understanding of numbers from hearing and seeing other people using them. Demonstrates increased intellectual maturity through drawing, though a picture of you shows the head extremely large, with no body attached to it and legs sticking straight out from underneath. Short-term memory advances – may be able to hold new information for a few seconds and then report it accurately back to you. Understands rules of behaviour and the reasons behind them if these are explained clearly. May confuse coincidence with cause and effect, linking two events that are not in fact connected.

- **Hand–eye coordination.** Holds small objects with a steady hand and moves them without dropping them from his grasp. Manages to grip scissors firmly and can cut through a large piece of paper. Uses a small rolling pin to roll modelling clay, then mashes it up to start again. Can unfasten large buttons (the larger, the better) by using fingers to open the buttonholes. Can hold toothbrush correctly if shown how, and can clean teeth after a fashion.

- **Movement.** Can propel a pedal toy such as a tricycle slowly along an even surface. Copes with walking up small slopes. Can jump from the second stair to the ground, with both feet together, after seeing you do this. Stands on tiptoes for several seconds without putting heels on the ground, and also walks forward on tiptoes. Enjoys dancing to music, twisting body and shaking arms and legs more or less in time to the beat. Climbs into chair at mealtimes and twists body to get comfortable.

From 2 to 4 years

3½–4 years

- **Language.** Humour emerges, much of it revolving around language, reflecting ability to go beyond a literal understanding of the spoken word. Increases the length of sentences by using 'and' as a link. May be able to match words of only two or three letters that are printed clearly on individual cards. Grasps basic language rules, such as plurals and verb tenses, and uses them in everyday speech.

- **Learning.** Improved short-term memory – can memorize, for example, a short poem or telephone number through repetition. Concentration increases, so will play at one activity or watch a television programme for several minutes before attention wanders. Organizational skills improve, so able to make a more systematic search for something. Uses imagination to create an image that isn't actually there, and is able to describe details of it. Reaches the first stage of genuine counting – for example, counts a row of small blocks up to the second or third block and makes an attempt to count on fingers.

- **Hand–eye coordination.** Is able to copy accurately many of the lines that make up written letters, but can't yet form complete letters. Can hold a piece of cutlery in each hand, and can drink from a cup. Enjoys mixing ingredients with a wooden spoon, rolling the mixture flat, cutting out shapes and putting these into the oven with your help. Loves challenging activities that involve hand–eye coordination, such as small jigsaws, and tries hard to achieve success. Can find and collect specific items from supermarket shelves by combining visual skills and hand–eye coordination.

- **Movement.** Has enough confidence to try out all the items in an outdoor play area, including climbing onto a swing and reaching much closer to the top of the climbing frame. Enjoys bouncing on a trampoline or bouncy castle. Can walk upstairs and downstairs putting one foot on each step at a time, using the banister or wall for support. Likes to kick a ball along the ground or pick it up and throw it; catching remains more of a challenge. Copies you to hop for one or two paces if concentrates and doesn't go too high. Combines physical tasks that each require concentration, such as carrying an object while negotiating the stairs.

Routine

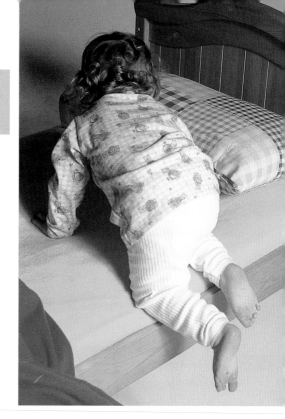

A stable daily routine is helpful for your child's development. Meals at regular times and a reasonably fixed time for bed each night enable her to structure her day, and this structure contributes to her overall sense of security and well-being. You'll find that she enjoys the familiarity of, for instance, her pre-bath and pre-bedtime routine because these actions signal what is about to come. Using a familiar routine when leaving her with another carer may help her adjust to her new surroundings quicker and more easily. Of course you need to be flexible; in general, though, routine is beneficial for your child.

Above: Building a bedtime routine can help your child to go to sleep at night happily.

What are the pros?
• **Advance planning.** Your child is happy knowing that she goes to nursery every morning, or that when she comes home she has a snack while watching television. In this way, routine helps her to plan ahead. She can organize her activities around her routine so that she gets the best out of each day.
• **Consistency.** Your child thrives best in a consistent environment. Of course, she likes change and excitement, but a routine fulfils her deep-rooted psychological need for stability.

Routine provides a secure foundation on which to build her daily activities.
• **Control.** If she has some choice in her routine – for example, she is allowed to choose when to play with toys or read a book – this predictable framework allows her to have some degree of control over her world. This is a terrific boost to her self-esteem.

What are the cons?
• **Resistance.** Children constantly test the authority of their parents and trying to enforce a routine can be both exhausting and frustrating. It is very hard to make a child do something if she does not want to do it, and you should question whether a particular aspect of your routine is absolutely necessary for your child's development.

• **Constraint.** Routine just for the sake of it can limit a child's freedom in a number of ways, limiting the amount of control she has over any given situation. Not only will she become bored with doing the same thing the same way day in day out, but she could easily become unsettled when, for some reason, the routine breaks down.

Keeping to routines

In order to have a routine that works, you should encourage your child to understand why it is necessary. You can increase her commitment by explaining the underlying purpose of any given rule. For instance, it's better to tell her 'I want you to eat your lunch now, otherwise you'll be hungry later on when we go to the park.' than to say 'Eat your lunch now because I'm telling you to.' The more she understands why the routine exists, the more likely she is to follow it.

Encourage your child to anticipate the next stage in her routine. For instance, during the morning remind her what the routine holds for her in the afternoon. Talk about the next part of the routine positively. And don't dismiss her complaints out of hand. If she insists that she is bored with her regular routine, ask her to consider ways in which it could reasonably be changed. For instance, there is no law that says she must play with her friends at a certain time each day. Ask her to suggest alternative ways in which her day could be organized.

If you agree to changes in her routine as a result, do what you can to stick to them. Emphasize that you support her

suggestions and that you expect her to adhere to them. She will be more satisfied with routines when she feels that she has played her part in forming them.

Unexpected changes

If there is a degree of flexibility in your routine, you child will be less unsettled by any deviation from the norm. Learning to cope with unexpected changes is part of the process of growing up, and she will learn to handle these minor interruptions to her otherwise organized life as her confidence steadily builds through varied experience.

Above: Being able to anticipate when to expect meals helps your child structure her day.

Sleep
Night fears

Although the majority of children may be sleeping regularly in their own bed and through the night by the age of two, there are some who don't. Even children who have been previously good sleepers can start throwing tantrums at bedtime as they try to carve out their own identity. Furthermore, a child who is an established sleeper may start to have disturbed nights resulting from toilet training or the occasional nightmare.

Sleepwalking

Sleepwalking is very common and tends to run in families. Like night terrors, sleepwalking occurs in the first third of the night, when your child is in deep sleep. However, it can be difficult to tell whether he is truly sleepwalking or is awake and wandering about. If you are unsure, watch what he does: sleepwalkers do only very simple things, so if he is carrying out a complex series of actions he is probably not sleepwalking. If you are sure your child is asleep during his nocturnal wanderings, it is important not to try to wake him. Instead, lead him gently back to bed, tuck him in and say your special night-time phrase, if you have one. Although sleepwalking can be spooky to watch, your child will not intentionally harm himself. However, he may trip over objects or fall down steps, so it is important to make sure his room is safe and the stairs are blocked.

Night fears may simply reflect your child's growing understanding of the world or may be triggered by real anxieties in his life, such as starting nursery or the arrival of a new baby. If your child is going through a period of change that may be unsettling for him, reassurance during the day will be a big help in making him more confident at night. Without spoiling him, try to build some fun events into his day such as a trip to the park and be sure to give him extra cuddles.

Nightmares and night terrors

These are different, although are often confused as being the same thing. Nightmares, which are generated during REM sleep (see page 38), are more likely to happen if your child is stressed or anxious and have no cause or real significance. Night terrors, however, can be traumatic to witness. Your child is unlikely to recognize you or want you to comfort him – he may even become more agitated if you try. However, your child will not remember a thing in the morning because night terrors occur in the deepest part of sleep, usually in the first few hours after going to bed. Although your child may appear to be awake and will seem very agitated and frightened, even screaming, he is in fact asleep. But as there is no dream occurring, when your child does wake of his own accord he will not be scared. On the contrary, waking up can provide immediate release from the night terror and he is likely to go back to sleep quickly.

Sleep
Common Problems

Q What should I do if my child wakes from a nightmare?

A Nightmares are common from the age of two right through until the teenage years: half of all five-year-olds have nightmares. They are generated during REM sleep, and are most likely to occur during the last two-thirds of the night. They are more likely to happen if your child is stressed or anxious; however, most nightmares have no cause and no real significance. Go in and reassure him, tuck him back in, say your special bedtime phrase, if you have one, and leave the room as soon as you can. If your child has recurrent nightmares, keep a diary to see if there is a pattern to them. Repeated nightmares can often be controlled, as they occur in the lighter stages of sleep: for example, if your child dreams he is being chased by a bird, suggest that you both catch it in a cage. This will put your child in charge of the situation and may help to put an end to that particular dream.

Q What should I do if my child suffers from night terrors?

A Although night terrors are disturbing to watch, your best response is to do nothing. If you do try to rouse your child before the episode has run its course, you may frighten her by your own anxiety. In addition, as night terrors aren't caused by a bad dream, your child won't remember the event the following morning. And therefore it will not cause her anxiety about going to bed on subsequent nights.

Q We have just started my child night toilet training, but this seems to have completely disrupted his sleeping patterns. He is often unsettled at night, waking frequently, although he has only the very occasional accident. Is this normal?

A Night training can throw even an established good sleeper out of his usual sleep pattern, especially if he has lots of accidents. The best advice is to wait until he is really ready: dry nappies in the morning and waking to go to the toilet at night are the important signs. Invest in a mattress protector and deal with any accidents with minimum fuss. Encourage him to go straight back to sleep again using your normal phrase, if you have one.

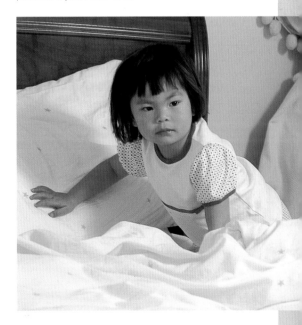

Above: When a child wakes up from night terrors she will have no memory of the event.

Eating
Foods to avoid

From the age of two to three, your child's eating requirements will not change dramatically from those of the previous year (see page 134). From three to four, you should double the recommended helpings of starchy carbohydrate foods and increase fruit and vegetables by another helping a day. By now you should be able to trust your child to eat what she needs.

Surveys indicate that 20 per cent of fat or overweight children become fat adults.

While it makes sense to give a child a snack if she is hungry between meals, it is also important to make sure you are giving the right kind of snack. Many ready-made junk foods are high in sugar and fat, but have relatively few nutrients. Although there is nothing wrong with junk food occasionally, too much on a regular basis can lead to bad moods, behaviour difficulties, weight problems and nutritional deficiencies. Read contents labels very closely and try to avoid those with a long list of additives and E numbers. If you make the meal yourself instead of using processed foods, you will know exactly what has gone into it.

Q What are additives?
A Most packaged foods contain additives such as preservatives, stabilizers, flavourings, colourings and antioxidants. Identified by an E number, these natural or synthetic substances are added to food to preserve it for longer, add flavour or just to make it look more attractive.

Q Are additives bad for my child?
A There is evidence that some additives, for example food colourings, can be linked to behaviour difficulties in childhood, particularly hyperactivity. Many parents and health professionals have found that when an overactive, impulsive child is placed on an additive-free diet, his difficult behaviour diminishes greatly. While this does not occur in every instance, overwhelming evidence suggests a definite connection with additives.

Q Can eating junk food increase my child's chances of becoming obese?
A Obesity is usually defined when a child's weight is more than 20 per cent over the standard weight for her height. While it could be a condition that runs in the family, there is no doubt that over-consumption of foods with a high fat or sugar content (such as fried foods, junk food, sweets and biscuits), coupled with under-consumption of healthy foods (such as fruit, vegetables and fish), contributes to obesity.

Positive parenting **Table manners**

Q My child seems to be developing some pretty disgusting eating habits, quite often chewing food with her mouth open and playing with her food at the table. It is very off-putting for the rest of the family and makes mealtimes unpleasant, which is a shame because this is quite often the only time we all sit together as a family. She behaves even worse on the rare occasions that we eat out, and I find the whole experience painful and embarrassing. I have considered making her eat her meals on her own, in a bid to discipline her. Is this a good idea?

A No. You would be much better advised to start teaching your child table manners. She is quite capable of learning them at an early age if you explain the purpose of them. It's better to give her praise for good eating habits than to reprimand her for poor manners. Don't give up on the family meal, which provides the best opportunity for your child to practise her table manners and to learn new ones by imitating the behaviour of older siblings and adults. Other table habits, such as taking turns to speak in conversation, passing items to each other and listening while others talk, also develop from the experience of family meals.

Strategies

• **Proper use of cutlery.** Encourage your child to hold her knife, fork and spoon suitably in each hand when eating a meal at a table.

Right: Family meals are a good time to teach younger children table manners.

• **Appropriate hand use.** Once she can use cutlery, discourage her from picking up food by hand during a meal, except bread and fruit.
• **Mouth position.** Strongly suggest that your child closes her mouth when chewing food – she may inadvertently let her jaw hang open while munching.

Eating out

• **Do your best to calm her** as you approach the restaurant.
• **Pick a child-centred restaurant,** so that any misbehaviour will go largely unnoticed.
• **Prepare her for the restaurant food.** She may be more willing to behave if she knows exactly what to expect on arrival.
• **Emphasize the importance of table manners.** Remind your child that there are others in the restaurant and encourage her to watch how they eat.
• **Choose child-sized portions.** Your child is less likely to play with her food if she is not overwhelmed by the amount on her plate.

GENDER DIFFERENCES

Influences on a child's development

There are no longer rigid views concerning how a girl or a boy should behave but subtle assumptions can affect a baby's self-concept.

Major gender differences in behaviour, clothes and play patterns emerge during the pre-school years. The development of a child's gender identity is due partly to biological influences (boys have a higher level of testosterone, a hormone that is linked to aggressiveness), partly to social influences (through watching the reactions of others towards boys and girls), partly to outside media influences, and is partly learned from you. Your attitudes to gender have a direct impact on your child.

Breaking the barriers

Despite real gender differences and stereotypical views on gender, the fact is that there is no good reason why a girl should not play football or a boy should not play with a doll. Of course, others might look disapprovingly at such unexpected behaviour, but that is simply an expression

Left: Playing with whatever interests them, regardless of gender, broadens their experience.

of their own fixed views. Your child should be allowed free choice in play and should not be limited by gender barriers.

In fact, breaking these barriers could be good for your child. Since play is crucial to your child's development, it stands to reason that the more varied her play experiences, the more enhanced her development will be. If she plays with toys and activities that are traditionally associated with boys, she simply broadens her experience. Diversity is good for your growing child, girl or boy.

Some parents describe their daughter as a 'tomboy' because she likes to wear clothes normally associated with boys. Again, this is simply a matter of personal preference. Maybe she wants to dress like that because she finds that boys' clothes are more comfortable or more colourful, or perhaps she just wants to be different from all her friends. Whatever the reason for her clothes preference, it won't do her any harm.

What can I do?

• **Encourage individuality.** Try not to be limited by society's views on gender. If that's what she wants, let your little girl play with a toy even though it's normally for boys, or your boy play with a 'girl's' toy. They are entitled to express their individuality through toys, games and clothes.

• **Talk with your child.** Both boys and girls benefit from being able to use words to express their feelings to someone else. If your child finds this difficult, have plenty of discussions with him so that he becomes used to chatting with you.

• **Don't fuss over gender issues.** The moment your child realizes that you are concerned about

her choice of clothes or toys, she'll probably use this as a means of grabbing your attention. Try to adopt a relaxed approach.

• **Avoid confrontations.** There is no reason to battle with your child because she likes to play football (or he is fascinated by his sister's doll's house). This is a normal extension of interest in a variety of toys.

• **Provide a good role model.** Since your child is strongly influenced by your own attitudes and behaviour, try to ensure that in your family home chores are not allocated on a gender basis. This broadens a young child's perspective.

Studies have found that girls tend to behave differently as soon as boys appear in the same room. For instance, they become less outgoing, talk in quieter voices and narrow the distance between themselves so that they are closer to each other.

Tantrums

The dictionary definition of a tantrum tells us that it is an 'outburst of bad temper or petulance', and clearly such outbursts can happen at every age. However, when most people talk about tantrums they are thinking about something very specific – the explosive bad temper displayed by young children. This behaviour is usually worst around 18 months to three years of age, still quite common up to five or six, and – or so conventional wisdom goes – not very common and gradually disappearing after that.

Are boys naughtier than girls?

It does seem that boys often demonstrate more of the behaviour parents find difficult – what psychologists call 'externalizing' behaviour, which involves 'acting out' and, from your point of view, acting up. Such behaviour includes aggression, defiance and over-exuberant physical activity. However, this may not all be due to a genuine sex difference. Parents may influence it by their thinking on what is 'masculine' – encouraging more rough play in their sons, for example, or being less accepting of tears as a response to frustration in boys than they are of anger.

What is typical?

Not all toddlers have tantrums, but life with some can resemble a war zone – 'No, no, no', 'I won't', 'Mine', 'Can't make me' – and the battles have a nasty habit of making normally calm, sane adults want to turn into toddlers themselves! It can be an uncomfortable realization for parents that their child is simply determined to get into a battle of wills, and any parent who has been confronted by a toddler who's determined to win a struggle knows just how hard it can be.

It is a fairly obvious but sometimes forgotten truism that a child doesn't have tantrums when she is on her own. A full-blown tantrum requires an audience. They are almost always conducted in relation to you or to someone very familiar. It takes two people to create a tantrum, so in that sense they are interactive, not simply reactive.

Inevitably, every toddler from at least 18 months to three years old and more, will rebel against your authority and assert her individuality some of the time – that is an absolutely normal part of being a toddler as she constantly tries to explore and learn where the boundaries are. Your child is almost bound to show some of the range of difficult behaviour, such as being stubborn and defiant (or what is called 'oppositional' by psychologists) as he is developing independence and autonomy. Tantrums are also a normal way of venting

Above: If handled properly, a child normally stops having frequent tantrums by the age of three or four.

feelings that are becoming overwhelming. A child this age will display some or all of the following:
- Resentment of any form of control
- A striving for independence, making more demands and being more defiant
- Swinging back and forth between independence and clinginess
- Wanting control and trying to control you, saying 'Sit there' or 'Don't touch'
- Generally having tantrums.

Ten facts about **tantrums**

1 Although anger is the emotion that is most obvious to parents, a tantrum is almost always combined with another feeling such as frustration or panic.

2 Tantrums are almost always conducted in relation to you, the parent, or someone else with whom the child feels safe and familiar.

3 Temperament plays a part. An active, strong-willed child may be more likely to have tantrums.

4 Some estimates say that one in five two-year-olds have at least two tantrums per day – but remember that this means that four out of five don't.

5 If handled successfully by parents early on, tantrums are likely to become less common as the child grows older, and the worst is usually over by age three or four years.

6 Tantrums often happen when a child's feelings are out of control.

7 An estimated three-quarters of all tantrums happen at home, but the worst tantrums often seem to be saved for public places, ensuring maximum attention for the child and maximum embarrassment for the parent.

8 Behaviour common in tantrums includes shouting, screaming, crying, hitting, kicking, stiffening limbs, arching back, dropping on the floor and running away.

9 In a really severe tantrum, a child can go blue in the face, be sick, even hold her breath until she is almost unconscious – but natural reflexes will make sure she starts breathing again before coming to any harm.

10 The majority of tantrums are an expression of loss of control – a response to feelings of frustration, helplessness and anger – and happen because of a child's lack of the skills needed to deal with these feelings.

Tantrum triggers

There are some things that can trigger tantrums in almost any child, regardless of their natural character. Below are some of the more usual circumstances, together with suggestions for avoiding a tantrum wherever possible.

Distraction action

There are a number of strategies you can employ in order to distract your child before or during a tantrum.

- **Diversion.** Even if you think a tantrum is starting to brew up, there is often time to divert your child. Quickly introducing a new toy, or pointing out something that is happening outside the window – 'I think I hear a bus coming – can you hear it?' – can work well, especially with younger children, though by three years or so they may have learned to see through this and will not be fooled as easily.
- **Substitution.** If you quickly offer a toy, your child will happily give up the keys you need. Other examples include offering paper when he tries to draw on the walls, or an old magazine to tear up when he attempts it on your newspaper.
- **Spotting a pattern.** If your child has a lot of tantrums, it can help to keep a written record of exactly what is happening beforehand, and what the circumstances are at the time a tantrum starts. For example, if it is often while you are making lunch, try letting him help you set the table, or organize him near you with an interesting toy or game before you start to prepare the meal.

Common causes

Tantrum trigger

Seeking attention

Wanting something he can't have

Wanting to prove he's independent

Inner frustration with his own limited ability to succeed at the things he tries

Jealousy

Challenging your authority

'Sheer cussedness'

Manifestation	Solution
Although tantrums are rarely done to manipulate parents, if the reward for a tantrum is massive amounts of satisfactory attention from the adults around him, it can provide a very good reason to have another one again soon!	**Try not to over-react or make a huge fuss when your child throws a tantrum,** but to act calmly, even if you don't feel like it.
Your child might insist that he wants an ice cream for breakfast or that you give him a cuddle when you are in the middle of preparing a meal.	**Be consistent and forceful when saying no.** If you want your toddler to be less negative, use phrases like 'You can have an ice cream later' instead of 'No, you can't have it'.
Your child may demand to wear a particularly unsuitable item of clothing, such as a T-shirt on a freezing cold day, or refuse to eat the meal you have prepared for him.	**Let him have choices whenever you can, over what to wear or eat, or what to play with.** Say 'Do you fancy fish fingers or beans on toast for tea?' or 'Shall we get out your bricks or your cars?'
Your child will display a determination to do things by himself, such as putting on his own clothes or finding the pieces of a puzzle on his own, only to find he gets stuck and in a muddle half-way through.	**Keep an eye on your child so that you are alert to any signals that he is becoming frustrated.** Give him time to solve the problem himself, but step in to help the minute he seems to be losing control.
Often directed at a brother, sister or another child, he will want a toy they have got, or a book they are reading.	**Encourage your toddler to take it in turns,** or try to distract him with a toy of his own.
Your child may suddenly reject an established bedtime routine, or refuse to go to nursery one morning, despite liking it there.	**Start to give your child time and warnings before moving on to new activities:** say 'Your bath will be ready in five minutes' or 'In 10 minutes we will need to put the toys away to go to nursery.' A timer can help him to understand that this is part of his routine and not you giving him orders.
A child just seems set on having a tantrum no matter what.	**Try to pinpoint the likely cause of the tantrum and offer your child the chance to take more control.** For example, if he hates to be forced to sit in his pushchair inside shops let him hold your hand and walk.

Tantrums
Common problems

Q My partner and I have been arguing more than usual lately and our little girl's tantrums have got worse during this time. Is this just a coincidence?

A No. The way you behave provides the most accessible example to your child. If she sees you flying into a rage or screaming with frustration at minor upsets, it is much harder for her to learn self-control. A child needs to see that adults can handle frustration and disappointments without falling apart – this is how she learns to deal with them. You can't expect your child to behave calmly if you are setting a bad example yourself.

Q I appreciate that my child wants to assert his independence, and is more determined than ever to try to do things for himself, but there is not always time for him to get his own shoes on before we go out, or to walk to the post box before the last collection. How can I persuade him otherwise?

A If you can, allow at least a few minutes for your child to try and acknowledge his angry feelings that are inevitably stirred up when you have to take over. Expect your child to be angry but remain calm yourself and try to encourage him that there will be other opportunities. Always find less pressured times for him to practise skills and give lots of praise for his efforts.

Q I battle every morning with my child over what she should wear. She doesn't always choose something suitable and I find myself forcing her into clothes against her will. What else can I do?

A It is true that small children choose what they like or whatever attracts their attention first, not necessarily something sensible. Ask yourself whether it really matters what your child wears on a particular occasion – maybe there are times when you could be more flexible. You could make your life easier by only offering choices that are suitable for the weather and occasion, and keeping others well out of sight.

Q There are times when my child's tantrum gets the better of me. I feel myself getting more and more angry and find it almost impossible not to lose control. I really do not want to behave irrationally or to shout at my screaming child, but what else can I do?

A On the occasions that you do feel yourself losing control, it may be safer to walk into another room and take some cooling-down time for yourself. Tell your child that this is what you are doing, and that you will come back soon to look after him. This is better than losing your temper, shouting and making an already bad situation worse. Alternatively, you could try putting your child in another room or designated place until he calms down. However, it is not always practical for very young children, who can't or won't cooperate with the idea. If the child has to be forced, it is likely to inflame his anger more and will only make the situation worse.

Positive parenting **Making humour work for you**

Q I often have conflicting reactions to my child's tantrums. Although I want her to behave and learn that she cannot always have her own way, I sometimes feel that I am overdoing it and taking life a little too seriously. Besides, some of the 'naughty' things she does are actually quite amusing. Am I wrong to occasionally see the funny side of things? Does this just encourage more bad behaviour from my child?

A Strangely enough, laughter can work especially well for toddler discipline and can be used to defuse tricky situations and avoid battles where everybody loses and feels bad. In fact, laughter is good news all round. It has been clearly shown in research to be good for the whole family. It lowers blood pressure, reduces stress, raises your spirits when you feel down and releases feel-good 'happy hormones' called endorphins. Even smiling when you're not feeling cheerful can fool your body into releasing these, so you end up feeling better!

Strategies

• If your child completely refuses to put on her shoes and coat, even though it is raining outside, say 'Well, I will just have to wear them instead, and be nice and dry,' then make a big performance of forcing your feet into the shoes and arms into the coat.

• Pretending your child's favourite toy wants her to do something can sometimes make it easier to persuade her.

• Using a funny song for requests often helps to amuse your toddler long enough for her to go along with it: sing 'Mary, Mary, quite

contrary, how does this seat strap go' as you're strapping her in, or 'This is the way we brush our teeth' as you quickly get the job done.

• Pretending you are going to eat your toddler's meal can be effective: saying 'It's my pasta, I want to eat it, it's mummy's favourite' works much better than insisting she eats up.

• Imaginary games often work well. If your toddler won't put on her sandals, instead of forcing them on and creating a huge fuss, try pretending you are the 'shoe shop lady'. Ask her to choose between some pairs lined up, saying 'Which pair would you like to buy?'

• Try using humorous games to avoid confrontation. You want her to tidy up some toys: try saying 'I bet you can't put more away than me – let's race.' It's important always to let her win for this to be fun.

Above: Remaining calm and using laughter to divert attention can prevent a full-blown tantrum.

MISBEHAVIOUR

Disciplining your child

Finding a fair but effective way to discipline your child can sometimes be hard – especially if you are feeling angry yourself.

Repeated misbehaviour from your child can drive you to distraction – the constant touching of fragile objects, or the repeated refusal to help you tidy up, can be a cause of frustration and annoyance. The failure of your small-scale punishments may tempt you to escalate their size, intensity and length. Whereas the first time you punished your child's misbehaviour was with denial of sweets that afternoon, by the tenth time she misbehaves you feel you would like to punish her by never letting her have any sweets ever again!

Above: Consistency in discipline should help your child achieve self-control.

However, it is important for the punishment to fit the 'crime', not your anger. Just as adults are not hanged for parking offences (even though their poor parking may have had a severely disruptive effect on the traffic), neither should your child be dreadfully punished for a minor misdemeanour (even though her actions triggered your own temper). If there is a mismatch between your child's misbehaviour and the scale of your response, she will have difficulty making sense of your discipline system.

Wherever possible, match misbehaviour and punishment thematically. For instance, if your child breaks her friend's toy in temper, she should replace it with one of her own; if she takes her sister's sweets without permission, she should make amends by giving her some of her sweets.

Although not always possible to achieve, this thematic linkage is very effective.

Consistency

Of course, you have to be flexible when it comes to your child's behaviour. Much depends on the circumstances and context of each specific incident. In addition, you have to bend the rules occasionally, perhaps if her negative behaviour is in response to provocation by another child. In general, however, aim for consistency in your approach to punishment.

Parents often become disheartened when they punish their child for misbehaving and then she repeats the action a few minutes later. This leads to self-doubt and the belief that their system of discipline does not work – after all, they reason, their child wouldn't misbehave if they themselves were effective parents. As a result, they try something else the next day when their child continues to act inappropriately, and when that does not immediately have the desired effect, they try something else.

This shift from one strategy to another destroys any pattern of consistency, reducing the potential benefit of the techniques. Give your system of discipline time to work, persisting with it for two or three weeks before giving up on it. Consistency is crucial for your child to achieve self-control, and she cannot reach that target when you change your approach from one day to the next.

Intention not outcome

The intention underlying an action is more important than the outcome – for instance,

it is less of a 'crime' when your child accidentally drops her bowl of cereal on the floor than it is when she deliberately flicks a spoonful onto the floor. Human nature, however, means that you might impulsively punish your child for the outcome and not for the underlying intention. Consider your child's motives and perception of her behaviour and take that into account before embarking on your response.

Five steps to **better behaviour**

1 Have a prearranged list. To make life easier for yourself, compile a list of punishments for common acts of misbehaviour – for instance, hitting her young brother means going to bed 10 minutes early that night.

2 Listen to explanations. Give your child a chance to speak to you. She may have a perfectly good explanation for her actions, even though you are unhappy with her behaviour.

3 End confrontations quickly. Once an incident of misbehaviour is over, leave it alone. Resist any temptation to keep referring back to it later in the day. Try to have a positive, forward-looking approach.

4 Learn from other parents. Each parent uses their own system of punishments. You can learn about other possibilities by talking to your friends about their approaches.

5 Check out your child's understanding. When the punishment episode is over, chat to your child to make sure she knows that this incident has finished. Restore a positive atmosphere.

Siblings
A new arrival

What a wonderful moment it is when you arrive back home with your new baby, safe and sound. Now you can get on with life as a two-child family. But things are different: your older child isn't used to sharing you with the baby. All that is required to help forge that vital connection between your older child and your new baby once you are back home is some thought, sensitivity and planning.

Above: The arrival of a new sibling can cause your older child to feel insecure and jealous.

You can help your older child in the following ways:

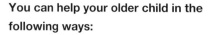

• Explain that you'll still love her just as much as ever and that the new baby will love her, too.

• Answer any questions she has openly and honestly.

• Involve her in the pregnancy and let her feel the baby move in your tummy so she can feel part of this very important family event.

• Let her buy a present for the new baby and make sure that the new baby has a present for her at their first meeting.

• Remember that your first child just needs to feel loved and valued, especially when the new baby is the focus of attention.

• Try to make some special time for your first-born on her own every day, to remind her that you love her as much as ever.

Three steps to a **happier home**

1 Encourage visitors to bring a small gift for your older child and make sure all visitors spend a few minutes chatting to your older child before rushing off to meet the baby. This gesture makes her feel that she benefits from the presence of her younger sister, too – that she's not the only one to get attention.

2 Remember that it's her new baby, too. Underlying all her mixed emotions at this early stage, she is still very proud of the new arrival and wants to show her off to anyone who is willing to listen. There is no reason why a child as young as two or three years should not lead friends and relatives to the baby's cot. A simple technique like this makes her feel very important.

3 Do your best not to show irritation or stress in front of your toddler in the early days, even though you may be exhausted and struggling with this new responsibility. Your older child will be watching you closely at this point, looking for signs that the baby is causing any disruptions to family life – her confidence is easily rocked after you return home from hospital. If she sees that you are relaxed, she feels relaxed as well.

Siblings
Common problems

Q My two-year-old appears loving towards the new baby and yet he cuddles her so enthusiastically that she bursts out crying every time. How can I encourage him not to be so rough?

A Your toddler's mixed feelings of affection and apprehension are showing through in the form of an uncomfortable cuddle that actually causes distress to his sibling. Watch him closely at those moments and remind him to be gentle. Give him lots of praise when he plays appropriately with the baby.

Q The minute I start to bath my three-month-old baby, my two-year-old starts to whinge and roll around on the floor. What can I do?

A Make sure your older child has something to do before you start bathing the baby. Give her a game or a toy to play with, or let her stay close to you so that she can watch you bath her younger sister. She is less likely to be attention-seeking when she is kept busy.

Q My two-year-old has seemed quiet and troubled since the birth of his younger sister. He does not admit to it, but I think he resents her for coming into his world. What can I do to make him accept her?

A Encourage him to spend a few minutes each day playing with his younger sister. Tell him that she loves him, or that she is proud of the way he colours in his pictures or builds his towers. He wants his younger sibling to look up to him.

Q Although fully toilet-trained and dry during the day, my three-year-old started to wet herself soon after our second baby was born. Is this normal?

A Yes, this is quite normal. Your child regresses to younger behaviour because she feels insecure. Don't get angry with her for wetting herself. Instead, give her lots of hugs and cuddles and make a special time for just you and her every single day.

Q Since our second baby was born, our four-year-old has become very attention seeking. Shouldn't he be past the stage where he can be affected in this way?

A Every child is different. Although your four-year-old is mature in many ways, he remains emotionally vulnerable – the fact that he has become attention-seeking demonstrates this. It is very likely that the birth of his sibling has made him feel insecure. However, you should also check out other possible sources of stress – for instance, he may have fallen out with his best friend, or he may be more tired from adjusting to the long school day.

Siblings
Sibling rivalry

The origins of sibling rivalry – that is, jealousy between children of the same family – usually lie in the first five years of life. When your first-born child is knocked off his perch by the arrival of the new baby, the resentment and jealousy often starts. Whereas before the birth your older child had you all to himself, he now finds that the new baby takes up a lot of your time and attention.

Your toddler may show his jealousy of brothers and sisters in a variety of ways. For example, a two-year-old may become moody around the time the new baby arrives; or a three-year-old might complain that his little brother constantly plays with his toys without asking. But sibling rivalry isn't just confined to the first-born child. There is research evidence that second and third children can resent a new baby, even though they are already used to living with others in the family. And younger children can be jealous of older siblings, which is why your 18-month-old toddler might burst into tears when he sees you cuddling his older sister; he wants all your love for himself.

If your child is around the age of two when your second child is born, he will probably express his jealousy by hitting his sibling rather than by complaining to you. Fortunately this pattern changes as he gets older, making such physical expressions of jealousy less likely.

Five facts about **sibling rivalry**

1 Virtually every child can feel jealousy towards their sibling, depending on the circumstances – even your mild-mannered son or daughter can feel negative about their brothers and sisters at times.

2 Sibling rivalry tends to be strongest when the youngest child is three or four years old. This means that having children aged, say, three and five years, may involve you in smoothing out frequent fights between them.

3 Fist fights are more common than verbal disagreements when one of the children is around the age of two or three. At this stage of development, a child is typically very quick to be physically aggressive towards his sibling.

4 When siblings aged three or four argue with each other, the disagreement usually revolves around a game or toy. They both want to play with the same item at the same time and haven't yet developed a mature ability to share.

5 Every child is different. You might have one child who is extremely passive and is prepared to let his sister do what she wants, whereas your other child might be ready to pounce on his sister every time she does something he doesn't like.

Sibling behaviour

Age gap	Likely behaviour
less than 2 years	• There is a strong possibility your children will grow up to be good friends, especially when the younger child reaches school age. • As your first child is still quite young when the baby is born, he is less likely to feel threatened by the new addition.
2–4 years	• Your older child's increased understanding means that he is more likely to feel annoyed with the new baby, so sibling rivalry may be stronger. • When you feed your baby, your first-born may feel jealous because he sees you both in such close physical contact. • Your first-born's daily schedule is different from the baby's – he stays up later and has his own friends, and this makes him feel like a special 'big brother'.
4 or more years	• You have lots of time to spend with your new baby because your older child is at school all day during the week. • Your older child can continue with his after-school activities despite the demands of his younger sibling. Arrangements can be made for him to get a lift from a friend's parents, for example. • Your older child might want to show off about his family's new addition, perhaps by telling his classmates or teacher.

Siblings: The significance of age

The age gap between your first and second children affects their relationship and, although each person is unique, findings from psychological research highlight the common effects. In most cases problems occur when the gap is between two and four years. The typical toddler likes to have everything his own way and he expects the world to revolve around him. From this perspective, it is understandable that he may be upset by the arrival of a new baby who needs plenty of attention, too.

Above: Around the age of two or three your child may express jealousy by hitting his sibling.

Siblings
Older siblings

It is not unusual for sibling rivalry to intensify when a younger child reaches the toddler stage, because that's when he starts to have practical effects on the life of the older sibling – for instance, when he takes her toys without asking, or tags along uninvited beside her. At this point in the family dynamics, the rivalry is not just because your time, attention and resources are limited, but also because each child has a real psychological need to develop his or her own unique identity.

Your five-year-old, for instance, has her own set of friends and they play their own types of games with their own set of toys. She also has her own taste in music, her own preferences in books and stories, and particular television programmes that she favours. The presence of her two-year-old brother can make her feel threatened – she may adore him, but she doesn't want to share everything because that dilutes her personal identity. That's why you hear the complaint 'Tell him to stop touching my things.'

Five steps to managing **sibling rivalry**

1 Take their complaints seriously. Listen to your children when they voice their moans about each other. To you, such complaints may seem trivial, but to your children they are serious. They need you to listen to them and to advise them.

2 Buy games that require cooperation. Although there may be a couple of years' age difference between your children, try to find a game that they can play together, such as football or a simple card game. Cooperation in play eases tension.

3 Go on family outings together. Such outings with young children under the age of five can be very stressful for everyone concerned – but they can also be great fun. Spending time together doing something enjoyable like this often adds strength to sibling relationships.

4 Encourage separate groups of friends. Each child has her own set of friends that she has made, and the older one certainly won't thank you for insisting she has to take her younger sibling with her – your younger child won't like it either.

5 Acknowledge their individuality. Your children have a lot in common with each other and it's wonderful when they share an interest together. But nurture their individual preferences, too, as this reduces competitiveness between them.

Siblings
Common problems

Q My five-year-old shares a room with his three-year-old sister but complains constantly that she plays on his side with his toys. How can I persuade my daughter to leave his things alone?

A Your child partly defines his role in terms of his personal space and personal possessions, and he wants this to be recognized. He resents his younger sibling's lack of respect. Explain to your three-year-old the rules of asking permission before using her brother's toys. Ask her how she would feel if he was always playing with her things. Encourage them to share or to take turns if interested by the same toys.

Q Does every parent have children who fight with each other all the time, or is it just my children who are like this?

A Sibling rivalry is so common in families that most psychologists would regard it as normal. Speaking to your friends about their family life will confirm this to you. Logic dictates that when there is a limited amount of time and resources available, each child competes for his own share and, not surprisingly, this is a recipe for jealousy between them.

Q Why is it that their arguments usually start over trivial incidents, such as which television programme to watch or what game to play?

A So often these arguments appear to be straightforward and trivial, and yet typically they have a deeper, hidden agenda. For instance, the real cause of your children's fight may not simply be that they both want to play with the same toy at the same time – rather, it could be that each wants to assert their territorial rights. It's often a matter of power, not possessions.

Q My children don't fight with each other at all. Does this mean they are repressing their feelings of hostility towards their siblings?

A Not at all. Although rivalry is common, there are some children who never feel threatened or annoyed by the actions of their siblings. That's a very positive characteristic and clearly your own children come into this category. Instead of worrying about repression, relax and enjoy their trouble-free relationships.

Above: Older children often take pleasure in 'looking after' younger siblings.

FEARS AND PHOBIAS

Helping your child to deal with them

Fears and phobias can be a big problem for some children and should be taken seriously rather than made into a joke.

When it gets more serious

A phobia is much less common than a fear – surveys estimate that fewer than five per cent of all children have a genuine phobia – and is different from a fear in a number of ways, including:

• **Severity.** A child with a phobia worries even when the focus of her anxiety is not present. For instance, a child who is afraid of dogs will be troubled when she nears one in the street, whereas a child with a phobia about dogs would be upset just thinking about these animals.

• **Resistance.** In most instances, childhood fears are temporary and often ease with some structured support and guidance. Phobias, however, are much more resistant to change, and they tend to last for years rather than months.

• **Impact.** Every fear has an effect on a child's life – for instance, she may try to avoid going to parties because she is afraid of meeting new people. A phobia, on the other hand, is more pervasive – for instance, she doesn't want to leave the house at all in case she meets an unfamiliar adult.

There is hardly a child who isn't afraid sometimes, depending on the circumstances. In fact, children can be afraid of almost anything at all. Fortunately, most childhood fears are mild, temporary and manageable – with some parental help and encouragement.

Common fears

Of course, every child is different, but here are some of the most common fears that occur in childhood:

• **Small animals.** Many children dislike small animals that move unpredictably – that's why animals such as insects and hamsters often create such terror in young minds.

• **Darkness.** Total darkness fills some children with terror – they become afraid the moment the light goes out at night.

• **Cats and dogs.** Memories of a snarling dog or scratching cat can make a child afraid whenever she sees one of these household pets.

• **Dirt.** Some children are very neat and fastidious. The sight of dirt on their hands or clothes makes them afraid and upset.

• **Water.** Nobody likes to get soapy water in their eyes during hair washing, but a child can be so afraid of this that she screams hysterically in the bath.

• **Injury.** While many children are daredevils without any fear at all, many others are frightened to explore at all in case they hurt themselves.

• **Failure.** A child can be so afraid of failing at something that she prefers not to try anything new at all – this protects her from the source of her concern.

• **Loss of love.** You know that you don't care for your child any less when you are angry with her, but she might fear that she'll lose your love at these moments.

• **Separation.** A child under the age of three or four years often shows real fear when she realizes her parent is about to leave her with another carer.

Spotting signs of fear

Children can express fear in many different ways and it can be difficult to read your child's behaviour. Of course, your child may simply tell you 'I don't like this, I'm afraid of it', but you may find that she demonstrates her fear through her behaviour rather than through her words. The signs of fear are not always obvious and they may include any of the following:

• A normally fluent child starts to stutter.

• Her appetite drops dramatically.

• She becomes lethargic and reluctant to play with her friends.

• She becomes disruptive.

• She starts to perspire profusely.

Five steps to **lessen anxiety**

1 **Take your child seriously.** You may find it amusing to think that she is terrified of an insect but the fear is very real to your child. Avoid ridicule – she cannot be joked out of it. Instead, let her see that you are sympathetic and there to help her. She needs to know that you are firmly on her side with your support.

2 **Give lots of reassurance.** Tell her repeatedly that she has nothing to fear, that she is totally safe and that everything will be fine. Do this as often as you need to, until her confidence starts to improve. Your reassurance boosts her emotional strength, eventually giving her the resolve to beat her fear.

3 **Aim for confrontation.** She won't learn to overcome her fear unless she tries to confront it. Make sure that she doesn't avoid the focus of her fear – for instance, she may ask to stay at home because your neighbour keeps a dog. Although avoidance might be an easy solution at first, it doesn't help her to deal effectively with her fear.

4 **Teach her to relax.** When you see your child tense up with fear, encourage her to unclench her hand and arm muscles, relax her facial expression and breathe more easily. Practise this regularly each day with your child at home. These physical changes help her to cope with her fear because they induce calmness.

5 **Tackle her fear with her.** Show your child that she can beat her fear by going through the dreaded event beside her. Your presence and encouragement give her the confidence to, say, climb up to the next level of the climbing frame. Watch how she draws psychological strength just from your presence.

Potty training
When to start

Potty training practices have changed considerably over the years. Mothers from previous generations were encouraged to start extraordinarily early – from as soon as they could sit up, or even earlier. These days we are much more relaxed about potty training: partly because we know far more about children's development and how their bodily control matures, and partly because disposable nappies have made life so much easier that there simply isn't the incentive to rush.

Are boys slower to train?

Research is now confirming that boys tend to be a little slower to gain control of their bladders and bowels than girls. According to American research, the average age for completion of potty training (day and night-time dryness) was 35 months for girls and 39 months for boys. There may be several factors:

- Boys' nervous systems mature later. Girls can begin to gain bladder control from the age of 18 months, whereas with boys it may not be until after 22 months.
- Women still tend to be the main carers, so boys do not see a same-sex role model as often as girls do.
- Boys appear to be less sensitive to the feeling of wetness against their skin.

Above: Always praise your child if she manages to use the potty successfully.

Is my child ready?
There is a gradual accumulation of indicators that your child is becoming physically, mentally and emotionally ready to be potty trained. He may be ready if:

- 'I can do it' becomes a regular refrain, showing that your toddler wants to become more independent.
- He has regular, formed bowel movements. He may go red in the face and gain a very concentrated expression when he's about to go.
- He has the dexterity to pull his pants up and down by himself.
- He's very interested when his father goes to the toilet and imitates his actions.
- He is developed physically so that he can walk and sit down on the potty.
- He knows what wee and poo are and may talk about them when you're changing his nappy.
- You notice that his nappy is dry for longer periods, up to three or four hours.
- He can understand what you are saying and follow simple instructions.
- He starts to demonstrate his need to go to the toilet by looking uncomfortable, holding onto himself or grunting.
- He becomes uncomfortable and complains if his nappy is dirty.

How to go about potty training?

Unfortunately, there isn't a totally right or wrong way to go about potty training, but there are two contrasting approaches that you can consider. Both are tried and tested and can be equally successful. The right choice for you and your toddler really depends on your personalities and lifestyle.

Method one

The relaxed approach

This approach may suit you if your child is young, or you'd prefer to continue your normal activities, or if you're laid back about the idea of potty training and you don't mind how long the whole process will take.

What to do

Start gradually, by taking off your child's nappy and popping him on the potty for a short time every day. He may not stay on for long and you might want to give him a book to distract him. Praise him if he does do anything, but do not scold him if he doesn't, or if he misses. Gradually increase the time your child spends without nappies over the next few weeks and then introduce pants. Once he's confident using the potty at home and his nappy has been dry when you've been out, you can venture out with him in pants.

Pros

- Your child feels under less pressure.
- You can get on with life as usual and don't have to devote your time to potty training.

Cons

- It takes longer.
- It's tempting to be lazy and leave your child to wee in nappies when it's difficult to get to a toilet.

Method two

The crash course

This approach will suit you if your child is older and showing signs that he's really ready to use the potty. You also need to be able to alter your life so that you can devote a whole week or more to staying at home and concentrating on potty training.

What to do

Clear your diary for at least a week. You should already have introduced your toddler to the potty and now you can bring out the grown-up pants. Put potties around the house and encourage him to sit on one if he needs a wee or poo. Congratulate any successes – and try to clean away any puddles with a smile. If you go out, say that you're going for a wee and encourage your child to sit on the potty too 'just in case'. Take a potty and a change of clothes with you. After a few days your child should be getting the hang of things and seeking out the potty on his own. If things aren't going well after a few days, take a break and try again in a month or so.

Pros

- It's quick.
- Your child gets clear messages about where to wee and when.

Cons

- It can be messy.
- You may both go 'stir crazy' if you're cooped up at home for a long period.

Potty training
Night-time

At around two and a half years old, your child's independence takes a huge surge forward. In particular, during this period in her life she becomes ready to gain bowel and bladder control at night. This is because she now has a higher level of self-confidence, is able to move from the bed to the toilet easily without requiring any help from you, already has experience of learning to become dry during the day, and is motivated to achieve this skill because she wants to be like a 'big girl'. Night training, however, rarely goes according to plan, so be prepared for occasional disappointments along the way.

Knowing your child is ready
It's probably wise to allow a few months for your child to consolidate all she's learned about daytime dryness before moving on to the next stage. In general, between the ages of three and four is a good time to try your child without a nappy on at night, although some may be ready much earlier. Signs that your child may be ready include:
• **Her nappy is dry when she wakes in the morning.** Bladder capacity increases greatly between the ages of two and four, so that children may be able to last most, or even all, of the night without going for a wee.
• **She wakes in the night** and asks to go for a wee.
• **She tears her nappy off in the night.** Toddlers who are used to lightweight, dry pants may become uncomfortable in a warm, soggy nappy and rip it off while they're asleep.
• **Her nappy leaks in the early morning.** As your child's bladder capacity increases she will pass much larger volumes of urine in one go.
• **She is keen to try without nappies.** Children usually know when they are ready to try without nappies.

Five steps to **dry nights**

1 Have a chat with your child about whether she wants to try without a nappy. If she does, then choose a night when you've nothing important on the next day and explain what's going to happen.
2 Be prepared for a few wet beds. Make sure there are clean sheets and pyjamas to hand, and buy a mattress cover to protect against any puddles.
3 Congratulate your little one every time she wakes with a dry bed. If she does have an accident, try not to be cross.
4 Don't encourage your child to drink vast volumes of liquid just before bedtime.
5 Try to ensure that your child empties her bladder just before going to bed and encourage your child to have a wee as soon as she wakes.

Potty training
Away from home

Whether you have decided on the intensive, home-based approach to potty training or the more relaxed style, you are eventually going to have to venture out of the house with your toddler. The first time you do this it can feel as if you're an action hero carrying a ticking time bomb, about to go off at any moment!

With time, you will become an expert at toilet spotting. If you can't see a public toilet you can always throw yourself on the shop assistant's mercy. In general, most supermarkets and large children's stores have toilet facilities. At the very beginning, it's sensible to have a potty to hand at all times. You probably thought life would get easier and your changing bag would become lighter once your child was out of nappies. This may eventually be true, but in the early days you'll need much, much more.

The essential **emergency kit**

• Potty. A portable potty is lightweight and convenient, but make sure your child is familiar with it. A busy pavement with lots of people walking past is not a good time to discover that your daughter will only sit on pink potties.
• Baby wipes and toilet roll.
• Carrier bag or nappy disposal bag, to tidy away any accidents.
• Change of clothes, including a couple of pairs of trousers or leggings, several pairs of pants and even socks.
• Plastic bag and towel for the car. Car seat covers are washable, but it's easier if you don't have to.
• Nappy pants. Keep these in reserve for when you and your child have had enough. They're also useful to pop on your toddler if she's tired and often falls asleep during car journeys.

Clothes for potty training toddlers

Out	In
• Dungarees	• Stretchy leggings
• All-in-ones	• Elasticated-waist trousers
• Poppers that do up under the crotch	• Skirts and dresses without tights
• Hand-wash or dry clean garments	• Bare bottoms in summer

Potty training
How did I go wrong?

No parent is perfect and everyone makes mistakes. But if you and your child are struggling with the whole potty-training process, the list below can help to identify where you may be going wrong.

Right: It is advisable to only start potty training if your child is happy to go without nappies.

The top ten mistakes and **how to avoid them**

1 **Losing your cool.** If you show anger or disgust, your child will pick up on it. Make sure it comes across that toileting is a natural process, accidents aren't the end of the world, and that the toilet and potty are there for when your child feels ready.

2 **Working to your own timetable.** It is easy to find reasons for potty training your child when it's convenient for you. This can work well if your child is also ready, but will only end in frustration and disappointment if he isn't.

3 **Making him sit on the potty for hours.** It's tempting to encourage your toddler to sit on the potty until he does something, but this can be both boring and uncomfortable.

4 **Nagging.** You want to be helpful and remind him to go to the toilet, but try not to overdo it. The occasional gentle prompt is quite sufficient.

5 **Being inconsistent.** If you sometimes allow your child to do a wee in his nappy pants, it will be difficult for him to understand that it's unacceptable on another occasion.

6 **Going over the top.** If, when your child is trying to do a poo, it makes you stop what you're doing and concentrate on him, he may well throw in a

few 'false alarms' just for attention. Try to encourage him in a calm and controlled way rather than giving him too much attention.

7 **Cutting down fluid intake.** In the beginning your child needs to go for a wee frequently to get the hang of it, so plenty of fluids are advisable. In addition, good hydration will help to prevent constipation, which can cause serious potty-training problems.

8 **Starting too soon.** There is no race to get your child potty trained. The only good reason for starting toilet training very early is because your child is ready.

9 **Putting it off.** If your child is asking to go to the potty, wanting to wear pants and aware when he is weeing or pooing, you should be getting on with it.

10 **Never surrendering.** You need to know when you and your toddler have had enough. If you find yourself getting angry or frustrated, or your child seems very resistant, then it is probably a sign that you both need time out. It's better to wait until you've both regained your patience and enthusiasm.

Potty training
Common problems

Q We've been trying to potty train our three-year-old daughter for six months. She's been getting worse and worse, and now she often refuses even to sit on the potty. Is there something wrong with her?

A There's almost certainly nothing wrong with your little girl: she's just resistant to potty training. It can happen because she started trying too soon, or because she felt under pressure to use the potty and began to get negative feelings about it. It may be a good idea to take a little time out and put her back in nappies for a while. Have a chat with her at bedtime when you are both calm and she's safe in a nappy. She may feel glad to have a rest from all the difficulties of potty training, in which case you can go back to it in a few weeks. If, however, she really wants to stay in pants then you can try again – but this time make sure she's the boss.

Q My son has been dry for six months but insists on using a nappy to do a poo. He just won't do it on the potty. Is this normal?

A This is a common problem. Children see their stool as an extension of themselves and don't want to 'let it go'. They especially don't like doing it on the toilet because it seems to fall away from them, and they hate the big splash! The good news is that your son is obviously aware and in control of his bowels, because he requests a nappy when he needs to go. The Enuresis Research Campaign recommends getting him to stand in the bathroom and poo into his nappy. The next stage is to coax him onto the toilet to poo (still with his nappy on). Gradually you can remove the nappy, or even cut a hole in it, until he's ready to go without. This process can take a long time and be very frustrating but it's important to be firm and praise any small successes.

Q My son is three and a half and shows absolutely no interest in potty training. We haven't really started trying because if we take his nappy off he has an accident. How long should we wait before seeking help?

A Perfectly bright and happy children can be very slow to potty train and you shouldn't be concerned until well after the age of three. Slow potty training can run in families and boys do tend to be slower than girls, so there's no cause to panic. Try taking his nappy off and putting him on a potty regularly. You may find that he surprises you and takes to it fairly quickly. If not, it would be worth consulting your health visitor or doctor for an assessment and some advice. If your child is not potty trained by the age of four he should be referred to a specialist.

Q Now that my daughter is comfortable using the potty (she's three and a half), I'd like her to try the toilet, but she just screams if we put her on it. What can I do?

A Many children find the toilet scary with its noisy flush and the splashing water. Although it's easier to flush the toilet than clean out a dirty potty, a toilet can seem very big to a little child and it's important not to rush or force your daughter into making the transition.

POSITIVE DISCIPLINE

Developing mutual trust and cooperation

Positive discipline means listening to your child's views, but not being afraid to set clear limits and boundaries to behaviour.

Positive discipline works by making sure your child wants to please you and to keep the good relationship you have built. When you develop trust and a willingness to cooperate in your child, you will both be on the same side. Your personality and the temperament of your child will influence the methods that work. A quiet, easy-to-manage child may need only gentle reminders for discipline. A more challenging child may need more hard work from you to encourage her to behave well.

It's a mistake to think that discipline is principally about the punishment of misbehaviour. In fact, the word 'discipline' derives from the Latin word which means 'learning' – in other words, you should aim to create a system of rules at home that enables your child to learn how to behave appropriately. Rote learning of rules, however, is not the most effective way of teaching your child good discipline. Always try to explain in simple terms the purpose of the rules you lay down for your child.

Working at positive discipline takes a lot of energy and no parent can get it right all the time. There will be days when you are too tired or too busy, and feel that you can't be patient or put in the effort that is required. All parents behave in ways they regret some of the time – scolding or smacking a child or getting close to a tantrum themselves. If this happens, the best thing you can do is to say you are sorry, kiss and make up, and try again. This teaches children to do the same.

Discipline versus punishment

'Discipline' is not the same as 'punishment'. Discipline involves teaching and guiding your child to behave in ways that are socially acceptable and fit in with your rules. There is no 'right way' that works for every situation. Punishment, such as smacking, is not an effective way of getting children to behave in the long term. Research has shown that it makes tantrums worse. It may appear to stop undesirable behaviour in its tracks at the time, but it doesn't prevent it in the future.

Negative discipline

Negative discipline – always expecting your child to be naughty and coming down hard on every small misdemeanour – can make your child and the rest of the family tense and unhappy. It can actually make some children more defiant and more likely to have tantrums. Also, continually trying to control your child's behaviour and forcing her to do as she is told means you can never relax and enjoy the fun aspects of parenting.

Strategies for positive discipline

• **Socialization.** Right from birth you should show loving responsiveness and a gradual setting of routines. As your child grows, you need to teach right from wrong, explaining the rules of behaviour and the importance of respecting others' needs and views.

• **Setting boundaries.** A child knows deep down that setting limits shows that her parents care. She gradually understands that the boundaries are for her well-being, and may regard too much permissiveness as indifference. It is normal for a child to test the limits and is a necessary part of becoming independent.

• **Natural consequences.** This means allowing your child to experience the consequences that would result from her behaviour if you did not intervene. For example, if she doesn't eat, she will feel hungry and if she doesn't wear a coat, she will feel cold.

• **Natural authority.** This involves using your voice and body language assertively. There is no such thing as a child who 'won't take no for an answer' – when you really mean it, your child will take notice. Try and speak or act as you would to stop her running into the road or touching a hot cooker.

Rewards

These are sometimes needed as extra motivation for a while for very difficult behaviour. They can be whatever your child would most appreciate – an outing or a new toy (hugs and kisses are great rewards too). However, you need to avoid creating a situation where your child will only do something in order to gain a reward.

Basic principles of giving rewards

1 **Time them carefully.** Never try to stop your child in the middle of an episode of misbehaviour by promising her a reward if she ceases to misbehave.

2 **Use them wisely.** Make sure there are times when you give your child a reward for her good behaviour even though she does not expect it.

3 **Keep them appropriate.** Try to avoid rewards that escalate too much in scale, or the rewards will become more important to her than the behaviour with which they are associated.

4 **Encourage reward-free behaviour.** Have times when you ask your child to do something for you without any promise of a reward.

5 **Reward effort.** Give your child a reward sometimes just because she tried hard to behave properly, whether or not she actually achieved her target.

Language
What is typical?

Your child uses language in ever more sophisticated ways during this phase of his life. This occurs partly through a better grasp of the rules of language, partly through his increased vocabulary and partly through his better learning skills.

Above: Always read books that your child enjoys rather than any that might make him afraid.

His sentences become longer, with a more complicated grammatical structure. He is more familiar with the concept of using conversation – taking it in turns to speak – and it is through this form of interaction that he strengthens and improves his verbal skills.

Although he won't understand individual words, at the age of three years, your child can begin to grasp that a book's title appears on the front page, that it is written by the author and that it starts at the front and finishes at the back. These facts are obvious to you, but not to your child. Understanding the nature of books is a fundamental pre-reading skill and it will also fire his enthusiasm.

2–2½ years	• He asks questions and listens attentively to the answers and has a vocabulary of several hundred individual words. He starts to use pronouns, such as 'he' or 'you' and prepositions, such as 'in' or 'on'.
2½–3 years	• He has a vocabulary of at least a thousand words and shows an understanding of grammar. He discovers that questions are a good way to gather information.
3–3½ years	• By three, he uses a string of four or five words to convey meaning, including adjectives to describe everyday objects or people. He can understand and carry out verbal instructions that contain up to three pieces of information.
3½–4 years	• As he approaches four, he may be able to match words of two or three letters that are printed clearly on individual cards. He grasps basic language rules, such as plurals and verb tenses, and uses them in his everyday speech.

Language
Common questions

Q Is it true that boys are somewhat slower in learning to speak than girls?

A Evidence from psychological studies confirms that, in general, girls acquire spoken language at an earlier age than boys and they also develop more complex language structures before boys. This is only a trend, though; it doesn't mean that every boy says his first word later than every girl. Much depends on the individual child.

Q At what age do children usually start understanding jokes?

A Your child probably first smiled from pleasure at around six weeks, but using language as a means of stimulating laughter starts around the age of two. Although your three-year-old's jokes may not strike you as funny – perhaps because they simply involve words in an unusual order – they make your child giggle, and your child's laughter is infectious.

Q Will my child's learning skills improve with frequent visits to the local nursery?

A Yes. It is very important for you to arrange regular contact with others her own age, at either a playgroup or nursery. The incentive of communicating with a friend in order to play together is strong enough to prompt better speech and more mature listening skills. Of course, she bickers sometimes with her peers when they play together, but for most of the time they prattle away happily to each other, sharing stories and experiences.

Q My child loves nursery rhymes and asks me to sing them with him over and over again. Is this good for his language development?

A Nursery rhymes are hugely beneficial and promote your child's language through repetition, through developing his awareness of rhyme, through demonstrating the poetic quality of language and through showing him that language has a fun element. Some nursery rhymes are tongue-twisters (such as 'Peter Piper') and are great for improving his mastery of different sounds and varied pronunciations.

Q Should I teach my child the meaning of words or should I leave him to learn the meanings himself?

A There is room for both strategies. His vocabulary increases just through talking and listening to you, or from mixing with his friends. However, you can also teach him words that he may find useful; he learns nouns more easily than adjectives or verbs.

Q When my three-year-old plays with a puzzle toy she talks to herself. Why?

A This is known as 'self-directing' speech because your child gives herself spoken instructions on how to complete the puzzle. In other words, she uses language to guide herself to the correct solution. Many adults do the same, except that they think the words instead of saying them out loud.

Language
Stimulation

Your child's speech and language become more complex from the age of two because she has a broader vocabulary, a greater understanding of grammar and an increased confidence in using language to express her needs.

Above: By pretending to be another person while dressed up, your child improves her language skills.

By the end of her second year, she is more animated in her use of words, phrases and sentences. She enjoys talking and is happy to tell you all her news. She combines words, gestures and facial expressions to make her accounts vivid and interesting. Her words flow more easily, with less effort. By the time she is four, her questions are more penetrating as she seeks more detailed information. She also applies the rules of grammar herself, though she doesn't always do this correctly.

How can I stimulate my child's language skills?

• Show interest in her endless tales and respond with questions to let her know you are listening and are interested.

• Involve her in pretend play, for example, dressing-up games. This sort of activity provides an opportunity for her to develop her language skills because she can pretend to be a completely different person.

• When she has finished watching a television programme or a video, chat to her about it and ask her basic questions.

• Emphasize prepositions in your speech. You can help her understand the meaning of 'in', 'on' and 'under' by demonstrating them.

• Choose stories that are more demanding. She is ready to listen to stories with more complex plots and multiple characters.

• Provide explanations. She is now at the age where she begins to understand explanations about why she should behave in a certain way.

• Encourage eye contact during conversation. Her attention is greater when she looks you in the eye as you talk to each other.

• Give more complicated instructions. Make a request that contains two or three pieces of information, for example: 'Go into the kitchen and bring me the blue cloth.'

• Play listening games. Get her to close her eyes while she is listening to a video or television programme with which she is familiar, and then ask her to identify the different voices she hears.

Positive parenting **Non-verbal communication**

Q At three years old, my child is quite able to express her views clearly using words. We chat all the time about what she gets up to and I always ask her whether she has had a good day or a bad day. Recently she fell out with her best friend and, although she told me she wasn't upset by it, her body language gave me the opposite impression. Can I use my child's body language to further her development?

A Body language never ceases to be an important form of communication (see pages 138–139). Some psychological estimates suggest that when you and your growing child communicate with each other, over half the meaning is transmitted non-verbally through body language. Your child tends to use body language to express her emotions rather than information. It's more sophisticated, varied and complex than in earlier years, so you have to work harder in order to interpret it.

What should I look for?

The various dimensions of non-verbal communication all interact with each other and you should therefore interpret the full range as presented by your child, not just one dimension in isolation. Main features of your child's body language at this age are:

• **Head position.** The way she holds her head could be upright and facing you, which suggests that she is confident and self-assured; or may be nodding or shaking, which indicates whether or not she agrees with you; or it could even be pushed forward at a rather menacing angle, which lets you know that

she's angry about something.

• **Facial expression.** Look at all aspects of your child's expression including her brow, eyes, mouth, and even her tongue. They all tell you something about her inner feelings. For instance, a relaxed, easy expression with mouth open lets you know that she's contented, while screwed-up facial muscles reveal that she is tense or angry.

• **Body distance.** If your child stands close and presses herself against you, the chances are that she feels very insecure, or very afraid, or very angry with you – you'll be able to identify the real emotion by studying other aspects of her body language at the same time, such as hand grip and breathing.

• **Body posture.** When she stands facing you square-on, with her hands on her hips, fists clenched and a tight facial expression, you can have no doubt that she is angry about something. Likewise, you know that when she slumps in a chair, legs stretched, arms hanging loosely by her sides and breathing easily, she feels contented.

Language
Common problems

Q My three-year-old still only uses single words, without forming short sentences. Is this normal at his age?

A The rate at which children acquire speech varies greatly. However, most children are further ahead with their language at this stage. The chances are your child's speech will develop normally and that there is nothing to worry about. But you may find it reassuring to have a chat with your family doctor about this.

Q What should we do about our child's lisp?

A Many children develop a temporary lisp while they acquire speech, substituting 'th' for 's', 'f' for 'th' and so on. In most instances this speech pattern disappears spontaneously as they grow older. Therefore at this stage you should do nothing in particular, except provide appropriate speech patterns for her to copy.

Above: Help your child to learn and remember nursery rhymes in small sections at a time.

Q My daughter, now three and a half, tends to chatter non-stop about anything and everything. Every so often, however, it is almost impossible to get one word out of her. What can I do?

A There may be times when you collect your child from nursery or playgroup, or perhaps a friend's house, only to discover that she is quiet and reflective. She simply doesn't feel like chatting to you. That's fine and should not become a source of confrontation between you. It could be that she is tired from her long day, or maybe she has fallen out with a friend and is in a bad mood. Whatever the cause of her reluctance to chat, give her space. She'll return to her usual talkative self within the next hour or so if you just leave her alone.

Q There are times when I am trying to explain something to my child that she suddenly shouts out, telling me to be quiet. Why does she do this?

A Quite often, this is an instinctive reaction to hearing something she doesn't like. Perhaps you won't let her have something she wants, or are trying to tell why she cannot do something. The best thing to do is to calm her, and continue to say what you wanted to say anyway. She eventually learns that you have as much right to speak as she has, even though she is unhappy with the message you convey to her. Once you've had your say, listen attentively to her response. In some cases, your child may be trying to slow you down because she is finding it hard to catch on.

Q I am really pleased with my child's progress in learning to speak, but he does tend to make a good number of mistakes. What can I do to correct this?

A You should expect your child to make mistakes with language. He's still learning and at times uses the wrong word in the wrong place or maybe uses an immature style of speech. Errors like this are perfectly normal and nothing to be concerned about. Instead of correcting each mistake, just say the right form to him as if confirming what he has said. For instance, if he tells you that 'Me wented to the bathroom', you could reply 'That's good, you went to the bathroom.' He'll pick up the correct phrasing from you. Sometimes his language contains mistakes that might be funny, but try not to laugh at him. Drawing attention to these errors makes him very self-conscious, possibly making him reluctant to talk so openly in the future.

Above: Reading your child books helps her to see how they work, which will help her with reading.

Q My child wants to learn nursery rhymes but seems to have difficulty memorizing them. How can I help her?

A The best way to memorize any rhyme, poem or song is in small sections at a time. It could be that your child tries to memorize too much all at once, finds this far too much for her limited memory capacity, and therefore only manages to retain part of it. Teach her a more effective strategy. Encourage her to repeat out loud perhaps only the first half of the line (making sure that each unit she memorizes makes sense on its own). Once she knows this fully after a few days, move on to the next small chunk. In this way, she slowly learns the whole poem.

Q I have started to read fairy stories to my three-year-old, but he seems disturbed by them. Is it true that they can scare him?

A Some stories have the potential to frighten your child. That's why it is important to choose carefully the books that you want to read to him, to ensure the content is appropriate for his age and understanding. He is unlikely to feel very positively about books and pictures if he experiences some that disturb him and make him afraid.

Learning
What is typical?

What a transformation in your child's understanding of the world around her! Your child's learning ability (also called 'intelligence', 'learning skills', 'thinking skills' and 'cognition') continues to grow rapidly during these remaining pre-school years. Her ability to learn new skills and concepts, to make sense of events around her, to use her memory accurately and to solve problems steadily improves.

As well as spending time with you, she loves the company of others her own age. Through playing and talking with her peers, your child learns a whole range of skills more rapidly than she could do on her own. By the time she reaches her third birthday, her memory has improved, she can interpret the meaning of her experiences, and she has a vivid imagination, sound use of language and higher level of concentration. By the time she is four, a genuine understanding of numbers develops and she considers concepts such as shape and colour in more detail than before.

What can my child do?

2–2½ years	• She sorts objects according to specific characteristics, ascribing human qualities to them as an expression of her active imagination. She begins to develop a broad sense of time.
2½–3 years	• She can compare two objects in terms of size or height and is able to remember the name of an object by repeating it to herself. She is now able to anticipate the consequences of her actions. For example, she knows that if she knocks her cup over the drink will spill.
3–3½ years	• She develops an elementary understanding of numbers and she begins to learn rules of behaviour and the reasons behind them. She may confuse coincidence with cause and effect, linking two events that are not in fact connected.
3½–4 years	• Her organizational skills improve, enabling her to make a more systematic search when she is looking for something. She at last reaches the first stage of genuine counting – for example, she counts a row of small blocks up to the second or third block and attempts to count on her fingers.

Learning
Common questions

Q Does progress in learning slow down as a child approaches the age of three?

A No, her rate of learning actually increases because she can think about concepts that were meaningless to her before. For instance, she starts to grasp the meaning of numbers and the significance of size and time. She may also recognize that letters and words have shapes, which is an early stage of learning to read.

Q Is television bad for my child?

A Your child can learn a lot from short, quality television programmes that present new information in exciting and challenging ways. The danger, however, is if he spends too much time staring aimlessly at poor quality viewing just because the television is on. Monitor his viewing so that you are aware of his viewing patterns.

Q When my three-year-old saw me roll a small ball of clay into a long thin piece, she insisted it now contained more clay. Why does she think in this way?

A Your child doesn't understand that the amount of clay remains the same no matter what its shape. She does notice that the thin shape is longer, however, and she mistakenly concludes that it must therefore have more clay in it.

Q Is it true that the youngest child in a family usually possesses more creative thought processes than the oldest?

A There is evidence that second-born and youngest children are often more creative thinkers than the first-born. Whatever the

Above: Placing items on a tray for your child to recall is a fun way to improve memory.

reason for this, you may find that your youngest thinks more flexibly than his older sibling, applying more innovative solutions to problems.

Q Do children this age understand about rules of behaviour?

A Yes. Your child may not like the rules that set limits on what he is allowed to do, and he may even try to break them, but he certainly understands rules about his behaviour. Always explain a rule to your child, especially the reasoning underlying it. He learns rules quicker when they are applied consistently.

Q Are some children naturally gifted and talented?

A There is no doubt that some children possess exceptional abilities in some areas of development. For example, musical ability is thought to be innate, and musically talented infants show this skill very early on, perhaps by playing tunefully with toy instruments. Yet virtually all children can learn new skills at every age, whether they are innately talented or not.

Learning
Stimulation

From the age of about two, your child becomes a much more active thinker, with a great deal more knowledge and grasp of concepts than before. He is now able to focus his attention more accurately and is less influenced by distractions. Led by his innate curiosity, the intensity of his questioning increases.

Above: Improve your child's memory by playing games – ask him to memorize five fruit in a bowl.

By the time he is three, increasing memory skills underpin much of his learning, and he can hold two or three pieces of information in his memory while he acts on them. Furthermore he starts to use imagery as part of his thinking. He is more able to discuss people, objects and toys that aren't actually there in front of him at the time, so he is no longer tied to what he can see. This opens up a whole new range of learning opportunities.

How can I stimulate my child's learning skills?

• When he is settled at an activity, tell him something to remember, perhaps a type of food or a piece of clothing. After several minutes, ask him to recall this item.

• Read him lots of stories and, now and then, ask him what he thinks will happen next.

• Show him recent family photographs. Ask him to identify the people and then ask if he knows where the picture was taken.

• As well as reading stories to your child, suggest that he makes up a story to tell you, encouraging him to use symbolic thought and to draw on previous experience.

• Give him sorting activities. For instance, ask your child to put his toy animals in one place and his toy people in another.

• Teach him to recognize his name in writing. Initially, he won't be able to tell the difference between his name and other words. Point it out to him, and ask him to find the same word elsewhere on the piece of paper.

• Show by example. Explain to him why you completed something in the way you did so that he learns this strategy.

• Clap out a simple rhythm and ask your child to repeat it – for example, two quick claps followed by two slow ones.

• Encourage him to use a desk. He'll soon discover that it is more comfortable to draw a picture or complete a puzzle while at a desk.

• Ask him to help you solve problems. For instance, ask him to think of the best way to store all the tin cans in the cupboard.

Positive parenting **Memory games**

Q My child shows signs of having a good memory. At two and a half he could play a simplified game of pairs and by three he can memorize five fruits and recount them five minutes later. Are there ways that I can encourage him to use his memory even more? Will it be beneficial to him?

A Your child's memory skills will certainly improve through practice and training, and the most effective way of achieving success with this age group is through playing memory games. All children love them and you can make them up yourself.

Strategies

• Place approximately six household objects on a tray in front of your child. Ask him to look at the tray and try to remember all the objects. Explain that you'll take the tray away, so he has to remember all the items he can. Remove the tray. You'll find that he probably recalls at least two or three objects, and quite possibly more. Once he has made his guess, let him look at the tray again.

• You can improve your child's performance at this activity by teaching him the strategy of rehearsal. When he tries to memorize the objects on the tray, suggest to him that he says the names of the objects out loud, over and over again. This technique – which you probably use yourself when memorizing, say, a new telephone number – will increase his recall of the objects. He'll be pleased with the results. Likewise, when you give him a simple instruction to carry out, ask him to repeat the instruction back to you. This

increases the amount of information stored in his short-term memory.

• An alternative to this game is to group together a series of familiar objects with different textures, such as a slice of bread, a small book, a teaspoon, a cup, a vest and so on. Let your child handle these for a couple of minutes and then remove them. After 10 minutes, place the objects in a bag and ask your child to guess what each object is just by touching it, without looking. He has great fun recalling as many items as he can.

Q I have trouble getting my child to commit anything to memory, because he has such poor concentration. What can I do to encourage him?

A To help improve his concentration, take him shopping with you at the supermarket. Hold up a particular food can and ask your child to find one exactly like it. Do this at the top of the aisle that contains the product. Encourage him to scan each row systematically as he walks along. If you see that he rushes down the aisle, missing items as he passes, suggest he slows down. Do this three or four times during any shopping trip – it's good practice for focusing his attention. You can also ask him to identify, say, red cars when you next go out driving with him.

Learning
Common problems

Above: Providing lots of stimulating games for your child improves his learning skills.

Q Despite having learned colours with relative ease, my three-year-old daughter often mistakes red for blue. She is quite insistent and there is nothing I can do to persuade her that the opposite is true. Why does she do this?

A A child this age has an amazing capacity to deny reality in the face of conflicting evidence, and there might be times when she is sure she is right about something even though you know she is wrong. If you find yourself trying to persuade your three-year-old that, for example, her new jumper is red not blue, calmly bring the jumper out to show her, patiently point out its real colour, and then change the conversation. The next time she talks about the jumper, she'll refer to it as red.

Q I have two children and the younger one has consistently proved slower to learn than his older brother. I have come to the conclusion that he simply isn't as bright as his brother and am reluctant to push him. Am I right?

A While it is true that some children are brighter than others, you must avoid falling into the trap of creating what psychologists call 'a self-fulfilling prophecy'. For example, if you think your child is not very clever, you'll expect less of him, and you'll accept lower achievements from him; this will probably de-motivate him, and sure enough your child's progress slows down. Your prediction becomes self-fulfilling. That's why it's vital to expect the most of your child's learning potential, and to continually provide a high level of stimulation for him.

Q My child, who's two and a half, is prone to sulking when she cannot complete a puzzle, or when she forgets what she wants to tell me. Should I do anything?

A As your child's thinking skills increase, she inevitably tries more challenging learning activities. In some instances she will fail to achieve her learning target, whether that's completing a large jigsaw puzzle or learning the sequence of the first five numbers. This can depress her self-confidence, thus reducing her willingness to learn new information in the future. Do your best to keep her confidence as a learner high so that she maintains an upbeat, positive outlook about her learning skills.

Q My child makes odd connections between events that are completely unrelated. For example, yesterday he thought the local shop was closed because it had rained that morning. Why does he do this?

A Your three-year-old may form connections between two events that occur one after the other, even though they are not linked. For instance, he may conclude that your car doesn't start because he is in a bad mood with you. You know the two are totally unconnected, but your child's lack of experience allows him to establish a cause-and-effect link in his own mind. When you see your child make this sort of mistaken relationship between two episodes, point out to him that they are not connected but occurred one after the other by chance. Advise him that things can happen together by coincidence.

Q Why is it that my child is more interested in other children's toys than in her own?

A It is simply that she is attracted by the novelty of those toys, because they are different from her own. Try reducing the number of toys that she has at any one time, so that when you bring different toys to her she is attracted by their unfamiliarity. Keep rotating her toys regularly so that she doesn't get bored with them.

Right: By the age of four children are often able to count using their fingers.

Q My child is almost three and I have been trying to introduce the concept of numbers. She doesn't seem quite ready for it, however. Is she too young?

A Genuine understanding of numbers usually doesn't develop until around the age of four or five, but you can lay the foundations for mathematics even at this age. When you walk with your child up and down stairs, slowly count each step. Saying the numbers 'one', 'two' and so on as you move draws her attention to these words. Do the same when you hand her sweets, or count the fingers on her hand before tickling her palm. After time she will start to imitate you, by repeating the number names herself.

Hand–eye coordination
What is typical?

As your growing child progresses through the pre-school years, hand control becomes increasingly important, not just because it helps her become more independent but also because it is linked to problem-solving and to learning.

Above: Playing with toys that have small pieces requires a child's maximum concentration.

By the age of two, improved hand–eye coordination enables your child to be more independent and to pick up and manipulate objects without having to ask you for help. As she approaches the end of this year, so many of the activities that were previously beyond her are now well within her abilities. For instance, her cup-holding skill, her use of cutlery, her effectiveness at picking up and carrying objects, and her ability to dress herself all help to make her much more self-reliant. She is prepared to do much more for herself as a result and from the age of three to four, her confidence really grows, for example, she plays more intricately with small doll's house furniture because she knows she can move the tiny pieces more accurately.

What can my child do?

2–2½ years	• By two she can thread large beads onto a lace, make a controlled mark when painting or drawing and has established hand preference.
2½–3 years	• She will try to cut paper with a pair of child-safe scissors, although finds it difficult. She can copy simple shapes you draw and carry out simple household tasks like putting cutlery on the table or toys in a box.
3–3½ years	• She can build a mini-tower of eight or nine blocks with wooden bricks. She can use a small rolling pin to roll modelling clay and can unfasten large buttons.
3½–4 years	• By now she is able to find and collect specific items from supermarket shelves and loves challenging activities such as small jigsaws.

Hand–eye coordination
Common questions

Q My son is two and a half and obsessed with dressing and undressing dolls but plays with very little else. Is that normal?
A Yes. Children this age often become fixated with one toy in particular. Yours has turned his attention to playing with dolls like this because his hand control has developed to the point where he achieves success every time. Encourage him to play with other toys too.

Q How many pieces should a child aged two and a half be able to replace in an inset board?
A As a rough guide, you could expect a child of this age to cope with a board that has six to eight different pieces. The difficulty of an inset board is also affected by the shape of the inserts – irregular, large shapes are harder to fit than small regular shapes.

Q My child can do inset puzzles with ease. Is this a good time to introduce jigsaw puzzles?
A Yes. Your child is probably ready to move from inset board puzzles to jigsaw puzzles, although the transition is challenging. Unlike inset boards, jigsaw puzzles have no outer frame to guide your child. Pieces can fit anywhere in any orientation, so there are more possible combinations than for the pieces of an inset board. Initially, buy your child a two-piece jigsaw only, one that has an easily identifiable picture. The picture, rather than the shapes of the pieces, will guide him. Once he has achieved a two-piece jigsaw, progress to a

Above: Finger painting is great fun and should be encouraged even if your child can use a brush.

three-piece then a four-piece, and so on. Build up the degree of difficulty gradually.

Q Is my daughter too old for finger painting now that she can hold a brush?
A Finger painting uses different parts of her hands and fingers compared to painting with a brush, so she should have an opportunity to take part in both activities (as long as you are prepared for the mess). It's also great fun, no matter how old she is.

Q Why does my child make such strange faces when she concentrates hard while playing with very small toys?
A The chances are that you do the same when, for instance, you try to thread a needle. Her twisted facial expression simply helps her focus her attention more on the job in hand, that's all. As she gets older, she will do this less and less. Also, children often go through phases of pulling a particular expression (especially if they see it annoys you!) then after a while, they just stop.

Hand–eye coordination
Stimulation

For the next few years, your child's continued progress with hand-eye coordination depends on the interaction between the stimulation and encouragement he receives daily, his physical and neurological development, and his motivation. These three different dimensions need to be carefully balanced before he can move from one stage to the next.

Improvements in hand–eye coordination typically occur steadily but slowly between the ages of three and four years, making them difficult to detect. Your child might need you to point out that he is now much more adept at cutting his food with a knife than he was, say, a couple of months ago. He needs you to draw his attention to these small steps forward.

How can I stimulate my child's hand–eye coordination skills?

• **Ask him to bring items to you.** He loves helping, so use this to boost his hand control. For instance, he can unscrew a jar to bring you a biscuit or open a box to bring you a button.

• **Show him how to use cutlery.** He already uses a spoon but try to teach him how to use cutlery in each hand. Start with a fork in one hand and a spoon in the other. This takes time to master.

• **Give him varied drawing and painting equipment.** Buy a range of coloured pencils, crayons and types of paper so that your child has choices when it comes to creative activities. Encourage him to vary the materials he selects.

• **Allocate responsibility.** He will love to be involved in your household routine, such as being responsible for dusting a tabletop, or for sweeping a rug with a small brush.

• **Take him to nursery or playgroup.** He will benefit from mixing with other children, from playing with them in novel ways, and from having access to a new range of toys.

• **Give him small tasks that combine personal responsibility and hand control.** When he tidies his toys encourage him to put them away neatly. Show him how to hold his toothbrush so that he can clean his teeth properly. He will try hard to achieve targets you set for him.

• **Play finger games.** Make up games involving finger and hand movements. For instance, his hands could be two spiders crawling up the wall, or his fingers could be the legs of a little person walking along the table top.

• **Play challenging visual games.** For instance, when you are out together, ask him to look for cars that are the same as yours or get him to tell you every time he sees a baby being pushed in a pushchair. The object you choose for him to identify is unimportant – it can be anything you like – just as long as he has to use his vision to locate it.

Suitable toys for your growing child

Age	Toy/activity	Skill
2–2½ years	Drawing with coloured crayons and paper	• To encourage him to hold crayons correctly.
	Toy tool set	• **To improve hand control.** Actions such as sawing, hammering and turning a screwdriver all provide excellent practice.
2½–3 years	Art and craft materials including coloured paper, child-safe scissors and glue	• **To learn new skills.** Cutting paper, scrunching it and sticking it down are all complex hand-control tasks that take time to master.
	Plastic tea set	• **Using real liquid,** this will encourage greater accuracy in pouring from one vessel to another.
3–3½ years	Colouring-in book	• Encourages greater accuracy when colouring in, by staying within the black outline.
	Modelling clay	• Hand–eye coordination benefits from practice making clay shapes, or rolling lumps of clay with a small rolling pin.
	Stacking bricks	• To encourage your child to experiment making different shapes and patterns.
3½–4 years	Sand and water play	• **To feel different sensations.** Children enjoy rubbing their hands in sand and squeezing the 'mud' out between their fingers.
	Clothes with Velcro fastenings and big buttons	• To encourage greater dexterity in the fingers.

Hand–eye coordination
Common problems

Q My child's hand strength doesn't seem to be very good. How can I improve it?
A The power in his muscles will increase spontaneously as he matures, so you don't need to do anything special at all at the moment. However, you could play a game in which he grips a small soft ball in his hand and then squeezes it repeatedly. You can also encourage him to play with construction toys so that he uses his hands more, which may help to build up their strength.

Q Although my child is under four, she insists on trying to button her coat by herself. This usually ends in tears. What should I do?
A Work in partnership with her, not in opposition. For instance, you can pull each button most of the way through, leaving her to tug the last section into place. This way she will feel that she is doing it herself and be delighted with her success. It also means that any confrontation is avoided.

Q My three-year-old has good hand control but prefers me to fetch and carry for her. How can I change this?
A Resist carrying out tasks you know she is capable of doing, even if she whinges. Eventually her desire for the toy or the piece of food will become so strong that she will get it herself. And when she does, be sure to reinforce her behaviour by telling her how clever she is and how delighted you are that she did this all by herself.

Above: Always encourage your child's efforts with pen and paper whatever level of ability he has.

Q My child is three and a half and, although she can hold a pen correctly, she cannot draw anything recognizable at all. Why is this?
A No matter how hard she tries, she simply does not have the muscular and neurological maturity to make such fine hand movements. Moreover, if you put your child under pressure, for example, to 'write neatly like your big sister', you run the risk of turning off her interest in writing altogether. Instead of pushing her, look carefully at your child's ability and encourage her to develop it further slowly.

Q When roused to anger, my child impulsively raises his hand and whacks the object of his wrath without thinking through his action. How can I stop him doing this?
A Such misuse of his hand-control skills is totally unacceptable and should always be discouraged. Make sure your child understands that you are angry at his aggressive action, explain that he should express his displeasure verbally not physically,

and ask him to consider what he would feel like if someone hit him in that way. You will probably have to repeat this process again and again until he gains better control of his impulses.

Q Now that my child mixes more with other children she compares herself to her peers. This can have a negative effect on her if, say, her pictures are not as good as theirs in her eyes. Is there anything I can do?

A A young child's enthusiasm for challenges involving hand–eye coordination will rapidly evaporate in the face of apparently better efforts by her pal standing next to her. And when she loses belief in her own abilities, she'll be very reluctant to paint, draw or write the next time an opportunity arises. All you can do in such instances is give her bags of encouragement. Your positive comments will always boost her motivation.

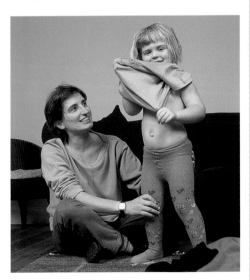

Above: Provide easy-to-manage clothes so that your independent child can dress herself.

Five top tips

1 Resist the temptation to compare your child. He will develop hand–eye coordination at his own rate. You may know other children his age who have better hand control than he does, but comparisons with them only make you anxious and dent his self-confidence.

2 Provide modelling materials. He can make any shape he wants from clay or playdough, and if he doesn't like what he has made, he can squash it and start again. As long as it doesn't dry out, clay or playdough can be used again and again.

3 Wiggle his fingers. Demonstrate how you can stretch your hands wide open and wiggle your fingers in the air. Your toddler will try to imitate you, although he'll find that he can't move his fingers in such a coordinated fashion as you.

4 Play 'pointing' games. Name specific objects in the room and ask your child to point to them. He'll then scan the area, spot the object you have named and point his index finger towards it. This type of 'I spy' game is great fun.

5 Use household items. His hand–eye control benefits when he plays with everyday items. Dried pasta, for instance, can be arranged into many different patterns, and flour and water combine into a sticky mixture that he can manipulate.

Movement
What is typical?

Your pre-school child consolidates and advances the physical skills she developed in earlier years. Coordination challenges that eluded her before – such as hopping, skipping and balancing – are now accessible to her and she can now attempt many of these activities. Of course she has a long way to go before she achieves total competence in these areas, but she is significantly more agile and athletic than before.

Between the ages of two and a half and four, your child grows around 8 cm (3 in) in height each year and puts on about 3 kg (6–7 lb) in weight. Her head size becomes smaller in proportion to the rest of her body, and her face broadens in preparation for her second teeth, which will start to come through in a couple of years. Neurological changes take place in the brain, spine and nervous system as well. The combined effect of all these normal physical changes is that your child becomes leaner and more agile, with less fat to slow her down, and she can take part in energetic physical activity for longer without tiring.

What can my child do?

2–2½ years	• By two she is able to jump a short distance off the ground from a standing position, walk up stairs without your support and can successfully manoeuvre herself around obstacles while performing another task.
2½–3 years	• She will attempt challenging balancing activities, such as walking along a log or hopping, and is able to negotiate ladders and slides on large outdoor play equipment. She runs fast with great confidence.
3–3½ years	• She can carry out more than one physical task at the same time through improved coordination. She can propel a pedal toy such as a tricycle, climb into her chair at mealtimes and stand on tiptoes for several seconds without putting her heels on the ground.
3½–4 years	• As she approaches four she has enough confidence to try out all the items in the outdoor play area and enjoys bouncing on a trampoline or bouncy castle. She can walk upstairs and downstairs putting one foot on each step at a time, using the banister or wall for support.

Movement
Common questions

Q Why is it that most boys seem to prefer strenuous outdoor play, while girls generally prefer to engage in more sedate activities?

A Nobody knows for sure why this difference occurs; some claim it is biological, while others say it is due to social expectations. Whatever the explanation, your child, whether a girl or a boy, should be encouraged to join in play activities involving balance, movement and coordination. Every child benefits from these games, irrespective of gender.

Q Should I discourage rough-and-tumble play because it is quite aggressive?

A Rough-and-tumble play may look aggressive and destructive, but it isn't. In fact, it's a very constructive form of play from a child's point of view because it develops his social and physical skills. If your child and his friends are happy playing this way – and it doesn't end in tears – leave them to get on with it.

Q My child is two and a half years old. Should she be able to hop?

A Most children do not develop the ability to hop until they are between the ages of three and four, but there is no harm in preparing your child for this skill. For instance, you could ask her to try balancing with one foot off the ground.

Q Compared to my friend's child, my child is fatter and slower. Will he start to thin out?

A He is already in the process of losing his 'puppy fat' – this happens as part of natural growth during this period. His attitude is more

Above: At this age your child will begin to learn to hop, skip, jump and improve her balance.

important than his body size at this stage. If he is enthusiastic, you have no need to worry.

Q At what age do children have a growth spurt?

A This rapid period of growth in your child's height, weight and body volume occurs at two points during childhood. The first takes place between birth and two years, and the second during adolescence. Her growth rate is steady between the ages of two and a half and five.

Q I've heard that children who grow faster are smarter. Is that true?

A Some studies have found that children who have very quick growth patterns in early childhood do tend to score slightly higher in school tests than children with a slower growth rate. Yet there are plenty of small children who are brighter than their larger peers. Growth rate is only one small factor.

Movement
Stimulation

Between the ages of three and four your child makes big progress in major movement skills such as jumping, running, climbing and balancing. His movement skills become more sophisticated and controlled and his learning ability also increases. He combines these two areas of development so that he can take part in a varied range of activities.

He is much more confident with activities involving movement skills, and knows that his balance, coordination and muscle strength is greater. He eagerly takes part in kicking, throwing and catching games, and by the time he is four, stairs are no longer a major hurdle.

How can I stimulate my child's movement skills?

• **Walk with him rather than strapping him into a pushchair.** Although your journeys will generally be slower, it'll be worth it as he'll be getting much more practice with his movement skills.

• **Ask him to put his toys into the toy box.** As well as giving your child a little bit of personal responsibility and independence, which he will be beginning to look for anyway, this regular task involves him in whole body movements, including walking, bending, balancing and placing.

• **Run alongside your child, holding his hand.** He'll make an attempt to move quicker when he has the security of knowing you're beside him to support him if she falls.

• **Outdoor play is crucial for the development of your child's movement abilities,** so take him to an adventure playground as often as you can.

• **Let him walk along a log. He'll probably fall over, so you will need to hold his hand as he walks along it.** This is a very difficult activity for your child but, as well as being exciting for him, it is a good way to encourage his balance and movement skills.

• **Use music to make movement activities more fun.** For instance, dance along with your child to his favourite music.

• **Play on a seesaw with him.** Moving gently up and down on a seesaw uses his leg muscles (as he pushes off), his arm muscles (as he holds on) and builds his confidence.

• **Let him seat himself.** He is now capable of climbing into his own chair at mealtimes and twisting his body until he achieves a comfortable position for eating.

• **Walk on slopes.** Make sure that you and your child don't only walk on perfectly flat areas. Strolling up a slight incline strengthens his leg muscles and builds up his stamina for movement.

• **Enrol him in a swimming class.** Your child may have already learned to swim, but whether he has or not, he'll benefit from instruction by a qualified swimming trainer. His confidence in the water will grow steadily.

Positive parenting **Finding a balance**

Q My youngest son is a bit of a daredevil and bursting with enthusiasm. His improved physical skills mean that he wants to run and climb around every potential play area (and it doesn't matter whether it's an 'official' play area, such as his bedroom or a park, or an 'unofficial' play area, such as the kitchen or the other side of the street). He delights in using his improved motor skills, even when the activity is potentially hazardous. What can I do to prevent him coming to harm without discouraging his efforts?

A It is not easy to strike a balance between protecting your child so much that he becomes afraid to take part in energetic play, and letting him go until he reaches a point where he is at risk. A combination of sensible guidelines about keeping safe, coupled with positive directions about how to have adventures without danger, is the most effective strategy.

Strategies

• **Make sure he has plenty of opportunities to explore safely,** so that he doesn't need to put himself at risk in order to achieve adventure and excitement. Well-structured outdoor play areas with swings and roundabouts, climbing frames and balancing logs are great fun and help to keep his curiosity stimulated – and the beauty is that they are designed with safety in mind.

• **Take him along to a leisure class,** such as swimming, gymnastics or any other type of sport. Choose a well-supervised class that offers a safe, secure environment. Energy and enthusiasm are encouraged in these activities, not frowned upon. Although your child might be reluctant to go along at first, he'll soon settle in once he realizes the fun that awaits him.

• **Give your child lots of praise when you see him play energetically but safely** – when you see him setting his own limits. Point out, for instance, how pleased you are that he only went halfway up the climbing frame because he wasn't sure how he would get down. Give him a cuddle when he remembers to walk along the street, instead of running wildly.

Q My three-year-old boy is timid by nature and is afraid to explore wide-open spaces in the park or adventure playground. I know he wants to play, but he is not bold enough to venture onto the climbing frame or even kick a ball. What can I do to encourage him and prevent him missing out on activities that I know he would find stimulating?

A Resist the temptation to push him too hard, too quickly. If he is genuinely afraid of hurting himself or of falling over, then he will freeze if pressurized to be more adventurous. Far better to use gentle, sensitive persuasion – sarcasm or ridicule about his timid behaviour will only make matters worse. He needs to feel that you are on his side, ready to guide him instead of laughing at him. Bear in mind that your timid child will be more willing to extend the limits of his physical skills when there is adult supervision. For example, he will be less afraid to learn to swim in a pool that has attendants and when you (or an instructor) are in the pool beside him.

Movement
Common problems

Q Lately my daughter has been coming to me in tears claiming 'I can't run like my friend'. She is two and a half and constantly comparing herself to others. Is this normal?

A Your child's increased social awareness can have a negative effect on her self-esteem, in that her confidence may drop when she realizes some other children are more agile than she is. If she gets upset, take her feelings seriously. It may be a small matter to you but it's extremely important to her. Give her a reassuring cuddle, comfort her until she calms down, tell her that she will improve as long as she continues to try hard, and remind her of all the other movement skills that she has already acquired.

Above: Some children lack confidence in physical activities and may need gentle encouragement.

Q My three-year-old is very determined. His imagination knows no limits and he dreams about scaling barriers, throwing the ball high in the air and running very fast. But whenever he discovers his physical limitations, he explodes with rage and frustration. What should I do?

A Above all, don't get annoyed when he loses his temper like this. Instead, remove him from the activity and calm him. Point out that the more he cries, the less he'll be able to complete the activity. Explain that other children find this very difficult too and suggest that he tries to achieve an easier task.

Q My child is afraid of climbing. Should I just put her on the climbing frame anyway?

A This will probably just terrify her further. Far better to encourage climbing ability slowly by starting with a small obstacle to climb, such as a cushion lying on the floor. Next, make the obstacle two cushions, gradually building up her confidence with more challenging feats. She'll tackle the climbing frame when she's ready.

Q I'm hopelessly uncoordinated and can't teach my child much in the way of movement. Will he lose out?

A Psychological research confirms that while parental interest in their child's movement skills has impact, children also learn about movement just from playing with others their own age. So do what you can to guide your child's physical activities and ensure that he has regular opportunities to spend time with his peers.

Q My child is three and a half years old and she insists on climbing all over the furniture. What should I do?

A Make it clear that climbing over the furniture is not acceptable. Point out to her the risk of possible injury to herself and the damage she could do to the furniture. At the same time, suggest a play area in which she can exercise her climbing skills freely.

Q My three-year-old is very boisterous when playing with his pals and there is one in particular that gets very upset at times. Should I stop my boy playing with him?

A Some children are naturally more exuberant during energetic play than others; they like to push the other children, wrestle with them, and roll on the ground whenever they can.

This is not intended as aggression, simply as play. However, a child on the receiving end of these acts of exuberance may become upset. Don't stop your child playing with others, but gently advise him that not all his friends may like such rough play. Encourage him to think about their feelings and to watch whether or not they seem to be having fun. This increases his sensitivity towards them.

Q My child is three and a half and cannot walk on tiptoes. Is there something I can do to help her?

A Yes. You can teach new movement skills if a child struggles to learn them spontaneously. With walking on tiptoes, for instance, your child's initial reaction to this challenge might be to rush at it, the end result being that she falls over and loses her confidence. Break the activity down into small stages. First, she should stand steady with both feet firmly on the ground and then raise her heels slightly. Once she is comfortable she can raise them higher, and so on, each time getting closer and closer to standing on her tiptoes. Eventually she will be confident about standing independently on her tiptoes. The next stage is to teach her how to walk in that position. Encourage her to move one foot forward just slightly, while the other is stationary. Then the forward step can become longer, and then she can start to move her back foot. In other words, gradually lead her towards mastering the movement skill. Be patient with your child. You'll find that she learns at her own natural pace.

Left: By the age of four your child will become more adventurous and enjoy using outdoor play areas.

Health issues
Basic first aid

This health section covers minor accidents only. First aid cannot be taught from a book, and to be able to deal with resuscitation, severe bleeding and burns or head injuries, you should enrol on a first-aid course. Otherwise you should get your child seen by a doctor or take her to an accident and emergency department. (See also pages 120–121 and 174–175.)

Q What should I do if my child faints?

A Typical signals that a child is likely to faint are dizziness, a slow pulse and a pale face, usually caused by a brief restriction in blood flow to the brain. A child may faint out of hunger, fear or pain, or if he is made to stand without moving for a long time. If your child faints, lie him down, raise his legs and support them. Loosen tight clothing at the waist, chest and neck. Ensure there is fresh air by opening a window and/or fanning his face. As your child comes round, so as not to frighten him, sit him up gradually and reassure him, but do not give him anything to drink until he is fully conscious.

Q What should I do if my child gets something stuck in her ear?

A It is quite common for young children to push objects, such as tiny parts of toys, into their ears. Or it is feasible that an insect may fly into your child's ear. In the event of either, sit the child down and examine the ear in a good light. If there is an insect in her ear, lay a towel over the child's shoulder and pour tepid water in to float the insect out. Never try to remove anything else from the ear canal. It is only too easy to push the object further down the canal and cause more damage. Reassure your child and take her to the accident and emergency department of your local hospital.

Q How should I treat a child with something in his eye?

A Particles of dust or grit often get into the eye and it is usually quite simple to remove them. However, anything embedded in the eye or sticking to the coloured part of the eye (the iris or pupil) must not be touched. If the particle is on the coloured part of the eye and does not move when the child blinks, cover the eye with a pad and bandage it into place. Treat as for an eye injury (see page 175). If the particle is on the white of the eye or under a lid, gently pull down the lower lid and ask the child to move the eye up, down and across until you see the particle. Tilt the child's head so the affected eye is on the lower side. Then pour a small amount of water from a jug into the eye to wash out the particle. If the particle is not washed out, lift it using a moistened folded corner of a tissue or a clean handkerchief. If the particle is under the upper lid, pull the upper lid down over the lower lid and ask the child to blink. This may remove it. If the particle remains in the eye, cover with a pad, bandage it into place and take the child to a doctor.

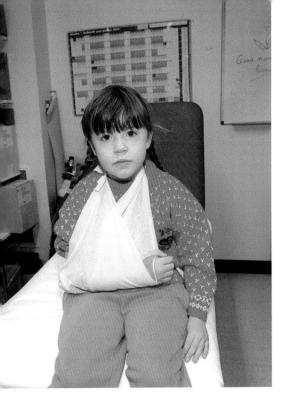

Above: If you suspect a broken arm after bandaging (see right), take your child to hospital.

Q How can I treat a sprained ankle?

A A sprain is a tear in the ligaments and tissues around a joint, which causes pain and swelling. The injury may be minor or it can be so extensive that it is difficult to distinguish it from a fracture. If there is any doubt, a sprain should always be treated as a fracture (see below). In the first instance, help your child to sit or lie down and support the leg in a comfortable resting position. Gently remove footwear and socks. Lay a cloth that has been wrung out in cold water over the ankle and put an ice pack, or a pack of frozen peas, on top to reduce pain and swelling. Wrap a thick layer of cotton wool around the ankle and bandage this into place to provide support and cushioning. Keep the ankle raised. If you think the injury might be a fracture, take your child to hospital.

Q What should I do if I suspect my child had broken her arm or leg?

A A broken limb may be obvious with swelling, distortion and extreme tenderness. Children who have a partial break in the bone (a greenstick fracture) may have less clear signs. Any child who has had an accident and then has tenderness over part of the bone should be investigated. Fractures involving the elbow are especially common in children. For a broken arm, sit the child down and support the injured limb. Place a pad of folded cloth between the arm and the chest. Gently move the arm across the chest to the most comfortable position and immobilize it using a triangular bandage or a headscarf. For extra support, tie a second bandage around the chest and sling. Take the child to hospital. For a broken leg, support the limb while helping the child to lie down. Immobilize the leg with your hands or a rolled blanket. Call an ambulance. Bandage for support only if the ambulance is going to be delayed – it is better to let trained personnel do this. Keep the child still, and do not give her anything to eat or drink. If you need to move her, first support and splint the broken leg, moving the good leg to the injured one.

If after an accident there is no danger to life, and professional help will be available quickly, the best course of action may be to wait for help to arrive.

Health issues
Growth

Q What are growing pains?

A Growing pains are burning or aching pains in the legs which usually occur at night. The cause is uncertain, but the pains are almost certainly not caused by the fact that the child is growing. Some children are especially prone to them, with girls suffering more than boys. The peak ages are three to five and again at eight to 12 years. Children who suffer other recurrent pains such as migraines or stomach aches also get more growing pains. The pains are never serious and eventually disappear on their own.

Q What are the implications of a growth hormone deficiency?

A If your child has growth hormone deficiency you will notice that growth tailed off after the first year of normal development. Your child may be overweight with a babyish face, but will be of normal intelligence. Growth is largely controlled by growth hormone output from the pituitary gland, which is located at the base of the brain. Some children grow very slowly and on investigation are found to have a growth hormone deficiency. One in three children with growth hormone deficiency are overweight because of an inefficient metabolism. If the condition is treated early enough, the child can reach full adult height. Without treatment a boy only grows to around 143 cm (4 ft 7 in) and a girl to 127 cm (4 ft 2 in). In most cases treatment involves the child being injected with a synthetic hormone replacement on a daily basis.

Q What should I do if I think my child is overweight?

A Your health visitor will measure your child and plot the results on a growth chart. As long as her weight curve runs roughly parallel to the percentiles, and is no more than two bands higher than the height curve, most doctors will not worry too much. If the weight curve rises more steeply than the height curve, she is putting on weight too fast. If this is the case, talk to your doctor or health visitor to rule out medical causes, but also think about your family's lifestyle. How much physical exercise does your child get? Does she eat or snack a lot? Find ways of bringing more exercise and better eating habits into your child's daily routine.

Although some doctors are doubtful about whether growing pains exist, any parent whose child has been awakened in the night by the pain is quite certain that they are not imaginary.

Health issues
Asthma

Dealing with an **asthma attack**

A child having an asthma attack finds breathing difficult and may be too breathless to talk or feed, or may breathe very fast. Stay calm and follow the steps below. If this is the child's first attack, go straight to step 4.

1 Stay calm and follow the emergency plan agreed with your doctor.
2 Give the bronchodilators immediately, using a spacer if available. Wait 5 to 10 minutes. If the breathing is no better, repeat the dose.
3 Hold the child, sitting upright if he is comfortable in this position.
4 If the two doses of medication have no effect, contact your doctor, ambulance/ accident and emergency department urgently.

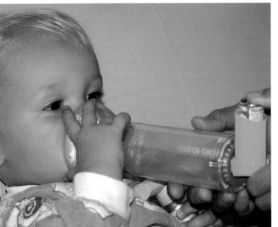

Above: Younger children may find it easier to use an inhaler with a spacer attached.

Q What is it?

A This common illness, which often begins in childhood, occurs when the small airways in the lungs, the bronchioles, become inflamed. As a result the lining of the airways swells and produces more mucus than usual, while the muscles in the walls of the airway tighten. The result is the characteristic wheezing when trying to breathe in and out and, sometimes, a persistent cough to clear the mucus. In most infants and toddlers, symptoms are triggered by virus infections such as the common cold, with the child staying well between colds. Asthma often runs in the family, especially in those with a predisposition to allergies. Symptoms can also start when the child comes into contact with allergic substances such as house dust, pollen, furry animals and feathers.

Q How can it be treated?

A Drugs for asthma are designed to be breathed in, so they work where they are needed, deep in the lungs. There are two main types: reliever inhalers (bronchodilators) and preventer drugs. The former relax the muscles in the airway walls; they usually come in blue inhalers to be used when an attack is coming on. Every child with asthma should always have access to a blue inhaler. The latter come in white or brown inhalers and are taken every day when the child is well. They damp down the inflammation of the airways and make the child less likely to over-react to allergens that are breathed in.

Health issues
Childhood infections

Q What is chickenpox?

A Caused by the virus *Varicella zoster*, chickenpox is a highly contagious infection, most often affecting children under 10 years old. It is transmitted in the fluid that oozes from the rash or in droplets in the breath. The virus takes 10–21 days to incubate and the patient is infectious from a day or two before the rash appears until the last spots have scabs. One attack of chickenpox normally gives life-long immunity, but the virus remains dormant in the body and can cause shingles later.

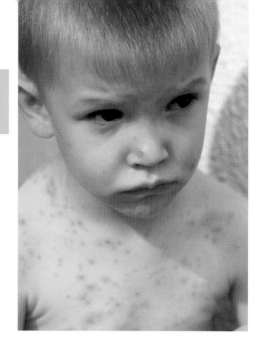

Above: Chickenpox can be identified from the small spots that turn rapidly into fluid-filled blisters.

Q What should I look for?

A Your child may be off-colour with a fever, appetite loss and possibly a sore throat. Tiny spots appear first on the scalp and face, then spread to the stomach, back, arms and legs. Within hours they develop into small fluid-filled blisters. The red skin around the blisters is less obvious on dark-pigmented skin. In three to four days the blisters form itchy yellow scabs which fall off after 10 days or so. Spots may continue to appear for up to five days.

Q Can I treat the infection myself, and if so what should I do?

A If you are confident that this is chickenpox and your child usually throws off coughs and colds easily, you can treat the infection yourself. Consult your doctor if your child feels unwell, if you are worried or if the spots redden and become sore, as they may need treating with an antibacterial cream. First check her temperature. If it is raised, give paracetamol.

Inform her nursery school and any pregnant friends. Stock your medicine chest with calamine lotion, antihistamine and bicarbonate of soda. Trim your child's nails to minimize damage by scratching and dab on calamine lotion, or a paste made from bicarbonate of soda and water, instructing her to press, pat or pinch rather than scratch. Make sure she has a daily bath in warm water in which a handful of bicarbonate of soda has been dissolved. Keep her cool and dress her in loose clothing without elastic. If she has long hair, put it up.

Q What is hand, foot and mouth disease?

A Hand, foot and mouth disease is usually a mild viral infection in which small blisters appear on the hands, the feet and inside the mouth. It has no connection with the foot and mouth disease that affects cattle and sheep. The infection is spread in droplets in the breath, especially when someone with the virus coughs or sneezes. The virus then infects the gastrointestinal tract. It can be transferred from faeces onto the hands for weeks after the infected child has recovered. Hand, foot and mouth disease takes three to five days to develop but only causes a mild upset in most children, lasting three to seven days. Your child will seem generally unwell with appetite loss and fever. Keep him away from other children until the crusts that develop from the hand and foot blisters have dropped off or until the fluid in the blisters has been reabsorbed. The child is most infectious at this stage and is likely to pass the virus on. Give your child paracetamol and undress him to underwear to calm the fever and make sure he has plenty of cool drinks.

Q Should I be concerned if my child gets mumps?

A While mumps itself is usually mild, frequently with no visible symptoms, the infection can lead to complications, including meningitis, encephalitis or permanent deafness in one ear. Normal symptoms of mumps include fever and possibly headache; reluctance to eat, swallow, even talk; swelling at the angle of the jaw. If your child becomes worse when you expected her to improve, you should contact the doctor. She may fully recover but develop a secondary infection a few days later. Contact your doctor immediately if your child shows any of the following symptoms: change in mood, becoming irritable or drowsy; reluctant to bend the neck forward; convulsions; unsteadiness or confusion; stomach ache or vomiting.

Q What is slapped cheek disease?

A Slapped cheek disease is a mild viral infection with rubella-like symptoms, including a bright red rash on the cheeks. The disease is spread by droplets that are transmitted on the breath and by sneezes and coughs. The incubation period is four to 14 days, and once the rash has appeared the child is no longer infectious. Slapped cheek disease is usually so mild that it resolves without treatment. However, like rubella, it can occasionally cause a miscarriage, so pregnant women should avoid all contact with known infected individuals. For some months following recovery, children may develop bright red cheeks again when excited or if exposed to bright sunlight.

Above: If you think your child may have mumps you should take him to the doctor for a check-up.

Health issues
Skin, hair and nails

Q What should I do if my child has ringworm?

A Ringworm is contagious, so you should keep your child away from nursery until treatment has started. He may have scalp ringworm, which can lead to patches of baldness, or trunk ringworm. In either case these are round patches of red, scaly skin, which spread slowly outwards, leaving pale, healed skin in the centre. In most cases the infection is treated with an antifungal drug, griseofulvin, as tablets or syrup, which the child needs to take for four to eight weeks to guarantee success. In addition to this, you can apply antifungal cream to the patches on the scalp and body. Always wash your hands after touching the child's ringworm patches.

Q What is scabies?

A Scabies is an infestation by a parasite, which burrows into the skin to lay its eggs. The eggs hatch and more mites emerge. The result is intense, but relatively harmless, irritation. Scabies is caught by skin-to-skin contact, and a child will become contagious as soon as she is infested by the mite, even though it can take a month or so before the first signs of scabies are evident. The infestation is usually treated with a prescribed insecticide lotion that must be applied all over the body, and especially around and under the fingernails, the soles of the feet, between the fingers and behind the ears. The lotion needs to stay in contact with the skin for at least eight hours, and one treatment is usually enough.

Above: Do not rely on medicated shampoos to get rid of head lice as they are often ineffective.

Q What is the best treatment for a wart?

A The best thing you can do with a wart is leave it to disappear of its own accord. However, this could take as long as a year, and in some cases two, and often a child will want to be rid of the unsightly growth before then. Warts consist of a surface of dead skin cells covering live skin cells that are infected with the human papilloma virus. They can be treated using a lotion, a gel or an impregnated plaster available from the pharmacist. Rub down the wart first with an emery board, then soak the skin in warm water for two to three minutes and pat dry. Apply the lotion, gel or plaster and let it dry. Rub down the surface of the wart and repeat every day. If home treatment has not worked after 12 weeks, take your child to a doctor.

Q What are headlice?

A Headlice are extremely common, especially among nursery and primary school children. As they like warmth, these insects, the size of a match head, live close to the scalp and cling to the hairs. When two children have their heads together the lice move rapidly from head to head. They make no distinction between clean and dirty hair, and live only on humans. The only way they can move is by crawling – they cannot fly, jump, or hop through the air. Lice lay their eggs (the empty shells of which are known as nits) close to the scalp and they glue them to the base of the hairs. Sometimes a child with nits does not have lice because the lice have all hatched and moved on to another person's head. The eggs take seven to 10 days to hatch and the louse grows by moulting its skin three times over the next seven to 14 days.

Q What should I look for?

A Your child will have an itchy scalp. You may see immovable white flecks on his hair, which, unlike dandruff, will not brush off easily. Your child will have a red rash on the back of his neck, caused by an allergy to the louse droppings. If you notice any of these signs you need to check your child's hair thoroughly (see below).

Q How should I treat lice?

A You can treat the condition naturally using a 'bug-busting' comb to remove the lice every three to four days for a period of two weeks in order to remove lice emerging from eggs before they spread. Alternatively you can use an insecticide. Do not rely on a shampoo to get rid of lice because it does not come into contact with the eggs for long enough to be effective. Note that children with asthma, eczema, dry skin or cradle cap should be treated with a water-based lotion and not an alcohol-based one. Your doctor or pharmacist can advise you on which is currently recommended.

Checking for lice or nits

- Wash your child's hair with a normal shampoo and apply lots of conditioner.
- Untangle the hair with a normal comb.
- Run a fine-toothed detector comb through the hair, starting at the roots and angling the teeth towards the scalp. Make sure you comb even the longest hair right to the tips.
- Make small partings and comb individual locks of hair separately.
- Check the comb for lice after each stroke and wipe it on kitchen paper.

Above: Combing your child's hair every three to four days is an effective way to get rid of head lice.

index

acknowledgements

General editor **Anna Southgate**
Executive editor **Jane McIntosh**
Project editor **Alice Bowden**
Executive art editor **Joanna MacGregor**
Designer **Ginny Zeal**
Senior production controller **Manjit Sihra**
Picture library assistant **Sophie Delpech**

Expert contributors include:
Jane Chumbley National Childbirth Trust
(NCT), teacher and health writer
Dr Jane Gilbert Writer, TV doctor and
broadcaster
Eileen Hayes Parenting advisor to the
National Society for the Prevention of Cruelty
to Children (NSPCC), writer and broadcaster
Jane Kemp Writer and early learning specialist
Sara Lewis Writer and cookery editor
Prisca Middlemiss Freelance medical
journalist specializing in family and child health
Dr Penny Stanway Doctor specializing
in child health, writer and broadcaster
Siobhan Sterling Television producer and
journalist
Nancy Stewart Early years play specialist
Clare Walters Writer and early learning
specialist
Dr Richard C Woolfson Child psychologist,
writer and broadcaster

Hamlyn would like to thank the following for the
loan of props for photography:

www.modernbaby.co.uk
00 44 (0)800 093 1500

www.jojomamanbebe.co.uk
00 44 (0)20 7924 6844

www.bloomingmarvellous.co.uk
00 44 (0)20 7371 0500

Many thanks also to all the babies and parents
who participated in the photoshoot for their
time, energy, patience and co-operation.

**Special Photography: © Octopus
Publishing Group Limited/**Adrian Pope

Other photography:
Alamy/Andrew Linscott 175;/Shout
245;/thislife pictures 177, 251;/David Wall
247
Bubbles/Frans Rombout 20, 249;/LoisJoy
Thurstun 179, 180;/Jennie Woodcock 117
Corbis UK Ltd/Laura Dwight 142;/Jose Luis
Pelaez 40;/Jennie Woodcock 11;/Jennie
Woodcock, Reflections Photolibrary 248
Getty Images/33, 76, 105, 134, 167;/Karen
Beard 29;/Patricia Doyle 204;/David Oliver
178;/Tosca Radiganda 207;/Stephanie
Rausser 223;/Tamara Reynolds 169;/Arthur
Tilley 156
Octopus Publishing Group Limited/David
Jordan 77, 137;/Peter Pugh-Cook 48, 74,
78, 86, 87, 97, 124, 130, 138, 144, 151,
168, 174, 184, 187, 188, 189, 193, 202,
209, 215, 216, 218, 220, 231, 233, 236,
237, 242;/Russell Sadur 8, 15, 16, 18, 24,
26, 31, 32, 36, 38, 44, 45, 47, 52, 54, 59,
72, 89, 92, 95
Mothercare/Stockist details: Mothercare
08453 304030 or www.mothercare.com 28
Photolibrary.com/Banana Stock 12, 13, 27,
34, 42, 43, 94, 96, 99, 100, 102, 108, 109,
114, 120, 133, 149, 154, 161, 162, 212
Science Photo Library/Ian Boddy
176;/BSIP, GIRAL 250;/Mauro Fermariello
56;/BSIP, Keene 60;/Dr. P. Marazzi 62;/Paul
Whitehill 127